ORDAINING WOMEN

ORDAINING WOMEN

Culture and Conflict in Religious Organizations

~ • • ~

MARK CHAVES

Harvard University Press
Cambridge, Massachusetts
London, England
1997

Library of Congress Cataloging-in-Publication Data

Chaves, Mark.
Ordaining women : culture and conflict in religious organizations
/ Mark Chaves.
p.   cm.
Includes bibliographical references and index.
ISBN 0-674-64145-0 (alk. paper)
1. Ordination of women—United States.   2. Women in Christianity.
3. Religion and sociology.   4. United States—Church history—20th
century.   5. Women clergy.   I. Title.
BV676.C46   1997
262'.14'0820973—dc21
97-12518

For
Alan and Joan Chaves
and
Ami

CONTENTS

ACKNOWLEDGMENTS

Many people have contributed to this book. Grants from the Louisville Institute and the Society for the Scientific Study of Religion supported much of the research and writing. These grants allowed me to benefit from the work of excellent research assistants, including Beth Caniglia, James Cavendish, Lynn Higgins, Min Liu, Sam Reimer, and Lori Wingate.

One major advantage of spending multiple years on a project is the opportunity to present pieces of it along the way. Earlier versions of several of these chapters were presented at Harvard Divinity School's American Colloquium, Duke Divinity School's Leadership Development Seminar, Notre Dame's Colloquium on American Religion, and the University of Wisconsin's Culture, History, Movements, and Politics Brown Bag. Still other versions of these chapters were presented at meetings of the Society for the Scientific Study of Religion, the Association for the Sociology of Religion, the American Sociological Association, the Social Science History Association, and the Chicago Area Group for the Study of Religious Communities. I know that I learned much from each of these discussions, and I hope that at least some of that learning is reflected in this book.

Special thanks are owed the individuals who read and commented on a draft of the entire manuscript: Virginia Brereton,

Andrew Gould, Andrew Greeley, William Hutchison, Fred Kniss, James Lewis, George Marsden, Martin Marty, John Meyer, Ami Nagle, and Martin Riesebrodt. Others offered particularly helpful comments on one or another of the chapters: Victoria Alexander, Gail Bederman, Kevin Christiano, Lis Clemens, Chris Coble, Nathan Hatch, Ed Lehman, Suzanne Marilley, Steve Warner, Catherine Wessinger, Judy Wittner, and Mayer Zald. Margaretta Fulton has guided this book to publication with graceful professionalism, and Elizabeth Gretz's excellent editing has smoothed many rough spots. The book is much better for all of these efforts.

The collective influence of the people named in the previous paragraph is greater than the sum of the parts. The observant reader will notice about an even mix of social scientists and historians among these individuals. I can testify that—even if the social scientists were somewhat more likely to encourage generalization and the historians somewhat more likely to encourage qualification—there was much more convergence than divergence in the reactions and recommendations of these two groups of scholars. If this book contributes to the developing interdisciplinary conversation between historians and sociologists, it is because these friends and colleagues have helped me to find both the right common language and the proper balance between generalization and qualification. I might have been able to write a book without the help of these people, but I would not have been able to write this book.

Very near the beginning of this project, Alice Jones generously shared with me the questionnaires from a 1987 National Council of Churches survey of denominational policies on women's ordination. Very near the end of this project, without reading a word of the text, Lyn Spillman helpfully offered the book's subtitle. I am grateful for both of these contributions.

At the beginning, middle, and end of this project—especially at its end—Ami Nagle provided love and encouragement that was always appreciated, if not always properly acknowledged. Thank you, and thank you again.

ORDAINING WOMEN

✎ · 1 · ✎

INTRODUCTION

Since 1970 women in the United States have become clergy in increasing numbers. According to the 1970 U.S. census, approximately 3 percent of clergy were female. That number rose to approximately 10 percent by 1990 and is likely to climb further. Today over 30 percent of students enrolled in theological schools are female. In some denominations the figure is 50 percent or higher (King 1994:79; Zikmund 1996:75; Marder 1996:287).

This influx of women into the clergy has prompted a fair amount of scholarly attention. Virtually all of the relevant empirical work, for good reason, has focused on the concrete experiences of women as they become (or try to become) functioning clergy, and on the concrete experiences of congregations and denominations as they face the prospect of women filling central leadership roles.[1] This book, by contrast, focuses on formal denominational policy regarding women's ordination. It begins with the observation that denominational policy regarding female clergy often fails to correspond to the actual practice of women in ministry. Denominational rules regarding women's ordination—whether those rules are inclusive or exclusive—neither reflect nor shape the tasks and roles women actually perform in congregations as closely or directly as might be expected. Rules and practices in this arena are only loosely coupled.

Denominational rules concerning female clergy therefore are not reducible to congregational- or individual-level practice; they require explanation in their own right. If rules about female clergy neither regulate nor reflect actual practice, then what do they accomplish? Why do people care so much about them? Why did some denominations ordain women so much earlier than others? What are the differences between early and late adopters of this organizational innovation? Who were the key actors in denominational conflicts over the formal rules? How has the social and organizational position of those actors changed over time? How has the character of the conflicts over these rules changed over time? If rules and practice are not tightly coupled, then how are they connected?

This book is about the granting of full clergy rights to women; it is about institutionalizing, or resisting, formal gender equality in American religion. For our purposes, I will say that a denomination ordains women or institutionalizes gender equality only when there is no official position that women are formally barred from occupying. This usage presents two potential sources of terminological confusion that should be clarified at the outset. First, mere ordination of women does not necessarily imply full clergy rights. Some denominations have ordained offices (for example, deacon, elder) that do not entail full rights of congregational leadership. Although I will use "ordaining women" as a shorthand for full clergy rights, readers should keep in mind that the focus throughout is on full formal equality for men and women within denominations.

Second, many denominations today assert that they are fully supportive of gender equality even as they formally deny women access to key leadership positions. Such denominations justify the exclusion of women with an ideology of gender-role complementarity: men and women are equal but different, and those differences warrant differential access to formal religious positions. Prohibiting women from certain positions, the argument goes, does not contradict the principle of gender equality rightly understood. This rationale notwithstanding, my focus here is always on the achievement of formally open access of all religious positions to women, and I will refer to arrangements falling short of this as manifestations of gender inequality even if advocates of the "equal but complementary" argument would reject this characterization.

Theoretical and Methodological Approach

Although many observers of American religion have noted the gap between rules regarding women's ordination and everyday practices, I am placing that gap at the center of attention. The phenomenon of formal rules only loosely connected to practice is common in organizations of all sorts, and focusing on this disjunction enables me to bring theory from the sociology of organizations to bear on the phenomenon of women's ordination.

In particular, this book draws heavily on the "new institutionalist" approach to organizational change (Powell and Di-Maggio 1991; Scott et al. 1994). Fundamental to this approach is the insight that organizational characteristics are often generated by an organization's efforts to respond to external, institutional pressures that may be related only tenuously to the organization's pragmatic activity. Such institutional pressures on organizations come in several forms. Legal or regulatory mandates, for example, may compel organizations to do certain things or look a certain way: the Federal Aviation Administration requires airports to have passengers walk through security devices, universities are obligated to form a standing committee for the protection of individuals who participate in research projects, primary schools must be in session for a certain number of days per year, and so on.

More subtly, normative pressure can lead organizational elites to make their organizations conform to certain expectations. Organizations gain legitimacy in the eyes of their various constituencies—clients, members, customers, sponsors—by conforming, or appearing to conform, to what those constituencies expect organizations of a certain type to look like. Organizational elites will strive to meet these expectations even in the absence of legal or regulatory mandates. Universities will tend to have a standard collection of academic departments no matter how small enrollments get in some of them; companies will tend to have research and development units even in the absence of evidence that such units enhance profitability; nonprofit organizations will tend to assign trustees to typical subcommittees (finance, membership) even if those subcommittees never meet or meet only to rubber-stamp staff initiatives. The basic idea is that some features of organizations exist because of institutional pressure emanating mainly from outside the organization. Whether the source is legal mandate or normative expectation about how a legitimate organization of a certain type should appear, significant aspects of organizations emerge in response to external pressure rather than in response to internal, technical needs.

Furthermore, it is often the case that the policies an organization puts in place in response to external pressure conflict with the pragmatic activity at the organization's technical core. Legal regulations may require safety rules that disrupt traditional, if unsafe, manufacturing practices; expectations for the rational justification of investment decisions may lead managers to present econometric analyses to stockholders "though no one may read, understand, or believe them"; social pressure for universities to show that they value undergraduate education may lead to the use of student course evaluations despite widespread skepticism that they measure effective learning or teaching.[2]

When faced with internal technical demands that conflict with external institutional demands, organizations commonly respond by "decoupling" one from the other. There are a variety of ways in which such loose coupling might manifest itself: "Structural elements are only loosely linked to each other and to activities, rules are often violated, decisions are often unimplemented, or if implemented have uncertain consequences, technologies are of problematic efficiency, and evaluation and inspection systems are subverted or rendered so vague as to provide little coordination" (Meyer and Rowan [1977] 1991:43). Thus safety rules are posted but not enforced; econometric reports are commissioned but not read; student course evaluations are duly collected and processed but not given much weight in faculty promotion decisions. The common thread across these examples is that loose coupling is produced when an externally generated organizational characteristic is at odds with an internal, pragmatic organizational activity.

Formal rules only loosely connected to on-the-ground practice, then, very likely reflect an attempt to make an organization conform to external standards rather than an attempt to solve internal pragmatic problems. Loose coupling suggests "the dependence of organizations on the patterning built up in wider environments—rather than on a purely internal technical and functional logic" (Scott et al. 1994:2). A formal rule or policy only loosely connected to actual organizational practice is very likely a rule functioning more as a signal to the environment than as a regulation governing internal operations.

I will argue in this book that formal rules about women's ordination are, in large part, generated by external pressure on denominations. I will also argue that these rules often are only loosely connected to on-the-ground congregational practice. The Roman Catholic Church, for example, famously does not permit female priests. At the same time, however, its clergy shortage has generated an acute need for someone to do the day-to-day work of running parishes. As a result, most of the three hundred priestless Roman Catholic parishes in the United States are "pastored" by women (Wallace 1992). The pragmatic requirements of the church generate loose coupling between rule and practice. Congregationalists, to mention an example with a different valence, first fully ordained a woman in 1853. But despite this early formal openness, women did not ever serve as pastors of Congregational churches in substantial numbers, and when they did serve, it was in the smallest congregations for the lowest pay. The resistance of congregants to female ministers generated loose coupling between rule and practice. Emphasizing loose coupling in this way should not be taken to mean that actual practice never reflects formal rules about women's ordination; sometimes it does. The point is rather that we should not assume that the two are tightly connected.

Given extensive loose coupling between rule and practice, formal rules about women clergy are best understood as a symbolic display that is part of a broader process by which denominations construct their public identities. For reasons that I will discuss, policies concerning female clergy often became laden with symbolic meaning. As such, a denomination's policy on women clergy has become an important part of its public identity, signaling to the world the denomination's location vis-à-vis certain cultural boundaries. A denomination's policy allowing (or prohibiting) women's ordination is better understood as a symbolic display of support for gender equality (or of resistance to gender equality) than as a policy either motivated by or intended to regulate the everyday reality of women inside the organization. Formal denominational policy regarding women's ordination, in other words, has a symbolic significance that is not reducible to the pragmatic internal operations of the organization. This book is devoted to explaining the dynamics by which those identities have been, and continue to be, constructed and maintained.

Methodologically, the analysis is historical and comparative. Previous work on women's ordination has tended to focus on very narrow slices of the denominational population. In addition to the numerous accounts of women's ordination within single denominations, extant comparative work mainly contains descriptive overviews of women's status and achievements. When explanation is offered, it usually is based on examination of a relatively small number of denominations.[3]

The limits of explanations based on small numbers of denominations often become clear when the perspective is broadened either cross-sectionally or historically. Mary Farrell Bednarowski (1980), for example, studied four nineteenth-century religious groups, all of which displayed openness to female religious leadership. These movements—Shakerism, Spiritualism, Christian Science, and Theosophy—also shared certain theological tenets: they deemphasized a masculine deity, tempered their doctrines of the Fall, denied the need for traditional ordained clergy, and denied that marriage and motherhood were the only acceptable roles for women. Bednarowski argued that there is a correlation and, possibly, a causal connection between the presence of these theological tenets and a denomination's openness to female leadership.

Broadening the comparison in various ways, however, reveals the limits of that conclusion. First, there were other nineteenth-century denominations, including Congregationalists, Methodist Protestants, Unitarians, and the Salvation Army, that ordained women yet did not share the theology of these four groups. Second, virtually all of the shifts in the direction of full gender equality that have occurred in the previous one hundred years have occurred without theological change toward the four characteristics Bednarowski emphasizes. Casting a wider cross-sectional and historical net thus renders implausible causal connections that appear plausible when only a few denominations are considered.

This is not to say that factors identified as important in studies of small numbers of denominations never hold up when the scope of analysis is broadened. Indeed, several variables identified by earlier observers (for example, denominational centralization) turn out to be very important influences on women's ordination policy. Other variables, however, that have seemed important when the focus is on a small subset of denominations (for example, the presence of a clergy shortage), turn out not to be important. The advantage of a broader comparative base is the ability to distinguish with greater confidence between the truly causal factors and the factors that only seem causal because they are viewed from too narrow an empirical perspective.

This book builds on but moves beyond earlier work by investigating women's ordination among a much larger set of denominations than have been included in previous efforts, and by systematically comparing—both across time and across denominations—policies on women's ordination and conflicts over those policies. Specifically, this book is based on a systematic quantitative study of the one hundred largest Christian denominations in the United States. Identifying the proper set of denominations required two major steps. First, all denominations that had clergy, some degree of national-level organization, and over three hundred congregations in 1992 were identified. Second, denominations in this group that were the result of mergers were traced backward in time in order to identify their organizational precursors. Once these precursors were added to the organizational population, 103 denominations were included. Relevant data were collected on 100 of these denominations, for a "response rate" of 97 percent. Although this population includes slightly fewer than 50 percent of U.S. denominations in 1992, these denominations contain approximately 85 percent of U.S. church members.

I will draw on these quantitative data throughout the book, sometimes reporting results obtained using a technique called "event-history analysis." Event-history analysis was used to determine the probability that a denomination would begin to ordain women in a given year. The idea behind this analytical technique is that each denomination in each year has an underlying probability of experiencing a defined event, in this case beginning to ordain women. The technique uses information about which denominations began ordaining women in what years to calculate the underlying probability for each denomination. More to the point, it allows one to calculate whether certain categories of denominations are more or less likely to ordain women earlier than others. Event-history results allow us to compare, for example, the likelihood that a sacramental denomination will ordain women with the likelihood that a non-sacramental denomination will do so. Or, to take another example, they allow us to compare organizationally centralized denominations with decentralized denominations regarding their respective likelihoods of ordaining women. As we shall see, these results can be very informative about the factors that make a denomination more or less likely to ordain women earlier rather than later.[4]

Although the results of this quantitative study support many of the arguments developed in this book, describing these results will occupy very few pages.[5] Instead I develop the arguments primarily by using qualitative material drawn from a variety of scholarly and denominational sources. These sources include responses from a 1987 National Council of Churches (NCC) denominational survey concerning women's ordination; telephone interviews with denominational officials and historians, used mainly to supplement the NCC survey concerning basic facts about denominational policy on women's ordination; published accounts of conflicts over women's ordination in a variety of denominations; and official and unofficial documents (for example, committee reports, minutes of debates at national meetings, commentary on denominational policy and practice) generated by the dozens of nineteenth- and twentieth-century conflicts over women's ordination in the United States. Whether the evidence is quantitative or qualitative, however, is of secondary methodological importance. Of primary importance is that, throughout, the evidence is used comparatively.

Plan of the Book

The first step in the argument is demonstrating the extensive disjunction between rules and practice concerning female clergy, a fact that is typical of rules that exist, at least in part, as signals to an organization's environment. Chapter 2 establishes the fact that loose coupling of rule and practice is a common feature of women's ordination.

Chapters 3, 4, and 5 examine the ways in which environmental, normative, and identity issues have shaped the meaning of women's ordination, and how they have influenced denominational policies on women clergy. Chapter 3 describes the range of environmental pressures on denominations. On the one hand, there is pressure emanating from outside the religious sphere—from the women's movement, for example. On the other hand, there is pressure coming from within the religious sphere but external to any particular denomination. In this regard, I will argue that interdenominational alliances influenced and continue to influence policies concerning female clergy.

The women's movement has affected intradenominational conflicts over gender in many ways. Perhaps most significant is that the rise of a broader women's movement changed the meaning of women's ordination. Largely because of the secular women's movement, women's ordination came to be understood as an issue of gender equality in a way that it was not in the absence of this social movement. Chapter 4 documents this changed meaning, a change that is fundamental to understanding the symbolic significance of women's ordination with which we still live.

Within the religious world itself, biblical inerrancy and sacramentalism are the most significant cultural boundaries when it comes to women's ordination. Chapter 5 concentrates on those types of denominations. Why are biblical inerrancy and sacramentalism so deeply and so tightly connected to resistance to female clergy? Chapter 5 argues that for both of these denominational subcultures, gender equality has come to symbolize the liberal modern world that they define themselves against.

The cultural and environmental factors emphasized in Chapters 3, 4, and 5 do not negate the importance either of activity inside denominations or of organizational structure. Intraorganizational change does not occur inevitably or automatically, as if organizations helplessly succumb to unyielding environmental pressures. On the contrary, organizational change is often the result of concrete conflict between advocates and opponents of that change, and internal structural features of organizations very strongly influence who is likely to win such conflicts (DiMaggio 1988). Some organizational characteristics will create an advantage for opponents of women's ordination; other organizational characteristics will benefit proponents. Chapters 6 and 7 begin to explore what occurs inside denominations by bringing the agents, or carriers, of organizational change—and the structural features that enable them to be effective—more into the foreground.

Chapter 6 argues that a denomination's level of centralization and the presence or absence of an autonomous women's mission society are key internal organizational features distinguishing between early and late ordainers of women. These factors are important largely because they structure intradenominational politics in ways that influence the ability of advocates to win women's ordination conflicts. The discussion of women's organizations, furthermore, adds to the argument developed in Chapter 5 about the strong resistance to women's ordination among sacramentalist and biblically inerrant denominations. These denominations are less likely than others to permit fully autonomous women's organizations. Because autonomous women's organizations have been major sites of gender-equality advocacy within denominations, discouraging the formation of such organizations means discouraging the emergence of actors likely to help bring about change in the direction of gender equality. In this way, I will argue, internal structural features of these denominations reinforce their symbolic resistance to women's ordination.[6]

Chapter 7 continues the focus on what happens inside denominations by analyzing four ways in which conflicts over women's ordination change over time. Change occurs in (1) the frequency of conflict; (2) the organizational location of actors pushing for change; (3) the tactics and strategies pursued by those actors; and (4) the extent of opposition to women's ordination. The basic story is that the same goal—women's ordination—is pursued by very different actors with different strategies at different points. This chapter identifies those actors and strategies and how they both change over time. I also will argue that the observed changes in intradenominational conflicts over this issue are driven largely by change in the cultural environment in which the conflicts occur. The chapter's goal is to pry open a bit more the organizational black box containing the conflicts that precede and produce denominational policies about women's ordination. At the same time, we will not lose sight of the fact that these intraorganizational conflicts do not occur in a vacuum. Indeed, like the formal rules concerning women's ordination, the systematic patterns observed in conflicts over those rules are understandable only by connecting them to what is happening in the social and political world in which they occur.

These chapters have their origin in a moment several years ago when I came across a list of denominations and the years in which they began to ordain women (Jacquet 1988). My attention was caught, and my curiosity piqued, by the fact that two major denominations—the Presbyterian Church in the U.S.A. and the Methodist Church—granted full formal clergy rights to women in the same year, 1956. Nineteen-fifty-six seemed a very odd year for any major religious body to institutionalize gender equality. The 1950s, after all, are commonly portrayed as the doldrums of the women's movement, well after the first wave of the movement had climaxed in female suffrage and almost a decade before its second wave would begin in earnest. How is it, I wondered, that two major denominations, and several smaller ones, began to ordain women in the 1940s and 1950s? A few hours of research confirmed that there was no rush of Presbyterian or Methodist women wanting to be clergy in the 1950s. Not for another fifteen years would significant numbers of women seek to be clergy in these, and other, denominations. Whatever prompted the policy changes of the 1950s, it was neither political pressure from an organized social movement nor a response to women banging on denominational doors. This was the first clue that denominations' formal policies about women's ordination are about something more than the need to regulate or respond to what women are actually doing inside religious organizations. It was the first clue that there was something moderately mysterious about formal rules concerning women's ordination. The mystery seemed worth unraveling, and this book is the result of that effort.

⌒ 2 ⌒

THE SYMBOLIC
SIGNIFICANCE
OF WOMEN'S
ORDINATION

A basic insight of contemporary organizational theory is that rules only loosely coupled to everyday practice are likely to have a source outside the organization—they exist more to respond to the environment than to govern internal operations. The first part of this chapter establishes extensive loose coupling between the rule and practice of women's ordination. The second part establishes that denominational leaders have, in fact, been quite aware that a major source of pressure to ordain women has been the changing normative climate regarding formal gender equality.

Loose Coupling

There are many clear indications that the granting of full clergy rights to women is uncoupled from day-to-day practice in which women do or do not function as clergy. Three kinds of evidence help us understand this phenomenon: (1) the disjunction between the timing of organizational policy changes and trends in the numbers of women actually seeking clergy status; (2) historical and contemporary evidence that, in denominations with restrictive rules, women still perform many of the same functions as men; and (3) evidence that in denominations with formal gender equality, women face many obstacles preventing the attainment of real parity with male clergy.

Denominational policy changes regarding women's ordination do not coincide with trends in the numbers of women seeking clergy status. Figure 2.1 tracks the presence of female doctors, lawyers, and clergy in the United States since 1880. The trend is similar for all three occupations. Except during World War II, the proportion of doctors, lawyers, and clergy who were female was very low from 1880 until 1970, after which the proportion of women started to rise steeply for all three professions.

The trend of organizational change in American religion is much different. Table 2.1 lists the denominations that began to ordain women between 1853 and 1987, the date at which they began, and the organizational event that marked the beginning of full clergy rights for women within each denomination. Figure 2.2 shows, between 1890 and 1990, the percentage of U.S. Christian denominations that granted full clergy rights to

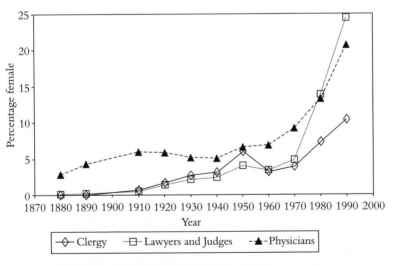

Figure 2.1 Women in three professions, 1880–1990
(source: U.S. Census Reports)

Table 2.1 Denominations granting full clergy rights to women

Denomination	Date began ordaining women[a]	Type of beginning[b]
Congregationalists	1853	C
Advent Christian Church	1860	F
Universalist Church of America	1863	C
Christian Church (General Convention)	1867	C
Salvation Army	1870	F
American Unitarian Association	1871	C
Church of God (Anderson)	1885	F
Disciples of Christ	1888	R
Church of the United Brethren in Christ	1889	R
Wesleyan Methodist Church	1891	R
Methodist Protestant Church	1892	R
National Baptist Convention, Inc.	1895	F
Pentecostal Holiness Church	1895	F
Pilgrim Holiness Church	1897	F
African Methodist Episcopal Zion Church	1898	R
Friends, United (Five-Year) Meeting	1902	F
Northern Baptist Convention	1907	F
Church of the Nazarene	1908	F
Baptist General Conference	1918	R
Cumberland Presbyterian Church	1921	R
Churches of God, General Conference	1923	R
Community Churches, International Council	1923	F
General Association of General Baptists	1925	R
International Church of the Foursquare Gospel	1927	F
Assemblies of God	1935	R

Table 2.1 (continued)

Denomination	Date began ordaining women[a]	Type of beginning[b]
Open Bible Standard Churches	1935	F
Evangelical and Reformed Church	1948	R
Presbyterian Church in the U.S.A. (North)	1956	R
Methodist Church	1956	R
Church of the Brethren	1958	R
United Presbyterian Church, North America	1958	M
African Methodist Episcopal Church	1960	R
Christian Congregation	1961	R
Presbyterian Church, US (South)	1964	R
Southern Baptist Convention	1964	C
Christian Methodist Episcopal Church	1966	R
Evangelical United Brethren Church	1968	M
American Lutheran Church	1970	R
Lutheran Church in America	1970	R
Mennonite Church	1973	R
Free Methodist Church, North America	1974	R
Evangelical Covenant Church	1976	R
Episcopal Church	1976	R
Reformed Church in America	1979	R

a. If congregations ordained women before they were organized into a national denominational structure, the date given represents the founding date of the national denomination. For example, a Northern Baptist congregation ordained Edith Hall in 1894, but the table gives 1907 because that is the year that the national organization incorporated as a denomination that permits female clergy.

b. C = Women's ordination begins because a congregation ordains a woman in the absence of a denominational rule prohibiting it, and the ordination is not overturned by a higher judicatory.

F = Women's ordination granted at denomination's founding.

M = Women's ordination begins because of merger with a denomination already granting full clergy rights to women.

R = Women's ordination begins with a denominational rule change.

women.[1] Unlike the individual-level trend in Figure 2.1, the organizational change tracked in Figure 2.2 occurs slowly but steadily across the denominational population during the twentieth century. In 1890 about 7 percent of U.S. denominations gave full clergy rights to women; today approximately half of U.S. denominations do so. Significantly, dozens of denominations made the organizational change permitting female clergy before there were very many women actively seeking clergy status.

The loose coupling is even more evident when we examine, denomination by denomination, the (non)relationship between rules about women's ordination and the female populations of seminaries. The (northern) Presbyterian Church in the U.S.A., for example, gave women full clergy rights in 1956. But in the period from 1948 to 1962, eight years before full status to six years after, the number of women receiving the bachelor of divinity degree annually from Presbyterian seminaries never exceeded nine. As in other denominations, the surge in female

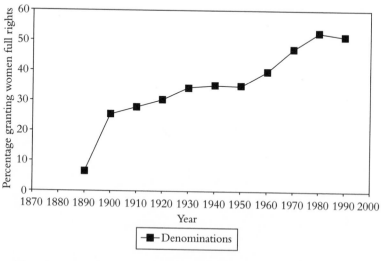

Figure 2.2 Denominations that ordain women

enrollment did not begin until about 1970. In 1976, 41 women received the professional degree, now a master of divinity, from Presbyterian seminaries (Taylor 1976). By 1987, 164 women were enrolled in professional programs in Presbyterian seminaries, representing one-third of the student population (Baumgaertner 1988:13). The increase in women seeking clergy training thus came after 1970, even though the denomination formally opened its doors to women in 1956.

At first glance, the Presbyterian trend—one that is typical for denominations ordaining women before 1970—might be interpreted as an organizational lag effect. It takes time for news of an organizational change to filter down and begin to influence individual behavior. But this interpretation loses force when we note that the post-1970 surge in women seeking seminary training occurred even within denominations that did not yet ordain women. The Episcopal Church did not grant full status to women until 1976, but by that year women already composed almost 14 percent of Episcopal enrollment in professional degree programs (Taylor 1980:11). Among the Southern Baptists, a denomination that no longer officially ordains women, more than 11 percent of seminarians were female in 1987 (Baumgaertner 1988:13). The increase in female enrollment is evident even within Roman Catholic schools of theology, where about one-fourth of the students currently enrolled are female (Wallace 1992:5).

Before 1970, then, women did not pursue the professional degree for clergy in significant numbers whether or not their denomination formally granted it to them; after 1970, women did pursue the degree whether or not their denomination formally granted it. This disjunction between when women began to seek professional training and status in significant numbers and when denominations began to grant that status illustrates the loose coupling between rule and practice regarding women's roles in American religion. It is important to distinguish clearly between the organizational phenomenon by which women are formally allowed to be ordained and the phenomenon of women actually becoming clergy in significant numbers. The organizational developments are different from the individual-level developments, and they warrant a separate explanation.[2]

Another way to see the loose coupling is to note that women have occupied and continue to occupy significant leadership roles within denominations and movements that formally forbid women to occupy such roles. This phenomenon is evident as early as the 1840s, for example, in the African Methodist Episcopal Church. Women had been preaching in this denomination at least since Jarena Lee requested (and was denied) a preaching license in 1809. Still, the denomination's General Conference defeated efforts to officially permit female preaching in 1844, 1848, and 1852. Jualynne Dodson (1996:128–129) observes, however, that these "negative votes of male authorities [had] little real consequence for preaching women." That is, women continued to preach despite the formal rules prohibiting it. The rules on female preaching did not catch up to practice until 1884, when the denomination granted preaching licenses to women. By this time women were not just preaching; at least two pastored their own congregations (Angell 1996).

The history of American Protestant fundamentalism provides another example of this sort of loose coupling. Four of the six most significant turn-of-the-century fundamentalist Bible institutes "provided Evangelical women with the training to preach, enter the pastorate, and teach Bible." They also "publicized preaching and pastoral experiences of alumnae and hired female evangelists in extension work" (Hassey 1986:30).[3] These schools did not maintain this openness to female clergy into mid-century, as formal exclusion of women from leadership roles became more deeply institutionalized within American fundamentalism. Yet Michael Hamilton (1993) found that this development of formal exclusionary rules did not necessarily reflect changed practice. Behind the strong rhetoric prohibiting women from engaging in public ministry, Hamilton cites numerous examples of women occupying public ministerial roles in local congregations, serving as faculty in Bible institutes, preaching to mixed-sex audiences at summer Bible conferences, serving as missionaries and traveling evangelists, and organizing their own special-purpose religious organizations.

It is true that fundamentalist denominations in this period resisted ordaining women, and they also resisted appointing them as trustees of national denominational organizations, but as we shall see, the same is true of actual practice within more "liberal" denominations of the period, even those that officially permitted ordained women. "At the local level," Hamilton (1993:180) concludes, "ministry opportunities for women in mainline churches were probably very similar to those in Fundamentalist churches." The noticeable differences in formal rules and rhetoric overlay essentially similar actual practices.

The phenomenon of practice that was more "liberal" than the rules did not go unnoticed by early observers. Fannie Mc-Dowell Hunter, a Holiness preacher, described the following scene in 1905:

> The writer was once present when a large body of preachers were in annual session. During that year, one of their pastors had invited a woman preacher to assist him in the revival services on his charge. She was greatly used of God in bringing the lost to Him. This body of preachers were in very plain terms expressing their disapproval of his course and of a woman being allowed to fill any pulpit within "their bounds." Different suggestions and resolutions were offered in order to prevent the repetition of such a course. At last it was settled in this way: "It is the *sense* (?) [*sic*] of this body that no woman be allowed to fill any pulpit within our bounds." Later on, before the session closed, the Presiding Officer introduces his wife to the audience, who, *standing in the pulpit,* proceeds to make a speech in favor of the "—— Society" of the Church, and from the pulpit very pathetically pleads with men and women to support it with their means and prayers. She met with the approval and applause of every member of that body. (Hunter [1905] 1985:95, emphases in original)

Hunter concluded the story wryly: "Consistency thou art a jewel."

Early proponents of women's ordination also used the fact of women's actual and effective ministerial activity as an argument in favor of ordination (Zikmund 1981:196). Women's ministerial activity was especially evident on the mission field, and so the disjunction between rule and practice was particularly salient there. An 1894 observer noted, "For while it is true that many Christians believe that women are enjoined from publicly preaching the Gospel, either at home or abroad, it is certainly true that scores of missionary women are at present doing this very thing" (quoted in Zikmund 1981:196).

Examples of women doing the functional work of clergy although they are denied the formal status are evident across denominations and religious traditions. Elaine Sommers (1983:93) has found evidence of loose coupling within the Mennonite Church of the nineteenth and early twentieth centuries: "Despite the fact that they may not have been ordained specifically to the offices, Mennonite women have done the work of evangelists, ministers, and teachers." And at least one woman served as a rabbi of Reformed Jewish congregations as early as the 1890s: "Because of her great learning and her devotion to Judaism, [Ray Frank Litman] often acted as temporary rabbi for western Jewish communities that had no ordained rabbis. The establishment of the first congregation in several West Coast towns resulted from her preaching" (Braude 1981:183).

Southern Baptist congregations have also demonstrated manifest loose coupling between formal rules and practice, even before 1980s statements against women's ordination by the National Convention. Leon McBeth (1981:516) observes that, while Southern Baptist congregations actually ordaining women may be relatively new, "one must guard against the erroneous assumption that their performing the functions of ministry is an equally new practice." In fact, "women have long been serving in various ministry roles in Baptist churches without ordination."

The case of the Evangelical United Brethren Church (EUB) is interesting because it reveals both the fact of loose coupling and the interpretive danger of assuming that rules truly reflect or govern practice. The EUB was formed in 1946 by the merger of the Evangelical Church, which did not ordain women, and the Church of the United Brethren in Christ, which had allowed women's ordination since the 1880s. The new church formally forbade female clergy, and at least one historian concluded from this that "the practice [of ordaining women] ceased with the creation of the Evangelical United Brethren Church in 1946. Several decades of ordained ministry by women was halted, and faded into history as the women already ordained passed from active service" (Will 1980:33).

But this is false; women's ordination was not halted by the merged denomination's formal prohibition. Examination of the actual practice reveals that "a number of women were ordained as elders in the Evangelical United Brethren Church despite a policy to the contrary supposedly established at the church's foundation." (In the EUB, ordination as elder was equivalent to ordination as clergy.)[4] At least twenty-three women were ordained between 1946 and 1968 (when the EUB merged with the Methodist Church), and at the end of that period another twenty-seven women were preparing for ordination. "Not only were the annual conferences ordaining women, they were actively encouraging them to prepare for ordination!" (Cooney 1988:25, 31).

Edwin Mulder (1989:235) has observed loose coupling within the Reformed Church in America. In 1975, four years before this denomination granted full clergy rights to women, "some classes [regional judicatories] which voted to receive women under their care as candidates for the ministry of the Word, had voted against the ordination of women to that office. Equally inconsistent was the empowerment of the Board of Theological Education to grant professorial certificates to women but not to consider them eligible for ordination."

Such loose coupling continues today. Investigators of contemporary religious groups with restrictive gender rules consistently observe gaps between rhetoric and practice, both with respect to women's roles in households and, more to the point, with respect to women's roles in religious organizations.[5] In the Seventh-day Adventist Church, which continues to deny women full clergy status, dozens of women work as clergy in congregations, some as sole pastors (Vance 1995; Dudley 1995:2). Laura Vance (1995:278) describes the "increasing discrepancy between General Conference policies and growing participation of women in pastoral service." This discrepancy was perhaps at its rhetorical widest in the motion passed by the 1989 Annual Council of the General Conference. The motion's first clause asserted: "We do not recommend authorization for women to be ordained to the gospel ministry." But the motion's second clause granted what the first seemed to deny: "Those who have, without regard to gender, been recognized as commissioned ministers or licensed ministers may perform essentially the same functions as an ordained minister to the gospel" (quoted in Vance 1995:278).

Chapter 1 observed that the vast majority of the approximately three hundred priestless Roman Catholic parishes in the United States are "pastored" by women (Wallace 1992). These women function as priest in almost every sense, including presiding at worship and distributing communion. They are often called "pastor" by their parishioners, by male priests, by diocesan administrators, and even by their bishops, despite the fact that this title is formally prohibited them. These women work mainly in small rural parishes, exactly the same low-status congregations most likely to have a female minister in denominations that formally grant women full clergy status.

Women also increasingly fill other functional clergy roles within the Roman Catholic Church. Dennis Geaney (1978: 149–153) interviewed Roman Catholic women with master of divinity degrees and found them engaged in numerous ministerial roles. They worked as Catholic chaplains at hospitals and colleges. They preached in parish churches and served as counselors and spiritual guides. One taught homiletics in a Catholic seminary. Indeed, females constitute more than 80 percent of nonpriests serving in paid ministry positions (not including schoolteachers) in U.S. Catholic parishes (Murnion 1994:12).

The 1840s example from the African Methodist Episcopal Church, described above, illustrated that African-American denominations that did not officially ordain women were not exceptions to this general historical pattern of loose coupling. The same is true for contemporary African-American denominations. Cheryl Townsend Gilkes (1993:238) reports, for example, that although the Church of God in Christ does not ordain women to be elders, pastors, or bishops, "women may 'teach the gospel to others' and may 'have charge of a church in the absence of the pastor.' " Only men may "preach" but women may "teach," a symbolic distinction without an apparent difference in practice. The public speaking of prominent women in this denomination "is indistinguishable from the most exemplary 'preaching.' "

Not incidentally, this aspect of the phenomenon—having a different label for the same activity when it is performed by women than when it is performed by men—can be observed elsewhere. Sommers (1983:97) observes that when women spoke from Mennonite pulpits in the first decades of this century, "Reporters preferred the term 'talk' rather than 'sermon.' " In response to an 1859 query asking if "the gospel permit of female preaching," the Church of the Brethren Annual Meeting "made a distinction between teaching, ministering, and prophesying . . ., deciding that a sister could prophesy but not teach" (Brubaker 1986:165). The Lutheran Church–Missouri Synod, in which the tension between rule and practice regarding gender has been most acute regarding the status of parochial school teachers, has tried in various ways to maintain symbolic differences between male and female teachers doing the same work. At one point, for example, male teachers held a "Diploma of Vocation"; female teachers held a "Solemn Agreement" (Todd 1996:141).

Loose coupling between rule and practice is thus ubiquitous among religious organizations that formally deny women access to some religious roles. Women in fact have more opportunities for religious leadership in such denominations than the formal rules would lead us to believe. There is much truth, it seems, to R. Stephen Warner's (1990) observation that religious organizations with restrictive gender rules may be the only organizations in our society that are more sexist in theory than in practice.

Loose coupling in denominations that grant full formal equality to women is the mirror image of that described above, and has been since the nineteenth-century beginnings of women's ordination. Close observers of women's ordination throughout the period have noted that liberal rules are often not matched by practice.

Writing in 1881, Matilda Joslyn Gage reported that "in the Unitarian and Universalist churches, which ordain women to preach and administer the ordinances, these women pastors are made to feel that the innovation is not universally acceptable" (Stanton et al. 1881:784). Cynthia Grant Tucker's (1990, 1996) research supports this claim. Although Universalists began ordaining women in 1863 and Unitarians began in 1871, Tucker (1996:80) reports that they "did so with little enthusiasm." Describing the experience of Unitarian and Universalist female ministers of the late nineteenth century, Tucker (1996:80, 87) writes:

> Seminaries were slow to let women enroll, and women who did enter programs soon learned this was no guarantee that churches would call them or pay them a living wage, or that their denominations would extend their institutional networks to bring them in and help them survive . . . When [women ministers] went to the annual gatherings of liberal clergy . . . they often were greeted by cold or incredulous stares from colleagues who seemed to regard them as aberrations and wished they would leave.

This situation was no different several decades later when, in 1935, "the general superintendent of the Universalist Church acknowledged that 'a tremendous prejudice against women ministers' made it almost 'impossible' to get a female candidate 'a hearing at any salary whatsoever' " (Tucker 1996:93). As late as 1974, only five of the approximately forty women clergy within the Unitarian Universalist Association pastored congregations, "and these few were working for *very* low salaries, some of them earning their substandard incomes by serving in more than one church" (Tucker 1996:94, emphasis in original).

Although a Congregational church was the first to ordain a woman when it ordained Antoinette Brown in 1853, "In 1889, over thirty-five years later, there were only 4 ordained Congregational women ministers listed in the national Congregational yearbook." A 1919 study of the sixty-seven female Congregational ministers found that "eighteen women were pastors of 'very small' churches, 14 were copastors with their husbands, 14 were religious educators or church assistants, and 21 were employed outside the churches." As late as 1950, in this denomination that pioneered opening its clergy ranks to women, only about 3 percent of its ministers were female (Zikmund 1996:68–69).

Practice less liberal than the rules was not, and is not, limited to Unitarians, Universalists, and Congregationalists. The African Methodist Episcopal Zion Church admitted Florence Spearing Randolph to full conference membership in 1898. Still, she was assigned only to congregations that were "small, poor, and struggling, with few members." When her congregation's situation improved, "she would be replaced by a 'nice young man' and reassigned to another 'problem' " (Collier-Thomas 1996:180). Georgia Harkness, associate professor of religious education at Elmira College, was the "outstanding clergy woman of her generation and the leader of the movement for equal clergy rights for Methodist women." She observed in 1924 that "not many more women are preaching in those denominations where ordination is possible than in those where it is denied" (quoted in Noll 1992:96–97). Consider also the committee of one hundred prominent women who met in 1929 to discuss women's status within the Presbyterian Church in the U.S.A. Although they supported efforts to grant women full equality within the denomination, "almost every woman committee member . . . admitted that 'she personally did not want to be a pastor or an elder, and would doubtless vote against a woman pastor in her local church' " (Bendroth 1984:126). The overall situation was no different twenty-five years later. A 1953 study of sixteen denominations carried out by the National Council of Churches' Department of United Church Women found that, even where women's ordination is permitted, "few women are ordained, and only a small proportion of them become pastors of churches" (*Christian Advocate,* Oct. 29, 1953:16).

Janet Riley's recollections of beginning divinity school in 1958 call attention to the fact of loose coupling within the Disciples of Christ. In that year, "a report prepared by the World Council of Churches stated that the Disciples [had] had official equality for women in every respect since the founding of the denomination." At the same time, "the dean of the Disciples House at [the University of Chicago Divinity School] had advised [her] that the Disciples provided financial assistance there only for men" (Riley 1989:219).

Denominations such as the Disciples, as well as those descending from the Congregationalists, Unitarians, and Universalists, often take pride in the early dates at which they began to ordain women. The historical record makes it clear, however, that even within these "liberal" denominations, truly inclusive practice toward female clergy was quite exceptional. As we will see in a later chapter, the pioneering place that these denominations occupy in the story of women's ordination is attributable more to their decentralized organizational structure than to any broad progressive spirit permeating the denomination. On the contrary, with respect to female clergy in the late nineteenth century, there does not appear to be substantial difference between the rank and file of "conservative" denominations and the rank and file of "liberal" denominations. Resistance to actual female clergy was the rule across the denominational population, even in denominations formally allowing women's ordination.

Early advocates of women's ordination recognized that changed rules would not necessarily result in changed practice. Moreover, they sometimes used that recognition to allay what they believed to be the fear of their opponents that positions of religious authority would be increasingly filled by women. Belle Bennett's speech to the 1910 General Conference of the Methodist Episcopal Church, South, provides an example. Arguing in favor of full lay rights for women (ordination was not yet on the table in this denomination), she assured her opponents that formally allowing women to vote and be delegates to Conferences would hardly change anything: "Put this measure on its passage, and let it go down to the [annual] conferences and come back to you; and eight years from now there will be one or two women in the General Conference" (quoted in Shadron 1981: 267–268). The measure nevertheless lost by a vote of 74 to 188. Why? In direct response to Bennett, "George R. Stuart maintained that the woman's emancipation movement in all its dimensions aimed at the destruction of the home" (Shadron 1981: 268). Here, in Stuart's response, we begin to see the symbolic significance of the issue. Formal rights for women were resisted not because they would result in actual women having actual power in this denomination but because such rights were associated with a broader woman's movement.

Recent research on female clergy has documented the fact that, not surprisingly, formal rules asserting gender equality still do not necessarily produce real gender equality. In a 1983 study of clergy in nine denominations, Jackson Carroll, Barbara Hargrove, and Adair Lummis found that women were more likely to work part time, and they were much less likely than men to have jobs as sole or senior pastors.[6] When women do have jobs as sole or senior pastors, they are significantly more likely than men to have jobs in congregations that are small, located in rural areas, and whose finances are precarious. Female clergy also earn lower salaries than male clergy (Carroll, Hargrove, and Lummis 1983:129–131).

All of these inequalities persist in the 1990s. A 1992 study of the active female clergy in the San Francisco presbytery within the Presbyterian Church found that "women clergy do not have the choices, the mobility, the positions, or the pay of their male counterparts" (Prichard 1996:49; see also Mills 1995:6). A 1990 study of United Church of Christ (UCC) clergy found that, while women made up 18 percent of UCC clergy, they constituted "52% of associate pastors or ordained Christian education staff . . . 38% of clergy in counseling or health care ministries [and] 29% of chaplains or missionaries." While women are over-represented in these "second-tier" positions, they remain underrepresented among senior or solo pastors of UCC congregations, only 13 percent of whom were women in 1990 (Zikmund 1996:74). A 1995 national study of Presbyterian clergy found the same pattern: 71 percent of male clergy were solo or senior pastors while only 37 percent of female clergy held comparable positions. From another perspective, 16 percent of solo or senior pastorates are held by women, while a majority of all associate pastor positions (53 percent) are held by women (Bruce and Marcum 1995).

Paula Nesbitt (1993:13) found evidence of sex segregation in the career tracks of males and females within the Unitarian Universalist Association and within the Episcopal Church, segregation that "disproportionately concentrates male clergy in high-level positions." And within Reformed Judaism, although women and men obtain similar entry-level jobs, "as the years go by, women make less money, they're more likely to work part-time, and they're far less likely to move into large congregations" (Marder 1996:272). A 1994 study of clergy in fifteen Protestant denominations found that, on average, it takes female master of divinity graduates more than twice as long as it takes male graduates to land a first job in a congregation—225 days for women versus 104 days for men. This same study establishes that, as recently as 1994, women who work in full-time clergy jobs earn significantly less than their male counterparts, even when controlling for education, labor force experience, congregation size, and type of position (Zikmund, Lummis, and Chang 1997).

As negative as these patterns appear, it is likely that the research on female clergy understates the differences in real opportunities faced by male and female clergy because surveys of functioning clergy do not include individuals who have dropped out of the profession. All of the thirty female seminarians whom Joy Charlton interviewed in the late 1970s expected to work in congregations. When she recontacted these women fifteen years later, half were no longer in parish ministry "and a substantial number of the others report serious consideration of leaving" (Charlton 1995:12). The recent experience of a University of Chicago researcher who attempted to collect data from male and female Episcopal clergy is instructive. Female clergy responded to her mailed survey at a much lower rate than did male clergy. Following her mailing with a telephone conversation, she "learned that a large proportion of the female clergy are demoralized and discouraged; they did not fill out my questionnaire about their career paths because they do not see themselves as having real careers in the church" (Blair-Loy 1994).

It is difficult to be certain how much of these career differences between male and female clergy represent continued discrimination against women and how much they represent the consequences of choices by women who bear primary responsibility for child care and household maintenance and who are trying to manage both church work and household work. Surveys of lay people, however, still indicate substantial resistance to female clergy even within so-called liberal denominations. Although majorities of lay people in denominations that ordain women say they would themselves accept a woman minister in their congregation, they also are willing to discriminate against female clergy in order to satisfy the large minority who object to female clergy. Few members, moreover, are willing to support affirmative action policies for female ministers (Lehman 1987: 321).[7] In one survey of lay people within a denomination formally open to female clergy, for example, while 69 percent thought a woman would make as good a pastor as most ministers they know, 82 percent thought that influential members of their congregation would be opposed to calling a woman minister (Lehman 1981:106).[8]

Loose coupling is thus evident as well in denominations that formally allow female clergy: congregation-level reality does not match the "liberal" formal rules. This means, not incidentally, that focusing on the formal rules concerning women in denominations leads to an overdrawn picture of denominational differences. Differences in formal rules across denominations hide substantial similarities in practice. "Liberal" and "conservative" denominations are not as far apart when it comes to actual practice as their very different formal rules would lead us to expect. Such similarities in practice—in the real opportunities and barriers faced by women across the denominational spectrum—suggest that there is a common set of market forces operating among congregations. When congregations are unable to hire a male minister, perhaps because of an overall clergy shortage or an inability to pay a good salary, they will turn to women to do the job. Turning to women, however, does not necessarily translate into granting them full formal equality.

The key point is that the market forces governing when women fill the functional clergy role occur whether or not the denomination formally grants clergy rights to women. The granting of official rights does not directly reflect what is going on in the day-to-day operations of the organization. There is, in sum, only a loose coupling between the day-to-day operations and the formal rules. This loose coupling prompts the question: if the formal rules do not directly govern or reflect internal practice, then what role are they playing? Organizational theory suggests an answer: the rules signal conformity to relevant parts of a denomination's environment. To paraphrase John Meyer, Richard Scott, and Terrence Deal (1981:153), denominations seem to be organizations that, at least with respect to formal gender equality, turn their backs on the technical core of their day-to-day operations in order to conform to their institutional environments.

Consciousness of External Pressure

The basic logic of environmental pressure on organizations is this: when an organizational practice or structure becomes com-

monly understood as a defining feature of a "legitimate" organization of a certain type, organizational elites feel pressure to
institute that practice or structure. If there is a cultural norm that
says, "In order for an organization to be a *good* organization, it
must have characteristic X," organizations feel pressure to institute characteristic X. A basic argument of this book is that external pressure for women's ordination is of this sort. The previous one hundred years, in other words, have witnessed cultural
change that increasingly favors formal gender equality. Denominations have felt pressure to conform to this expectation.

A look at debates inside denominations over the issue of
women clergy makes it abundantly clear that, except in some of
the earliest instances of women's ordination, denominational
elites have experienced the pressure to ordain women as coming
predominantly from outside their denominations. Consciousness
of the external source of this normative pressure is evident in
official denominational reports on the subject of women's ordination and in more informal debates on the subject recorded
both in minutes of denominational meetings and in newspapers
and pamphlets. Individuals inside denominations have been and
continue to be very much aware of the ways in which rules
about women's ordination are developed in response to normative pressures emerging from a denomination's cultural environment.

Official reports on the subject very often begin by noting that
we live in a time of increased rights and responsibilities for
women and that this situation raises the issue of women's ordination for the church. A 1922 statement on women's ordination
issued by the Central Conference of American Rabbis, the representative rabbinical group of Reform Judaism, began, "The
very raising of this question ['Shall Women be Ordained Rabbis?'] is due, no doubt, to the great changes in the general position of women, brought about during the last half century or
so. Women have been admitted to other professions, formerly
practiced by men only, and have proven themselves successful"
(reprinted in Melton 1991:303). These rabbis were conscious of

the fact that they were discussing the question of female clergy primarily in response to developments outside their own denomination rather than in response to a movement of women who themselves wanted to be rabbis.

Consider also this 1970 report prepared by a subcommittee of the Commission on the Comprehensive Study of the Doctrine of the Ministry of the Lutheran Church in America:

> In order to place its report to the commission in proper perspective, the subcommittee on the Role of Women in the Life of the Church found it imperative to make three basic statements. One, the evidence is overwhelming that the effects and the implications for women of the world-wide revolution in the economic, political, and social structures of secular society are profound, pervasive, and immediate. . . The point has now been reached where a responsible church has no choice but to participate in the movement toward a greater freedom of thought and action for women. . . Here and there a lone woman appears ready to make a test case after she graduates from a theological seminary. Most of the evidence, however, seems to lead to the conclusion that women who wish to work for the church do not make a great point of insisting upon ordination. The crux of the matter is justice. (reprinted in Melton 1991:85, 93)

This example illustrates both sides of the argument about the importance of environmental pressure. On the one hand, it points to the strong external pressure, pressure that leaves "a responsible church [with] no choice but to participate in the movement toward a greater freedom for women." On the other hand, it explicitly notes the near absence of any real internal pressure, that pressure coming only in the form of the occasional "lone woman" who actually wants to be a minister. This is an organization conscious of the fact that it is responding much more to the expectations of the secular environment than to problems generated by its day-to-day operations.

These examples are from denominations that went on (eventually) to change their formal rules in favor of full clergy rights for women, but denominations that continue to restrict women's access to positions also invariably recognize the external pressure to do otherwise. The Prefatory Note of a 1916 Lutheran tract written to oppose female voting in congregations makes this point:

> Any one who takes the stand which is taken in this tract will find that he is unpopular. The emancipation of woman, sex equality, and all that is connected with these fundamental ideas have gone so far throughout the world that it seems impossible that there will soon be a turning back. Thoughtful men are dreading the feministic movement of our times . . . If the secular State for reasons of its own adopts woman suffrage, the Church for reasons of its own may decline the same. (Dau 1916:2)

Consider also the 1984 Southern Baptist resolution prohibiting female clergy:

> Therefore, be it *Resolved,* That we not decide concerns of Christian doctrine and practice by modern cultural, sociological, and ecclesiastical trends or by emotional factors; that we remind ourselves of the dearly bought Baptist principle of the final authority of Scripture in matters of faith and conduct; and that we encourage the service of women in all aspects of church life and work other than pastoral functions and leadership roles entailing ordination. (Melton 1991:236)

There is much to observe about this resolution. In the present context, however, the key element is that it forbids female clergy explicitly in opposition to "modern cultural, sociological, and ecclesiastical trends."

These examples are not atypical. Denominational debates and reports on the subject of women's ordination virtually always acknowledge the external pressure for gender equality. The difference between those that do ordain and those that do not is that, in the former, recognition of the normative pressure leads to the conclusion that they need to follow suit while, in the latter, recognizing the growing legitimacy of gender equality leads them to conclude, in effect, that they must resist. But virtually all acknowledge that the pressure to make the formal change is coming largely from the outside rather than being driven primarily by dynamics internal to the denominations. Whatever their differing responses to the issue, denominations have experienced external pressure to ordain women.[9] The combination of loose coupling, on the one hand, and consciousness of the external sources of the pressure to ordain women, on the other hand, strongly supports the basic idea that a denomination's formal policy permitting female clergy should be understood in large part as a symbolic marker signaling orientation to, support of, and cooperation with a broader norm for gender equality. Similarly, a denomination's formal policy against female clergy should be understood as a symbol of resistance to this norm of formal gender equality.

At the same time, this combination of loose coupling and consciousness of external pressure should not be taken to mean that formal, national rules have no consequences for internal practice. Changing the formal rules to permit female clergy certainly has organizational consequences beyond symbolic display to the environment. Denominations that already ordained women by 1970, for example, experienced larger increases in female seminary enrollment than did denominations that did not yet grant full clergy rights to women. As a result, the functional clergy role may be feminizing in these denominations faster than in denominations that withhold formal status from women.

Perhaps more important, the presence of a formal rule permitting female clergy provides an organizational opening for those who advocate a deeper institutionalization of gender equality within the organization. For example, within the United Presbyterian Church, a denomination that had ordained women since 1956, the 1970s saw the creation of new denominational organizations (for example, the Council on Women and the Church) that "gave priority to assisting women in their preparation for and placement in pastorates" (Boyd and Brackenridge 1992:294). This kind of development was widespread in the 1970s and 1980s. In denominations that already have formal equality, efforts at internal change can thus concentrate on establishing and implementing a variety of equal-opportunity programs and policies rather than on forcing changes in formal rules. The administrative infrastructure of the denomination, such as clergy placement services, can then be used to extend gender equality. In this way, officially permitting female clergy channels conflicts over gender equality in particular directions, not unlike the ways that legal rules channel broader collective action into certain standard forms of organization and tactics (McCarthy, Britt, and Wolfson 1991).

The same is true for national rules prohibiting female clergy. Such rules can be used to legitimate local attacks on functioning female clergy, perhaps when such women are perceived as too successful or too directly competitive with males for available jobs. After the African Methodist Episcopal Church voted in 1884 to forbid pastorates to women, one female pastor was pressured to return the thirty-five dollars her local conference had given her the previous year. Another functioning female minister in this denomination "did not receive a pastoral charge after 1885" (Angell 1996:101–104). Formal rules granting full equality matter, but they matter more because they define and present opportunities for legitimate social action inside the organization than because they straightforwardly govern or reflect internal practice. As we have begun to see, the formal rules themselves reflect external pressure more than internal practice.

There is much more to say about the sources of external pressure toward gender equality in general and women's ordination in particular. Some of these sources, such as the secular women's movement, are easy to identify. Others, such as the influence that denominations exert on one another, are less obvious. The next three chapters examine the various sources of pressure to institutionalize—or to resist—gender equality within American religion.

·. 3 .·

EXTERNAL
PRESSURES

If rules about women clergy are best understood as reactions to environmental pressure to institutionalize, or resist, gender equality, then it should be possible to specify the sources of that pressure. It is useful to distinguish between two sorts of external pressure on denominations. On the one hand, there is pressure emanating from outside the religious sphere altogether, pressure that is pushing mainly in the direction of greater gender equality in religious organizations. Included here is pressure coming from the state and pressure coming from an organized women's movement. Also included is the more subtle normative pressure stemming from the fact that support for formal gender equality has become increasingly widely diffused in American society during the twentieth century, and denominations have lagged considerably behind other types of organizations in institutionalizing it. These sources of pressure are of varying importance to the institutionalization of formal gender equality in American religion.

On the other hand, there is pressure coming from within the religious sphere itself but external to any particular denomination. I refer here to the fact that denominations influence one another in their decisions about women's ordination. Although pressures from outside the religious sphere push denominations mainly in the direction of gender equality, ecumenical pressures can go either way, depending on the part of the religious institutional environment to which denominations are most oriented. Denominational alliances and the subcultures they support are therefore important sources of variation regarding women's ordination. In this chapter, I will discuss the way that interdenominational alliances influence policies concerning female clergy. In Chapter 5, I will discuss the particular significance of denominational embeddedness in either the biblically inerrant or the sacramentalist worlds.

In an important sense, it is impossible to draw a clear line between "internal" and "external" influences on women's ordination. Although I will argue that the women's movement, for example, is a source of "external" pressure on denominations, it exercises this pressure largely through women and men inside denominations who, influenced by the outside movement, advocate, either individually or collectively, greater equality within religious organizations. Similarly, although I will argue that ecumenical concerns represent another sort of "external" pressure, that pressure exists only to the extent that people inside a denomination care about their relations with other denominations. What these forces have in common, then, is not that they are wholly "external" to denominations. Rather, they all concern, in one way or another, denominations' interactions with their environments. Labeling these forces "external" is perhaps best understood as a shorthand way to call attention to the extensive interplay between what goes on inside religious organizations and what is happening outside.

The crux of the argument is this. Virtually all denominations have experienced broad external pressure to institute gender equality, pressure coming both from the women's movement and from the increasing legitimacy of gender equality in American society. At the same time, structural and cultural boundaries have significantly shaped the way in which denominations have variously responded to this felt pressure. Denominations are embedded in different cultural environments, and these differences affect denominations' formal rules about women. Indeed—a point to which I will return—rules about women's ordination have become one of the primary markers of a denomination's cultural location. For most denominations, the original impetus to ordain women came via political and normative pressure rather than via pragmatic concerns stemming from the organization's internal affairs. Some denominations welcomed this pressure toward formal gender equality; others resisted it. This chapter begins to explain those differences.

Pressures from outside the Denominational Field

THE STATE

Because of the state's authority to develop and enforce regulations stipulating various details of organizational structure and behavior, government action is often a crucially important influence on organizational policies, rules, and change. A common finding in research on organizational change is that organizations respond to state pressure in many ways. Neil Fligstein (1987) found that corporate merger behavior changed after the Celler-Kefauver Act of 1951. Stephen Mezias (1990) found that adoption of the "flow-through method" for reporting the investment tax credit among Fortune 200 firms increased substantially after 1964 legislation defined this accounting method as acceptable. Gerald Davis (1991:587) argued that the rate at which Fortune 500 companies adopted the "poison pill" method of guarding against hostile takeovers "leaped" after a key court case clarified ambiguity concerning the legality of the practice. These examples illustrate that the state, because of its capacity to regulate the environment in which organizations operate, exerts a powerful influence on the diffusion of various institutional practices across organizational populations.

Although a powerful actor in other organizational fields, the state plays almost no direct role in the case of women's ordination in the United States. Still, there are two ways that attending to the state helps to place women's ordination in a broader context. Focusing on the state helps to explain why formal gender equality has diffused so much more slowly among religious denominations than among other types of organizations in the United States, and it helps to explain certain features of cross-national variation in the timing of women's ordination.

In the United States, formal gender equality began at similar times within the fields of religion, medicine, and law. The first fully ordained woman was Antoinette Brown, ordained in 1853 (Zikmund 1981:206). Medical schools and law schools began to open their doors to women in the late 1860s (Bonner 1992:28; Morello 1986:44). The first woman sought certification from a state medical society in 1852, and in 1869 Iowa became the first state to admit women to the bar (Walsh 1977:xv; Weisberg 1977:486).

Despite the similarly timed origins of formal gender equality in these three fields, the diffusion of formal, if not actual, equality was much quicker in law and medicine than it was in religion. By 1972 every law school in the country admitted women on an equal basis with men. By 1944, 90 percent of U.S. medical schools admitted women, and the last holdout opened its doors to women in 1960 (McAnarney 1977:10). This complete diffusion of formal gender equality in law and medicine is not limited to professional education. As early as 1917, all but four states admitted women to the bar (Morello 1986:36). In the 1890s, only seven hospitals in the United States regularly accepted women to internship programs. In 1941, 15 percent of internship programs admitted women, up from 8 percent in 1921. Spurred by the demand for doctors created by World War II, almost 50 percent of internship programs admitted women by 1943 (Walsh 1977:221, 224, 233). By 1976 a female medical school graduate had "accessibility to virtually every [residency] program. In fact some specialties that were unenthusiastic about women ten years [earlier] actively seek her application" (McAnarney 1977:53). Within law and medicine, the basic story is one of near complete diffusion of formal gender equality by the last quarter of the twentieth century.

The picture within religion is much different. Even today only about half of U.S. denominations grant full formal equality to women. As noted by Robert Wuthnow (1988:228), this difference is largely attributable to the fact that, because of the First Amendment, law schools, medical schools, bar associations, and hospitals are all much more directly regulated by the state than are religious schools or organizations. Mary Roth Walsh (1977:271) comments, with respect to medical schools, that "affirmative action requirements accompanied by the threat of the loss of federal funds have proven to be a useful weapon in the drive to open more medical school places to women." Religious organizations are not subject to this same sort of regulation.

Institutional distance from the state is key to explaining why the diffusion of gender equality has been so slow among religious organizations. Indeed, it probably is a more important variable than differences either in the numbers of women seeking previously male roles or in the resistance of "clients" or "constituents" to female practitioners, neither of which may vary substantially across the three fields. Recall here the essential similarity of medicine, law, and religion when we compare the historical trends in the proportion of women who are doctors, lawyers, and clergy. Religious organizations, as a population, are slower than other types of organizations to institute formal gender equality because of their greater autonomy from the state. In American society, religious organizations' relative immunity from state regulation means that they are able to display their gender conservatism in ways that other organizations cannot.

A second way in which attending to the state helps to place women's ordination in a broader context involves cross-national variation. Nations vary, of course, in the extent to which governments regulate religious organizations within their borders, and this variation in state-church relations is among the key factors predicting early or late adoption of gender equality by religious organizations. More specifically, among Western liberal societies, religious organizations more institutionally tied to the state have tended to ordain women earlier than denominations not tied to the state. Governments have the power to legislate and enforce equal access to positions within religious organizations over which the state has direct authority.

State influence on women's ordination is clearest among Lutheran denominations. The state churches of Norway, Denmark, and Sweden all are Lutheran, and those churches are administratively part of the government in ways that other state churches (for example, the Church of England) are not. We would expect, therefore, that these Scandinavian Lutheran churches granted full clergy rights to women before Lutheran denominations in the United States. This is indeed the case. The Norwegian Parliament opened all state positions to women in 1938. By definition this included all positions in the state church, although "provision was made that a woman ought not be made pastor of a congregation unwilling to have a woman as pastor." In 1947, the Danish Parliament "removed any legal barrier to the ordination of women" despite the fact that only two of the nine bishops were in favor of the action (Lynch 1975:184). And in Sweden, as a result of "pressure . . . put on the Church Assembly by the government," women were first ordained in 1960 (Field-Bibb 1991:91; see also Stendahl 1985). By comparison, no U.S. Lutheran denomination ordained women before 1970. It seems that variation in state-denomination institutional ties affects the timing of this organizational change.[1]

The preceding paragraphs suggest that state action is important for understanding both cross-national and, within the United States, cross-sectoral variation in the institutionalization of formal gender equality. This book, however, is focused most directly on variation in gender equality among U.S. religious denominations—an organizational population relatively immune from state action. Consequently, external pressures more subtle than state regulatory action will be central to our story, and it is to these I now turn. Still, it is worth noting that the relative absence of state pressure has led U.S. religious organizations to behave differently both from U.S. organizations in other fields of activity and from religious organizations in other societies.

THE WOMEN'S MOVEMENT

Over the past 150 years, the women's movement has been a significant source of direct pressure in favor of women's ordination. The nineteenth-century women's movement explicitly and actively targeted religious denominations. Although the movement's broader agenda of social change became increasingly overshadowed by efforts to win the vote, opening the clergy to women was an early goal. For example, the announcement for the 1848 Seneca, New York, convention—a meeting widely considered the beginning of the movement—included religious rights among the agenda items:

> Woman's Rights Convention.—A Convention to discuss the social, civil, and religious condition and rights of woman, will be held in the Wesleyan Chapel, at Seneca Falls, N.Y., on Wednesday and Thursday, the 19th and 20th, of July, current; commencing at 10 o'clock A.M. (Stanton, Anthony, and Gage 1881:67)

And one of the twelve resolutions passed at the convention referred specifically to the church:

> Resolved, That the speedy success of our course depends upon the zealous and untiring efforts of both men and women, for the overthrow of the monopoly of the pulpit, and for the securing to women an equal participation with men in the various trades, professions, and commerce. (Stanton, Anthony, and Gage 1881:73)

Of the eleven sets of resolutions from state-level women's rights conventions published in the first volume of the history of women's suffrage edited by Elizabeth Cady Stanton, Susan B. Anthony, and Matilda Joslyn Gage (1881:808–855), six include resolutions calling for equal access of women to clergy status, and another three imply as much by calling for equal access to "the various civil and professional employments" (1881:821). Of the sixteen national meetings of the National American Woman Suffrage Association held between 1885 and 1900, the position of women in the churches received explicit attention during at least nine of them (Anthony and Harper 1902:58–359).

In addition to its organized aspects, the nineteenth-century women's movement influenced denominational policies on female clergy via another mechanism: it inspired small numbers of individual women to seek ordination. In a related development, the temperance movement inspired women to seek out pulpits from which to preach their message of reform. Numerous nineteenth-century debates over female clergy arose because an individual woman was permitted to speak about temperance during a worship service, or because an individual woman wanted to become ordained. In Chapter 6, I discuss the importance of internal organizational structure for determining the outcome of these early debates. Here the point is simply that nineteenth-century women's movements exerted pressure on denominations through the ambitions of individual women as well as through their more organized channels.

The movement goal of gender equity in religion continued to find organizational expression even after the first wave of mass mobilization had subsided. The interdenominational Association of Women Preachers, later the American Association of Women Ministers, was founded in 1919 and has published its newsletter, *The Woman's Pulpit (WP)*, continuously since that year. Although the initial purpose of the association was "to develop the spirit of fellowship among women who are preaching" (*WP* 1922(2):1), that goal soon was joined by another:

> The original purpose [of the Association] was to bring women who preach into fellowship with each other . . . Another purpose that developed as we planned and prayed was to secure equal opportunity for women in the ecclesiastical world. Our Association can honestly claim the obtaining of the license for women to preach in the Methodist Episcopal Church as a direct result of

> our work, and it is working toward some other things that will
> be revealed later. (*WP* 1923(4):3)

Early in its life, the association made advocating gender equality
in U.S. religious organizations one of its major purposes. It has
continued this work to the present day.

The Association of Women Preachers represents an organizational expression of the women's movement that is within the
institutional field of denominations yet outside any single denomination. Another similarly situated group was the Commission on the Life and Work of Women in the Church, a World
Council of Churches (WCC) commission formed in 1950 and
made into a permanent unit, the Department on Cooperation
of Men and Women in Church and Society, in 1954. Among
this department's mandates was "to encourage the churches to
accept the contributions of women 'to a fuller extent and
in more varied ways'" (Parvey 1985:143). This department
worked to raise awareness of the issue of gender equality among
the council's member denominations, mainly through the preparation and publication of three major reports (Bliss 1952; Bam
1971; Parvey 1983). According to Judith Hole and Ellen Levine
(1971:374), "As a result of the Council's work, over the years
many denominations have granted women the right to ordination." Whether or not the efforts of these interdenominational
organizations can be credited with actual changes in gender policies of denominations, it is clear that they carried the women's
movement's goal of gender equality directly into the organizational world of American religion. It also is clear, not incidentally, that they helped to keep that agenda alive between the two
major waves of the broader movement.

Second-wave feminism was, of course, much broader in its
goals and in its mobilizing than was the first wave of the women's
movement. It left untouched virtually no organizational field,
including religion. The National Organization for Women established an Ecumenical Task Force on Women and Religion
in 1967 (Hole and Levine 1971:390). In 1969 a women's caucus

was formed within the National Council of Churches (NCC) with the words:

> We begin our statement with an affirmation of support for the movement to liberate women in the United States . . . especially for [those who have] chosen to gather into the church . . . We will not be able to create a new church and a new society until and unless women are full participants. (quoted in Hole and Levine 1971:375)

Since then, groups devoted either to winning full clergy status for women or, in denominations that already grant full status, to advocating enhanced opportunities for female clergy, have formed inside many denominations (Wuthnow 1988:228–235).[2] The presence of such pressure groups has not been limited to the more "liberal" denominations. For example, the Evangelical Women's Caucus was organized in 1975, two years after a meeting of "influential" evangelicals "denounced the sin of ecclesiastical sexism" (Bendroth 1984:133). In addition to the formation of new women's groups, long-standing women's religious organizations, such as Church Women United, redirected their efforts toward movement goals during the 1970s (Hole and Levine 1971:393).

Second-wave feminism, unlike the movement's first wave, also helped to mobilize great numbers of women to pursue careers that previously had been closed to them. This development, of course, included but was by no means limited to the religious sphere (see Figure 2.1).

The point here is simple but important. Throughout the twentieth century, the women's movement—both through interdenominational organizations such as the WCC commission, the NCC caucus, and the Association of Women Ministers and through pressure groups forming inside denominations themselves—raised the issue of women's ordination in a way that was impossible for denominations to ignore. From its beginnings, the women's movement has attempted to influence the major institutions of society and has explicitly targeted churches as an organizational site for movement activity. Because of the pressure of this social movement, virtually every denomination has been forced to grapple with the question of full clergy rights for women, whether or not there were very many women inside the denomination who actually wanted to be clergy.

We would therefore expect that denominations were more likely to institutionalize formal gender equality during the two waves of the women's movement. At the same time, there is good reason to expect that second-wave feminism will have had a stronger effect on denominations than did the movement's first wave. Although the early phase of the nineteenth-century women's movement pursued broad goals, the movement became more narrowly focused on suffrage as time went on (Buechler 1990:90). More recent feminism, by contrast, has consistently maintained a far-reaching agenda of social change and, as noted, it has enjoyed greater levels of mass mobilization.

Close inspection of the dates at which denominations first instituted formal gender equality bears out these expectations. The proportion of U.S. denominations that ordained women jumped from only about 7 percent in 1890 to more than 25 percent in 1900. Nine denominations granted full clergy rights to women during the last two decades of the nineteenth century. Some of these nine were founded as national organizations in this period, and they instituted gender equality, at least in the form of the absence of any exclusionary rules based on gender, from their beginnings. This is true, for example, of the Church of God (Anderson)—founded in 1885—and the National Baptist Convention—founded in 1895. Others of these nine changed their rules during this period to explicitly allow women to be ordained, as did, for example, the Disciples of Christ (in 1888), the Church of the United Brethren in Christ (in 1889), the Wesleyan Methodist Church (in 1891), the Methodist Protestant Church (in 1892), and the African Methodist Episcopal Zion Church (in 1898).

Not until second-wave feminism was there another burst in which many denominations began to ordain women. Indeed, more denominations began to ordain women during the 1970s than during any other decade in the past 140 years.[3] No fewer than seven of the largest denominations in the United States began to ordain women during the 1970s, and all of these actions represent true rule changes in the direction of gender equality. The second most active decade in this regard was the 1890s. Six denominations began to ordain women during that ten-year period, three of these beginnings being organizational foundings.

These patterns indicate that denominations were more likely to change their rules in the direction of gender equality during both waves of the women's movement than during other periods. The organizational realities behind these numerical trends support this conclusion. As we saw in the previous chapter, denominational elites were very much aware of the pressure placed on them by the women's movement, and they often attempted to respond to that pressure. Indeed, some of the organizational changes toward gender equality that occurred between the two waves of the women's movement can also be attributed to events that were set in motion during the movement's first wave. These events sometimes took decades to work their way through denominational governance structures to become official policy. This theme will be taken up again in Chapter 6, when we focus on the importance of internal organizational structure to women's ordination.

Although virtually all denominations felt pressure toward gender equality emanating mainly from the women's movement, not all denominations, obviously, succumbed to that pressure. Even the restrictive rules of denominations that do not ordain women, however, can be understood as a response to the external pressure in favor of gender equality generated by the secular world. Even official policy statements *against* women's ordination cluster during the two waves of the women's movement. A 1984 study of Lutheran churches worldwide found that three-quarters (eleven out of sixteen) of those that had adopted an official policy prohibiting female clergy took that step during the 1970s (Maher 1984:14). In the face of a strong women's movement, some denominations have even imposed new restrictions on women's access to religious positions, erecting or reerecting barriers that had been down for decades. In 1880, when two women asked the General Conference of the Methodist Episcopal Church to allow them to be ordained, the Conference not only denied their request but also voted to prohibit women from receiving preacher's licenses, a practice that had been officially approved in this denomination since 1869 (Gifford 1987a:9). The Seventh-day Adventist Church acted similarly in 1975 (Lawson 1995). Denominational policy on women's ordination has clearly been influenced in large part by the presence of a broader women's movement. Even the reassertion of gender-exclusive policy has sometimes been in response to that effort.

THE INCREASING LEGITIMACY OF GENDER EQUALITY

Another source of pressure on denominations, the increasing legitimacy of gender equality, was present even during periods of relative quiescence for the organized women's movement. Increasing acceptance of gender equality in American society has been produced by several long-term social trends. Myra Ferree and Beth Hess (1994:2–9) point, among other factors, to the steadily increasing participation of women in both the labor force and higher education. In 1920, 27.4 percent of women were in the civilian labor force compared to 57.3 percent in 1991 (Ferree and Hess 1994:4). In 1900, women composed 35 percent of the undergraduate population and received 6 percent of doctorate degrees. In 1991, the comparable numbers were 55 percent and 37 percent (Ferree and Hess 1994:7).

There is substantial evidence that these changes in what women were doing were accompanied by changes in values and attitudes about gender equality. James A. Davis tracked public opinion trends from the early 1970s to the late 1980s. He found that "the net trends were distinctly positive [that is, in the liberal direction] for race, free speech, and sex/gender" (Davis 1992:

266). In the early 1970s, 62 percent of American adults disagreed with the statement, "Women should take care of running their homes and leave running the country up to men." Seventy-four percent of respondents said they would vote for a woman for President if she were nominated by their party and were qualified for the job, and 65 percent approved of a married woman's earning money in business or industry even if she had a husband capable of supporting her (Davis 1992:297). The comparable figures in the early 1990s were 83, 89, and 79 percent, respectively.[4]

This liberalizing trend is not unique to recent decades. Popular opinion already supported gender equality to a large extent by the early 1970s. Tom Smith used data from over a dozen different survey organizations to document trends in public opinion between 1945 and 1987. Trends were most strongly in the "liberal" direction "on such topics as race relations and women's rights that concerned equal rights for all" (Smith 1990:502).

Available survey evidence thus strongly supports the idea that gender equality has become increasingly normative in American society since World War II. Although we do not have reliable survey data before that time, recall that the social trends underlying these changes in attitude—increasing numbers of women in the work force and in higher education—began in the late nineteenth century. It is likely, then, that the norm of gender equality started to become increasingly accepted in the United States in the latter part of the nineteenth century. The two waves of the women's movement certainly hastened the diffusion of a norm of gender equality, but the underlying social trends pushed that diffusion along even during periods of relative inactivity for the organized movement.

As described earlier, this norm of gender equality has been increasingly institutionalized in formal organizational policies, although it has been more quickly institutionalized in organizations more directly influenced by the state. The relative distance of American religious organizations from the state means that denominations have lagged behind other types of organizations in instituting formal gender equality. This situation creates another source of normative pressure for denominations.

Organizational theorists have pointed out that the pressure for an organization to adopt a practice increases as more and more organizations in the relevant environment adopt the practice. As an organizational practice becomes more widely diffused, its legitimacy increases, and it becomes more and more difficult to resist as individuals come to believe that a "good" organization will, almost by definition, incorporate that feature. This phenomenon has been observed in the spread of civil service reform among cities (Tolbert and Zucker 1983) and in the spread of the multidivisional form among corporations (Fligstein 1987).

Perhaps as early as the 1920s, and certainly by the 1950s, it was clear that, with respect to formal gender equality, religious organizations were lagging behind organizations that educated, controlled, or employed other types of professionals. The *Woman's Pulpit* complained in 1923 ([4]3) that "no calling has offered so little to women in the way of recognition for the same amount of ability and preparation as has the ministry." In 1932 ([2]2), it observed that, in a *Good Housekeeping* article on eminent women in twenty-two different fields, "theology was conspicuous by its absence." It seems likely that this lag produced extra indirect pressure on denominations to ordain women, pressure that would increase as the years went by, and pressure that contributed to the ubiquitous sense among denominational elites that the world around them was changing in ways that required a response.

Although the experience of external pressure toward ordaining women has been well nigh universal, denominational response to that pressure has been far from uniformly positive. Some denominations institutionalized gender equality very early, others later, still others not yet. This variation suggests that the direct political pressure of the women's movement and the indirect normative pressure of a climate in which gender equality is increasingly legitimate cannot fully explain observed patterns of diffusion and resistance to women's ordination. To do that, we need to attend to factors that variously influence denominations' official response to the external pressure that they all experienced.

Pressures from within the Denominational Field

This section, along with Chapter 5, focuses attention on the creation and maintenance of social boundaries within the denominational world. These boundaries define denominational subcultures that, in turn, influence the policies of any denomination. To focus on these subcultures, then, is to focus on influences external to any one denomination but inside the denominational sphere as a whole.

These denominational subcultures have two mutually reinforcing aspects. One is the web of interdenominational organizations—such as the National Council of Churches, the National Association of Evangelicals, and so on—through which subsets of the denominational world interact and mutually influence one another. We can think of this as the structural aspect of boundaries within the denominational population. The fact that denominations become members of some interdenominational organizations and avoid becoming members of others creates a pattern, or structure, in the communication and influence networks in which denominations are embedded. A denomination's position in that network structure constitutes an important influence on how early it ordained women, if it ordains women at all.

The cultural aspect of boundaries within the denominational world is also very important in shaping policies about female clergy. Symbolic boundaries separate denominations from one another. These symbolic boundaries are clearly related to the network ties formed via memberships in interdenominational organizations. Denominations join some organizations and avoid others partly because they perceive themselves as culturally similar to some groups of denominations and culturally different from others. But cultural boundaries are not reducible to network ties. Cultural boundaries within the denominational world, in other words, are partially independent of the direct structural links that denominations may or may not share as a result of common patterns of membership in interdenominational organizations.

With respect to the issue of gender equality, the most important symbolic boundaries within the denominational world are the boundaries that distinguish biblically inerrant denominations on the one hand and that distinguish sacramentalist denominations on the other hand. Chapter 5 will explore the significance of these boundaries for women's ordination. Here I focus on the structural aspect of denominational connections to one another.

INTERDENOMINATIONAL NETWORKS

At least since James Coleman and his colleagues' (1957) classic study of the diffusion of tetracycline prescribing through communities of physicians, sociologists have investigated the ways in which social structure affects the diffusion of various practices among individuals. More recently, sociologists have begun to study how interorganizational network structure influences the diffusion of organizational practices. Davis (1991), in a study mentioned earlier, found that having ties to prior adopters of the "poison pill"—a shareholder rights plan that makes hostile takeover more difficult by increasing the costs an acquiring company would have to pay—increases the rate at which a Fortune 500 company will itself swallow the pill. Pamela Haunschild (1993: 564) studied merger and acquisition behavior among U.S. firms. She found that "firm managers are imitating the acquisition activities of those other firms to which they are tied through directorships." The basic idea is that organizational action is influenced by other organizations in the environment. Not all organizations, however, have equal influence; rather, organizations are influenced more by those with which they have direct social ties.

It is clear from debates over the issue of women's ordination that denominations are both aware of and not indifferent to the practices of other denominations when it comes to women's ordination. But denominations are not equally aware of all other denominations. Rather, they appear to be most influenced by the behavior of denominations to which they are most closely tied via common membership in interdenominational organizations or via discussions of a possible future merger.

There are two ways to see this kind of network effect in action. First, there is the common practice of reviewing the policies of others when a denomination is considering the question of women's ordination. In this regard, denominational reports on the issue often include a section devoted to whether or not other denominations ordain women. But these reviews do not equally weigh the policies of all other denominations; instead, they weigh more heavily, and sometimes even are limited to, denominations most closely linked to themselves. The Presbyterian Church in the U.S.A. compares itself explicitly only with other Presbyterian churches; a Lutheran Council report compares its member denominations' policies first with other Lutheran policies and then with non-Lutheran policies, but gives greater weight to the Lutheran comparisons; the Episcopal Church considers the practices of the Roman Catholic and Orthodox churches more relevant than the practices of other denominations.

In addition to the common practice of denominations' investigating how other organizations handle women's ordination—that is, in addition to the attempt to see what the environment considers legitimate practice—there also are the occasional direct attempts by denominations or interdenominational organizations to influence other denominations on this issue. This practice constitutes a second, more direct, manifestation of the general phenomenon by which denominations may influence one another's policies on female clergy. After the Christian Reformed Church (CRC) voted to ordain women in 1990, for example, the North American Presbyterian and Reformed Council (NAPARC), an interdenominational organization made up of six denominations, wrote to the CRC:

> In harmony with the stated "purpose and function" of the NAPARC to "exercise mutual concern in the perpetuation, retention, and propagation of the Reformed Faith['] (Constitution III:3), the North American Presbyterian and Reformed Council calls upon The Christian Reformed Church to reverse the action of the 1990 Synod leading to the opening of the offices of minister and ruling elder to women. (Christian Reformed Church 1991:533)

The Christian Reformed Church received similar communications from the Reformed Church in New Zealand and from the Christian Reformed Churches in the Netherlands. The latter considered the 1990 decision to ordain women "so serious it may jeopardize our ecclesiastical fellowship" (Christian Reformed Church 1991:170). The Orthodox Presbyterian Church wrote to say that, "In all candor, your handling of this matter may affect our relationship with you in the future" (Christian Reformed Church 1991:218).

In 1992 the Christian Reformed Church in fact reversed its 1990 decision to ordain women. External pressure to do so certainly was not the only reason, and perhaps it was not the most significant reason. But that external pressure was present, and it was noticeable. At the very least, such direct efforts to influence a denomination reinforce that denomination's perception of what others expect from its policies about women.

Another example of this sort is drawn from among the many instances of Roman Catholic spokesmen pointing out to other denominations the negative consequences for future union if a denomination were to ordain women. This passage is from the Roman Catholic cardinal Basil Hume's 1978 address to the General Synod of the Church of England, a synod at which the ordination of women was debated:

> There is an ancient practice in the Church of God whereby the faith and its formulation, tradition and ministries are matters to

be decided in consultation with other local Churches. Now that our dialogue is progressing and we move in the direction of closer collaboration on the basis of mutual communion between the Churches, it would—to take an important example—be a matter for deep concern were the Anglican Communion to proceed further with the ordination of women without taking very seriously the position of the Roman Catholic Church, our brothers of the Orthodox Church and of the Old Catholic Church regarding so momentous a change. (quoted in Field-Bibb 1991:139)

Note the similar pattern of argument in both the communications to the Christian Reformed Church and the cardinal's address to the Anglican Synod: if your denomination grants full equality to women, it will threaten your close association with us. Here we begin to glimpse the significance of formal rules about women. These rules function as symbolic markers of membership in and loyalty to one denominational subculture or the other.

Explicit attempts from the outside to influence denominations by raising the ecumenical consequences of women's ordination are paralleled by the use of such arguments in internal debates on the subject. Accounts of denominational debates over women's ordination are filled with such references. Lists of reasons against ordaining women very often include ecumenical considerations, as in this 1920 "Report on the Official Relation of Women in the Church" produced within the Presbyterian Church in the U.S.A. by a Special Committee on the Official Relation of Women in the Church:

Among the arguments advanced by those opposed to any change in the present usage of the Church, in addition to the Scriptural, are these: That woman's sphere is the home. That her family duties would interfere with her functions as minister and elder. That her ordination would result in lowering the dignity of the office. That it would afford an excuse for men to shirk *their* duties. That it would retard, and perhaps defeat the hoped for union of the Presbyterian Church in the U.S.A. with other Presbyterian bodies; that it would keep men away from the Church; that it would lend countenance to and accelerate a dangerous feministic movement. (reproduced in Melton 1991:180–181, emphasis in original)

This is a typical catalogue of reasons offered for not ordaining women. One of the interesting aspects of such lists is that the contents by and large do not vary much either among denominations or across the decades. Essentially similar reasons are offered for and against ordaining women in 1990 as were offered in 1890. The point I wish to emphasize here is that ecumenical considerations are often among the reasons.

The direction in which ecumenical considerations seem to push, however, varies both over time and across denominations. The handling of the issue in a 1970 report prepared by the interdenominational Lutheran Council in the U.S.A. is instructive. After reviewing the practices of Lutheran denominations around the world, the document contains a section called "What Will Others Think?," which examines the practices of non-Lutheran denominations. This section of the report concludes:

> The ecumenical factor should not be given undue weight, though, in the decision. When Swedish Lutherans decided to go ahead with the ordination of women, there were fears it would hurt their relations with the Church of England, but it hasn't . . .
>
> The greater ecumenical problems for Lutherans in this regard may be intra-Lutheran rather than inter-denominational . . .
>
> Since arguments neither for nor against ordination are conclusive, a variety of practices is permissible within a common confession . . . A decision by one church to ordain them, while another chooses not to do so, should not endanger their fraternal relationships. (reproduced in Melton 1991:172)

Whereas Presbyterians in 1920 saw only negative ecumenical consequences of ordaining women, Lutherans in 1970 faced a more complex world with more ambiguous ecumenical meanings attached to gender equality.

It is not the case, however, that all denominations uniformly experienced the interdenominational environment as one that shifted increasingly in the direction of encouraging women's ordination, as the Christian Reformed Church example shows. Another example, this one from the U.S. Episcopal Church, illustrates the same phenomenon. A 1972 report of a Special Committee of the House of Bishops on the ordination of women closes by noting that "the ecumenical issues implicit in the main question are of significance." Though acknowledging that an increasing number of churches grant full gender equality, the report goes on to say:

> Yet those churches [in which all ministerial orders are open to women] together do not number nearly as many Christians as those in the Roman Catholic and Orthodox Churches; and it would be reckless to imagine any swift change in Roman Catholic discipline, and probably even more so with respect to Orthodoxy . . . We agree that it would be idle to say that a decision to ordain women as priests or Bishops would make no difference in our ecumenical engagements. (reproduced in Melton 1991: 58–59)

Unlike the Lutheran Council's perception of its 1970s environment, the relevant denominational environment of the 1970s Episcopal Church, like the 1990s environment of the Christian Reformed Church, seemed more unambiguously hostile to women's ordination.

In sum, denominations engage in a kind of structured watching and influencing of one another. The direction of this influence, however, varies substantially depending on a denomination's position in the interdenominational network—depending on whom it turns to for purposes of comparison. The social structure of the denominational population—the patterned connections indicating which denominations are more closely tied to which other denominations—will therefore affect denominations' formal policies on women. If rules about women clergy are largely symbolic display to relevant environments, and denominations are embedded in denominational environments that send different signals on this issue, then identifying a denomination's position in the overall denominational world should help to explain its relative openness or resistance to ordaining women.

In addition to the qualitative support for this argument already described—evidence from internal discussions that denominations do, indeed, differentially weigh the practices of denominations to which they are differently connected—a quantitative exploration of this hypothesis is also possible. One of the great advantages of the event-history technique described in Chapter 1 is that it permits the incorporation of time-varying information into the analysis. In the case at hand, for example, the logic of the argument implies that a denomination's connections to other denominations *and* those other denominations' practices concerning female clergy will together influence policies. But both a denomination's connections to other denominations and those other denominations' policies concerning women's ordination change over time. Event-history analysis allows us to see whether or not a denomination's policies on women's ordination are influenced by changes in the network and by changes in the practices of denominations within the network.

To investigate this, denominational networks were defined by comembership in interdenominational organizations, such as the National Council of Churches or NAPARC. These data were developed as follows. First, existing interdenominational organizations were identified at ten-year intervals beginning in 1915, yielding forty-six organizations. Second, attempts were made to identify the denominations that belonged to each interdenominational organization for each year ending in a five that the interdenominational organization existed. Such information was available for thirty-four of the interdenominational organizations, and it is these thirty-four organizations that constitute the network. Third, this organizational membership information, together with knowledge about when each denomination began to ordain women, was used to calculate, for each denomination in each year, what proportion of that denomination's interorganizational ties were to denominations that had already begun to ordain women.

The results of this analysis paint the same picture as did the qualitative evidence: the more a denomination was connected to denominations that already ordained women, the higher the probability that it would begin to ordain women itself in a given year. To get a sense of the magnitude of this network effect, consider the results for a given year, 1950. In 1950, if we ignored network connections and randomly selected a denomination from the set of denominations that did not yet ordain women, the odds against that denomination's beginning to ordain women in that year were about 130 to 1. Those odds vary quite substantially, however, depending on the denomination's network position. If we picked a denomination that did not yet ordain women but for which 100 percent of its network ties—denominations with which it has formal relations in interdenominational organizations—were to denominations that already ordained women, the odds against that denomination's beginning to ordain in 1950 drop to about 25 to 1. If that denomination had only 50 percent of its ties to denominations that already ordained women, the odds increase to about 75 to 1. If none of a denomination's ties were to denominations already ordaining women, the odds against doing it that year leap to about 220 to 1. The magnitude of this effect is not reduced when other variables are controlled.[5]

The results here are straightforward: denominations are influenced by the particular denominational environments in which they are embedded. Those environments do not completely determine a denomination's action, to be sure. Even a denomination completely embedded in an environment in which no other group ordains women still has some chance of itself ordaining women. But such a denomination has a much reduced chance of ordaining women, because it would have to do so by fighting against the expectations of its immediate organizational environment.

It would be a mistake to leave the impression that the influence of denominational networks on women's ordination is a one-way street. Concrete interdenominational networks reflect, as well as cause, commonalities across denominations. Whether or not to ordain women is not just a policy decision on which denominations look to their networks for guidance. It also is one of the policy decisions that denominations use to construct their networks and alliances. When interdenominational influence fails to affect a denomination's policy on women's ordination, ecumenical floundering often follows.

The American Lutheran Church's (ALC) 1970 ordination of women, for example, provoked an immediate negative response from the Lutheran Church–Missouri Synod, with whom the ALC was engaged in ecumenical dialogue and negotiation. Eight resolutions, "some insisting that the state of fellowship with the ALC be terminated," were submitted to the Missouri Synod's 1971 convention, which expressed its "strong regret" over the ALC's action and "voted to ask the ALC to reconsider its decision." Instead, the ALC reaffirmed its decision in 1972. Friendly relations between these two denominations did not survive such disagreement over women's ordination, among other issues. In 1981 the Missouri Synod's "state of fellowship" with the ALC, "under official protest since 1977 because of the ALC's decision to ordain women, was finally broken" (Todd 1996:269, 270, 283).

This chapter has emphasized how denominational subcultures, once they exist, influence the policies of a particular denomination. But fully understanding the relationship between women's ordination and denominational subcultures requires attending more closely to the construction of denominational subcultural boundaries and how women's ordination is implicated in that construction. Chapter 5 examines the two most important denominational subcultures regarding policies about female clergy—the world of biblical inerrancy and the world of sacramentalism—in order to show that resisting women's ordination has come to be a prominent marker of the boundaries separating these denominational worlds from the "liberal" world.

The next chapter, however, returns to the influence of the women's movement on women's ordination by examining what is perhaps the most important of those influences: the way in which the women's movement transformed the meaning of women's ordination into an issue of gender equality.

ᷓ · 4 · ᷓ

THE CHANGING
MEANING OF
WOMEN'S
ORDINATION

Conflicts over female preaching and women's ordination have occurred in American religion since long before the rise of the secular women's movement in the middle of the nineteenth century. Since the beginning of the nineteenth century, there have been three constellations of such conflicts (see Figure 4.1).[1] Two of these constellations—one in the 1880s and one in the 1970s—align temporally with the two waves of intense activity connected to the women's movement. The earliest constellation, in the 1830s, was produced by the intense religious activity associated with the Second Great Awakening. Historians have long noted that women were actively involved in a wide range of religious activity during this period, including preaching (see Billington 1993), and Figure 4.1 shows that this activity generated conflict. Of particular interest here, however, is that the 1830s conflicts were understood by participants quite differently than were most of the conflicts of the 1880s and later. Even though earlier and later conflicts all were, and are, over the same concrete issue—whether or not women would be recognized as legitimate religious leaders—post-1870 conflicts were more

Figure 4.1 Frequency of conflicts over formal female access to religious positions (each X = one conflict)

likely to be understood as conflicts over a principle of gender equality. This chapter documents this changed meaning of women's ordination and seeks to explain why it occurred.

Students of collective action have recognized that social movements do more than mobilize material resources, analyze political opportunities, and strategize about how to wring concessions from their targets. Movements also provide new interpretations of practices—new frames (Snow et al. 1986). When organizations come into contact with social movements, therefore, we may expect that organizational actors will be more likely to understand internal practices in movement terms, and this will be true even if the practices themselves, and conflicts over those practices, are not new. This seems to have occurred with the cause of women's ordination, to which the secular women's movement lent its gender equality frame. Although it may be difficult for late twentieth-century observers to think of conflict over women's ordination as an issue of anything other than basic gender equality, that fusion of practice and idea is a cultural achievement, and it is an achievement of the liberal wing of the nineteenth-century women's movement.[2]

Establishing the Changing Meaning of Women's Ordination

Before the Civil War, proponents of female preaching almost always based their arguments more on the extraordinary abilities of the few women who wanted to preach or on the special religious sensibilities of women or on the practical need for effective workers for Christ than on the principle of gender equality. Catherine Brekus (1996b:39) summarizes the views of antebellum female preachers within Methodism by saying that "very few of these women ever demanded complete equality to men," and very few were involved with the women's rights movement. "Instead of demanding political or legal equality to men, [female preachers] continued to laud the virtues of female subordination."

As historians have argued in various ways, early to mid-nineteenth-century women's religious activity usually was justified in terms that did not undermine, at least not in the short term, the prevailing "Cult of True Womanhood" (Welter 1966). Preaching women of this era (and their advocates) did not tend to rest their arguments on a principle of gender equality, even while they were in fact expanding the arena of legitimate female activity.

Consider first the example of Sarah Osborn, a woman central to a Newport, Rhode Island, 1760s revival:

> They crowded her house for special meetings, where she read to them from selected books and the Scriptures, or gave them individual advice. Mrs. Osborn proceeded with great caution, insisting that all who attended her meetings had the permission of masters or parents, behaved in an orderly fashion and retired at a reasonable hour, but she was still unhappy with her role. "She trembled with fear that if she encouraged their meetings at home, it would be going beyond her sphere." She persevered in the work but remained anxious, "fearing to go beyond her line as a woman" and insisted that all formal preaching was undertaken by her minister. (Billington 1993:172)

Osborn was not atypical of New England preaching women of this era. Louis Billington (1993) reviews the self-defenses offered by late eighteenth- and early nineteenth-century female preachers, and he notes that all "emphasized both publicly and privately the overwhelming compulsion of their calling and yet the fear and dread which it produced in them" (176). Although the women described by Billington offered other justifications, especially biblical ones, for their activity, they apparently did not connect that activity to a principled concern for gender equality.

Writing in 1849, Jarena Lee, an African Methodist Episcopal (AME) preacher, justified her call in this way:

> For as unseemly as it may appear now-a-days for a woman to preach, it should be remembered that nothing is impossible with

God. And why should it be thought impossible, heterodox, or improper for a woman to preach? seeing the Savior died for the woman as well as for the man.

. . . If then, to preach the gospel, by the gift of heaven, comes by inspiration solely, is God straitened: must he take the man exclusively? May he not, did he not, and can he not inspire a female to preach the simple story . . . As for me, I am fully persuaded that the Lord called me to labor according to what I have received, in his vineyard. If he has not, how could he consistently bear testimony in favor of my poor labors, in awakening and converting sinners? . . . I firmly believe that I have sown seed, in the name of the Lord, which shall appear with its increase at the great day of accounts, when Christ shall come to make up his jewels. (reprinted in Ruether and Keller 1981:213–214)

Lee justified her call by pointing to the fruits of her labor and by emphasizing God's freedom to call whom God will. Although she offers an argument based on a sort of religious equality when she points out that "the Savior died for the woman as well as for the man," claiming that men and women are equal before God when it comes to access to salvation is not equivalent to claiming that men and women are equally deserving of access to occupational roles. Lee's defense of her own preaching does not invoke this latter notion of gender equality, something that was not atypical among nineteenth-century AME female preachers. Jualynne Dodson (1981:277) notes that these women indeed wanted to be fully included in their denomination. However, it was "not feminist claims for the rights of all women, but their sense of their own special call [that] led them to challenge male domination of the Church." These women wanted to preach, but they apparently did not see the struggle to be allowed to preach as part of a larger struggle for women's rights.

Phoebe Palmer, a Methodist evangelist of the 1840s and 1850s, offers another example. Anne Loveland (1993:48) points out that "Phoebe explicitly dissociated her viewpoint from the cause of 'Women's Rights' " even while she advocated women's right to preach. Palmer believed that "the proper sphere for most women was the home" and that preaching was something "a few exceptional women" might do. Loveland concludes, "Phoebe was not proposing 'a change in the social or domestic relation.' " For Palmer, there should be room in the church for the "few exceptional women," but her justification for female preaching is clearly not in terms of gender equality. Indeed, that frame is explicitly rejected.[3]

The manner in which the Church of the United Brethren in Christ handled the issue in this period is also instructive. This denomination began receiving requests to recognize female preachers in the 1840s (Will 1980). In 1859 the Upper Wabash Conference issued a female preacher the following letter of recommendation:

> Whereas, Sister Lydia Sexton is regarded among us as a Christian lady of useful gifts as a public speaker; and
> Whereas, She has been laboring among us in the gospel of Christ; therefore,
> Resolved, That we, the members of the Upper Wabash Annual Conference, of the church of the United Brethren in Christ, do hereby recommend her to the churches as a useful helper in the work of Christ. (Sexton [1882] 1987:403, reprinted in Will 1980:29)

The conference allowed her to preach because of her demonstrated talents and skills and because she thereby would be a "useful helper in the work of Christ." There is not a hint that this event was understood in terms of a broader concern for gender equality.[4] This is substantially different from how later conferences and denominations frame their decisions—both pro and con—about women clergy.

Many other examples can be cited. Sarah Righter, who began preaching in Brethren congregations in 1828, does not mention equal rights in her justification for female preaching (Brubaker 1986:164–165). "Even Maggie Newton Van Cott, who in 1869 was the first woman to be granted a measure of official recognition from the Methodist Episcopal Church . . . did not claim her right to preach by virtue of her equality with men before God. She was not concerned with women's equal rights but only with her call from God" (Gifford 1987a:7; Hardesty 1991:109). Hannah Reeves, who began preaching in the United States in 1831, did not seek equal rights, nor did her biographer, writing in 1870, include gender equality among his reasons for supporting female preaching (Brown [1870] 1987:11–12, 17–18, 317–321). Jocelyn Moody (1995) has reviewed the writings of several antebellum African-American preaching women. Several themes are prominent when these women discuss their preaching, including their sense of a direct and personal authorization by God and the precedent of biblical women who preached, but not, apparently, a universal norm of gender equality. And Harriet Livermore, who preached in the U.S. Congress four times between 1827 and 1843, "never defended women's equality on the grounds of 'natural' rights." Livermore "never showed the least bit of interest in feminist political activism," and her preaching was characterized by a "reluctance to proclaim women's full political, religious, and social equality on earth as well as in heaven" (Brekus 1996a:396, 399).

As the nineteenth century moved on, but especially after 1870, the issue of female clergy came to be more and more understood as an issue of gender equality. Again, several examples illustrate the contrast.

Louisa M. Woosley was ordained to the ministry of the Cumberland Presbyterian Church in 1889. She wrote her own defense of women's ordination, published in 1891. Woosley connected women's ordination to the basic equality of women and men. She also was conscious of the connection to broader social change regarding women's proper activity. In her own words:

> The women of today, with all their advancements, have much to do in order to establish their capacity to work on an equal plane with the man, and still to maintain with gentle dignity the bright lustre of their true womanly nature. It only remains for woman to take hold boldly of the rights of progress, and to guide

her destiny to the highest plane of success. (reproduced in Hudson 1990:225)

Or:

Great moral revolutions are shortly to transpire, and . . . good men and women will soon stand side by side in the defense of the gospel . . . Then let America's women press forward to higher attainments; for, if Christ is ever proclaimed universal King, it must be done by the united voices of men and women. (reproduced in Hudson 1990:226)

Mary Lin Hudson (1990:224–225) concludes that Woosley "believed in the equality of women with men." For her, Christ's redemption "allowed Christians to understand and practice equality between the sexes." In the 1880s and 1890s, then, women's ordination is defended not just in terms of biblical or spiritual warrant, though these arguments remain common. It also is increasingly defended in terms of the principle of gender equality and in terms of its connection to a larger movement for "advancement" and "progress."

Janet Riley (1989) reviewed debates over women's ordination within Disciples of Christ periodicals of the 1880s and 1890s. Advocates of women's ordination, in addition to the usual biblical justifications, also invoked the principle of gender equality. T. W. Caskey argued in 1892 that "when Bro. Briney proves his right to be pastor of the church at Knoxville, I will prove that the church had an equal right to call Sister Briney." An 1893 letter from "three girls aged 19" began, "I believe a church is at liberty to select the very best material it has for any sort of church work, whether spiritual or temporal without regard to a sex line" (quoted in Riley 1989:227, 229).

David Jones (1989) found among Disciples advocates of women's ordination the same link between gender equality and progress that Woosley articulated among Cumberland Presbyterians. "In an 1892 article in the *Christian Standard*," he writes, "Persis Christian demonstrates even more clearly this linking of the advance of civilization with the advance of women's rights in general. For her, the question of women preachers has become a matter of justice" (Jones 1989:209).

This same shift in rhetoric can be seen among conflicts over access of women to religious positions short of full clergy status. Within the Methodist Episcopal Church, South, for example, Belle Harris Bennett, president of the Woman's Home Mission Society in 1906, thought that the struggle to allow female representatives in church governing bodies represented "God's [hand] leading to awaken a great body of women in the South to the religious teaching of Christian scriptures concerning the essential equality of man and woman" (quoted in Shadron 1981: 266). Over time, more and more "southern Methodist women began to acknowledge the connection between their struggle in the church and the political woman's suffrage movement outside" (Shadron 1981:269). In 1928 the denomination's Woman's Missionary Council report stated:

> Until equal opportunity in industry, in public service, in the professions (especially the religious vocations . . .), is secured . . . there is a continuing need for united effort for woman by woman, which can best be directed through permanent organizations . . . When men and women have attained equality, both theoretical and actual, in church, state and society, then the day of the separate organization for women anywhere will be over. (reproduced in Shadron 1981:275)

By this point, in this denomination, the connection between female access to religious positions and a broader movement for equal rights has become about as explicit as can be.

B. T. Roberts, founder of the Free Methodist Church, provides another example. *Ordaining Women,* which he published in 1891, contains the usual biblical arguments in favor of women's ordination. Indeed, he wrote in his preface that he "purposely avoided all appeals to sentiment and to 'the spirit of the age,' and based [his] arguments mainly on the Word of God" (Roberts 1891:8). Still, it is notable that Roberts believed the Bible to promote the principle that women have an equal right with men to religious positions. Just as "the Church did, for ages, misinterpret the teachings of the Bible on the subject of slavery, so it may now fail to apprehend its teaching on the questions of woman's rights" (13). And "though Christianity has greatly ameliorated the condition of woman, it has not secured for her, even in the most enlightened nations, that equality which the Gospel inculcates" (16). Roberts concluded his treatise with six propositions, the first of which is this: "Man and woman were created equal, each possessing the same rights and privileges as the other" (158). This is the crux of the difference: although advocates of female clergy found biblical support for their position from early on, it became more and more common in the closing decades of the nineteenth century to express that support in terms of a principle of gender equality.

Other, more brief, examples may be cited. At the 1884 African Methodist Episcopal General Conference, the question of licensing women to preach was introduced by a bishop who asked the denomination "to give notice to all that we have risen to that height where sex is no barrier to the enjoyment of some of the privileges of the Gospel Ministry" (quoted in Angell 1996: 100). The 1893 United Brethren General Conference welcomed women delegates to a national church body by saying, "Since the world began, until now, it is not probable that in an ecclesiastical body of such functions and proportions as belong to this General Conference have women been recognized on an equality with their brethren" (quoted in Gorrell 1981:243). Within the Christian Methodist Episcopal Church (CME), advocates of equal access for women to lay positions open to men also used equal rights arguments. A "stirring speech in behalf of the rights of women" was made at the 1892 General Conference, and, in 1896, the bishops wrote that "the women of the CME Church . . . are very much discouraged and have about decided that the CME Church will never accord them equal rights with their brothers" (Lakey 1985:417–418). And a Josephine Butler, in 1892, wrote about "Woman's Place in the Church" in the *Magazine of Christian Literature*: "When the Church or the Churches, become more deeply humble; when they have realized even more than they do now, their desperate need of the help of woman *as man's equal, absolutely,* in her relation to spiritual things, they will grant the freedom we ask" (quoted in Zikmund 1981:195, emphasis in original).

By the middle of the twentieth century, this equal rights frame was ubiquitous in debates about women's ordination. In 1953 the Presbytery of Rochester petitioned the General Assembly of the Presbyterian Church in the U.S.A. to ordain women by saying, "Let us follow the spirit of our Master and no longer discriminate against any person because of sex." The 1956 General Assembly, in its approval of female ordination, included this justification:

> Whereas, there is an increasing cooperation between men and women in business, industry, government, professional life and the Church, whereby each makes room for the other to develop his or her special potentialities, and each recognizes the other as a partner on equal footing; . . .
> Whereas, the Reformed doctrinal view, as it pertains to the place of women in the Church, as well as the Reformed view of the ministry, set forth: . . . That it is proper to speak of equality of status for men and women in the Church and its ministry. (reproduced in Melton 1991:187–188)

A 1970 report prepared by a subcommittee of the Commission on the Comprehensive Study of the Doctrine of the Ministry of the Lutheran Church in America said this:

> Full recognition of the ministry of women in the "building up of the community of Christ" [is] based upon the following considerations: . . . Gifts, talents, abilities . . . are not differentiated according to sex. The differences are between individuals and not the sexes. Therefore, full equality must be extended to members of both sexes for the full development and exercise of whatever capacities they may possess. . . This is the basis for full equality of women in our society (politically, economically, socially) without negating the fact that they are women. This applies then

equally to the life and work of the church. (reproduced in Melton 1991:86)

And in 1973 this passage was part of a "Statement on Behalf of the Ordination of Women," signed by sixty bishops of the Episcopal Church:

> As has so frequently happened in the history of civilization, human societies have developed rules and traditions to enshrine the rights and responsibilities of a ruling or dominant segment of each age. In so doing, such rights have denied equal access to other segments of that time. Finally, and inevitably, the sense of justice prevails, and it becomes essential to see that all human rights are available to all human beings. . .
>
> So we affix our names as evidence of this conviction in favor of the ordination of women, in profound trust in divine guidance, to let this Church know that this issue of moral justice and theological justification must not rest until all have known equal treatment in their search for vocation. (Melton 1991:63)

These examples illustrate the point: this gender equality frame for conflicts over women's ordination, almost completely absent in the 1830s and becoming noticeable in the conflicts after the Civil War, is today the dominant way in which these conflicts are understood.[5]

Explaining the Changing Meaning of Women's Ordination

It seems clear that the meaning of these conflicts shifted in the late nineteenth century. The primary cause of this shift, I will argue, was that these conflicts were now occurring in the context of a social movement advocating gender equality as a goal. The gender equality frame was a women's movement frame that was brought into religious organizations and thereby changed the meaning of conflicts over women's ordination. Four different sorts of evidence support the idea that this shift in meaning was produced by the interaction of these organizations with the women's movement.

First, consider Sarah Grimké. She used the language of equality and rights in the 1830s, and is therefore an exception to the generalization that 1830s advocates of female clergy did not frame their arguments in a language of equal rights (Gifford 1987a:5). In 1838, for example, she published "Letters on the Equality of the Sexes and the Condition of Women," which included several passages concerning female access to public religious positions. One letter, part of a response to an 1837 attack by Massachusetts Congregationalist clergymen on public speaking by females, argued that Jesus taught that "men and women were *created equal;* they are both moral and accountable beings, and whatever is *right* for man to do, is *right* for woman" (reprinted in Rossi 1973:308, emphasis in original). Unlike most others promoting female preaching before the 1870s, Sarah Grimké connected this issue to the principle of gender equality.

Grimké understood this issue differently than did most of her contemporaries because she was closer to the center of the social and cultural milieu that would produce the nineteenth-century women's movement. Most early nineteenth-century preaching women were not close to this context. Billington (1993:169–170), who has studied early nineteenth-century preaching women in the Northeast, finds that "these women were overwhelmingly the daughters of small farmer-artisans, possessed a common school education, and had grown up in a small-scale Yankee Protestant world." Sarah Grimké and her sister, by contrast, were, by the 1830s, abolitionists active in the Garrisonian wing of the movement (Rossi 1973:282). It was in this milieu, and partly because of the Grimkés themselves, that a "feminism of equal rights" developed and was prominently applied to women in churches (Marilley 1995:chap. 2).

There are complexities and ambiguities surrounding the relationship between Garrison and a feminism of equal rights: To what extent was Garrison's support of gender equality a political maneuver to secure female support for his wing of the abolitionist movement? What is the relative importance of Quaker theology versus secular liberalism in the development of an equal rights ideology among Garrisonians? Whatever the answers to questions like these, it is clear that it was in this urban, educated, abolitionist milieu that the idea of equal rights for women came prominently together with the idea that women should be permitted access to official religious positions. Marilley (1995:31) comments, "The Grimkés assumed the burden of proving why women's rights constituted equal rights, an equation inspired partly by Garrison and partly by their determination to inform the ministers that it was inappropriate to put women in subordinate positions."

A second way to see the importance of the women's movement to the understanding of women's ordination as an issue of gender equality is to observe that, after the 1870s, individuals connected to the women's movement were prominent among those advocating women's ordination within denominations. Such individuals almost invariably advocated women's ordination in terms of gender equality. Examples abound: Anna Howard Shaw, denied ordination by the Methodist Episcopal Church in 1880 but later ordained by the Methodist Protestant Church, became president of the National American Woman Suffrage Association (NAWSA). Antoinette Brown, ordained in a Congregational church in 1853, married into the Blackwell clan (as did Lucy Stone) and participated in national meetings of the NAWSA (Anthony and Harper 1902:128). Olympia Brown, ordained a Universalist minister in 1863, was an active worker for women's rights (Hardesty 1991:104). Marcia M. Bassett Goodwin was one of the strongest advocates of women's ordination among the Disciples of Christ. "In 1869, she helped organize a woman's suffrage convention in Indianapolis; in 1872 she published a monthly suffrage column in the *American Housewife*" (Bailey 1979:200). Ann Allebach, ordained by the General Conference Mennonite Church in 1911, had moved from Green Lane, Pennsylvania, to New York City in 1893. She took courses at New York University, Columbia, and Union Theological Seminary, and she became active in the suffrage movement. Moreover, her "deep conviction about equal rights and obligations for each citizen involved her in many humanitarian organizations" (Cummings 1978:9). Late nineteenth-century Unitarian female ministers on the western frontier (that is, Iowa) were well connected to the broader women's movement and understood their access to ministry in terms of equal rights for women and men (Tucker 1990). Amanda Way was a licensed Methodist preacher from 1870 until 1880, when the Methodist Episcopal Church disallowed such licenses for women. She called the first Indiana women's rights convention (Hardesty 1991:109).

Similarly, during the movement's second wave the most prominent proponents of women's ordination were connected to and influenced by the secular women's movement. As a result, the equal rights frame for women's ordination became ubiquitous after 1970. Again, examples abound: the 1974 General Synod of the Reformed Church in America considered a report entitled "Feminism in the Church," which challenged the church "to commit itself to greater sensitivity to feminist issues" (Mulder 1989:234). A key event in the 1970s conflict over women's ordination within the Episcopal church was the 1970 Graymoor Conference, organized by women active in the Episcopal Peace Fellowship. This "conference had grown out of the secular women's movement" and included participants who were "young, militant feminists who felt peripherally connected to the church but very wounded by it" (Hiatt 1983:577).

The contemporary movement for women's ordination within the Roman Catholic Church also has clear ties to secular feminism. Mary Jo Weaver (1995:112–115) reports that the Women's Ordination Conference (WOC) had its origins in a 1974 meeting called by a Catholic laywoman "to ask whether the ordination question ought to be raised during International Women's Year." That meeting led to a much larger, national, conference at which "an equal rights perspective" was one of two dominant themes.[6] By 1978 the WOC "took a more consciously feminist approach," opposing the traditional view "on the basis of structural renewal and an interpretation of institutional sexism as sinful.''

These connections add further support to the basic thesis of this chapter: social proximity to the secular women's movement changes the meaning of women's ordination. Although conflicts over female preaching and women's ordination occur with or without a larger women's movement, conflicts that occur in the context of this larger movement are more likely to be understood as conflicts over the principle of gender equality.[7]

A third way to see the significance of the women's movement for the changed meaning of women's ordination is to note how often women's ordination comes to be connected not just to gender equality but to other developments regarding women. Not only do post-1870s conflicts more often use the language of gender equality, but this frame also tends to appear in conjunction with explicit acknowledgment of social change regarding women's roles and the women's movement as developments that require a response. Consider this 1920 resolution brought before the General Conference of the Methodist Episcopal Church:

> Whereas, Today the principle of equality of opportunity for women is being recognized in all fields of activity; and
> Whereas, This General Conference has gone on record as urging political equality for women . . .; therefore be it
> Resolved, That the General Conference approve ecclesiastical equality for women. (reproduced in Noll 1992:93-94)

Several examples described in Chapter 2 also illustrate this point.[8]

A fourth indicator that social distance from the women's movement is a key influence on the meaning of conflicts over female clergy is this: post-1880s conflicts that are *not* framed in terms of gender equality tend to occur in denominations, such as Pentecostal and Holiness denominations, whose populations are less urban, less educated, and more southern. That is, later conflicts that are not understood as conflicts over a principle of gender equality take place in contexts less influenced by the women's movement. In 1905, for example, Fannie McDowell Hunter published brief autobiographical statements from eight contemporary female preachers within the holiness movement of Texas, Alabama, Tennessee, and Kentucky. Despite the relatively late date and the fact that by this time the issue was commonly framed in terms of gender equality, none of these women discussed the issue in those terms, although Hunter herself did (Hunter [1905] 1985:62–93,96).

This correlation between distance from the women's movement and reluctance to understand female ministry in terms of gender equality is still evident today. Susan Kwilecki interviewed fifty-three Pentecostal clergywomen in the 1980s. She describes their activities like this:

> Very few supported themselves from clerical income alone. At the same time, the ministry was more than a sideline for the forty who devoted full-time to church work; the twenty-one who had founded or pastored churches single-handedly; the seventeen assistant or copastors; and the eleven full- or part-time travelling evangelists. And as church officers, all fifty-three had qualifications and duties that distinguish them from laypersons. (Kwilecki 1987:60)

Clearly these women were active clergy.

Yet very few of these women understood their activity, or the issue of female clergy, in terms of a principle of gender equality. One of these women, who had begun preaching against her husband's objections and who had "revived two dead congregations" and "began a third congregation in a tent," said this: "I just don't believe in [the women's liberation movement] . . . because the Bible says that man is the head of the house, and I just don't believe that a woman is equal to a man . . . When a woman puts herself out there ahead of a man, she's stepping out of the will of God" (quoted in Kwilecki 1987:57). Another told Kwilecki that her ministry had "nothing to do with woman's liberation" (65). The "overwhelming majority" of Kwilecki's respondents objected to gender-neutral language referring to God, and even the thirteen respondents who seemed consistently "egalitarian" in their thinking about female ministry "tempered egalitarian with patriarchal opinions" (59, 65).[9]

Rather than understanding their own activity in terms of gender equality, these 1980s Pentecostal preaching women primarily understood themselves in ways that are reminiscent of the early nineteenth-century defenses of female preaching described above. Kwilecki reports that "many clergywomen felt that in their personal calls, they had been given directly by God a public task and spiritual authority over men; but they were nonetheless bound by the scriptural rules for their sex . . . Like female Christian leaders in prefeminist eras, the subjects of this study generally claim the authority to minister on the basis of personal inspiration from God, which, they say, mitigates women's natural incapacity for leadership" (58, 66–67). These women understood their own activity as exceptional, not as an instance of a general principle of gender equality.

Elaine Lawless (1988) observed the same phenomenon among the Pentecostal women preachers and pastors that she interviewed. She summarized the point by saying that a Pentecostal female preacher or pastor "must work to make certain her independence and outspoken stance do not appear as a denial of the traditional female role as good wife and mother. Most especially in this vocation, her credibility must not be shaken by any suggestion that she is a feminist or that she is in any way a threat to the status quo or is making a statement about women's 'rights' " (Lawless 1988:68). The women she talked with "decry the feminist movement and deny that they have chosen a strong feminist stance against the dictums of their world" (66).

These contemporary preaching women illustrate this chapter's central point: the greater the social and cultural distance from the larger women's movement, the less likely it is that women's ordination will be understood in gender equality terms. Only a small minority of the Pentecostal women interviewed by Kwilecki had a college diploma and, while most had taken Bible courses, "only nine had degrees from Bible institutions or seminaries." Eighty-five percent lived in Florida or Georgia, and most were working- or lower-middle class (Kwilecki 1987:59–60). "Virtually every one" of the women Lawless interviewed was "born into a very poor family," and virtually all "were raised in rural counties in Missouri and grew up on farms or in very small towns in rural areas" (Lawless 1988:69). When the issue of female clergy arises in a context that is distant from—or hostile to—a larger movement for gender equality, that issue is less likely to be understood in those terms, even by female clergy themselves.

There is much more to say about the changing meaning of women's ordination. Two additional points are worth mentioning here. First, an increasingly salient gender equality norm generated conflict and change regarding women's ordination even between the women's movement's two waves of mass mobilization, and even in the absence of women who wanted to be ordained in any substantial numbers. In this context, the 1956 actions of the Presbyterian Church in the U.S.A. and the Methodist Church, mentioned in Chapter 1, become less mysterious. Recall that both of these denominations granted full clergy rights to women in 1956, well before there were more than a handful of either Presbyterian or Methodist women seeking full clergy status. Why, then, did they begin ordaining women when they did? Once women's ordination became fused with the principle of gender equality, denominations began to ordain women more to institutionalize formal gender equality than to permit or encourage women to become clergy. These rule changes—and others during the 1940s and 1950s—occurred because, by the middle of the twentieth century, permitting women's ordination meant promoting the principle of formal gender equality.

Second, the symbolic connection between women's ordination and gender equality was made at least as eagerly by opponents of women's ordination as it was by proponents of women's ordination, and it appears that recognizing this connection generates additional opposition to female clergy. This point is explored further in Chapter 7.

For now, however, the key point is that denominational policies about women's ordination carry a symbolic meaning well beyond their pragmatic consequences for religious organizations. Denominations not yet ordaining women after the policy comes to mean "gender equality" resist something more than actual females in pulpits and at altars. They resist modernity. More accurately, they resist a part of modernity in which the liberal agenda of elevating individual rights is of paramount importance. John Meyer, John Bolin, and George Thomas (1994:25) call this agenda the "Western cultural account," a central element of which is the notion that individuals have distinctive moral standing *qua individuals* and not as members of "natural" groups (for example, families, races, genders, classes) that possess certain "natural" rights and functions.

The next chapter develops this argument further by examining the connections between sacramentalism and biblical inerrancy, on the one hand, and women's ordination, on the other hand. These are the two denominational subcultures that resist women's ordination most strongly. As the next chapter will show, this resistance to women's ordination is part of a deeper struggle against the liberal modernity that is symbolized by full gender equality.

⤳ · 5 · ⤳

INERRANCY, SACRAMENTALISM, AND WOMEN'S ORDINATION

Two groups of denominations are particularly resistant to women's ordination: denominations practicing sacramental ritual and denominations endorsing biblical inerrancy. Sacramental denominations are those, including the Catholic, Episcopalian, Eastern Orthodox, and, to a lesser extent, Lutheran churches, in which the communion ritual is not merely a symbolic remembrance of a meal long ago; it actually changes bread and wine into body and blood.[1] Similarly, in more sacramental denominations, baptism is not merely a ritual joining of a group; it is an act that makes an individual acceptable to God and literally confers salvation. Biblically inerrant denominations are distinguished by an official assertion that, to take the Conservative Baptist Association as an example, the "Old and New Testaments are regarded as the divinely inspired Word of God and are therefore infallible and of supreme authority" (Jacquet 1989:54).

The resistance of these two types of denominations to women's ordination is clear. Sacramentalist denominations, such as the Roman Catholic Church and the several Eastern Orthodox denominations, and biblically inerrant denominations, such as the

Conservative Baptist Association, are prominent among denominations still not ordaining women today. Moreover, inerrantist and sacramentalist denominations that today do permit female clergy have tended to make this change much later than denominations that are neither sacramentalist nor inerrantist.

Of the eighteen largest sacramental denominations that have existed during the previous one hundred years, only four (22 percent) have to date begun to ordain women.[2] This level of resistance is far stronger than among nonsacramental denominations, 46 percent of whom began to ordain women over this period. Equally significant, the four sacramental denominations that began to ordain women—the Episcopal Church, the American Lutheran Church, the Lutheran Church in America, and the Evangelical Covenant Church—all did so rather late in the period. The Lutheran Church in America and the American Lutheran Church both granted full clergy rights to women in 1970; the Episcopal Church and the Evangelical Covenant Church both officially permitted female clergy only in 1976. The average year at which these four denominations began to ordain women is 1973, with none of them granting full clergy rights to women before 1970. Among nonsacramental denominations, the mean date for beginning to ordain women is 1918. Overall, the odds of a nonsacramental denomination that did not already ordain women beginning to do so in 1950 are about 100 to 1. The odds that a sacramental denomination would begin to ordain women in that year are about 410 to 1, indicating that nonsacramentalist denominations are more than four times as likely to begin to ordain women in a given year than are sacramentalist denominations.[3]

Biblically inerrant denominations are similarly resistant to formal gender equality. Only 28 percent of biblically inerrant denominations have ordained women since the 1850s, compared with 55 percent of denominations that do not hold the Bible to be inerrant. Among those inerrant denominations that have ordained women, the mean date at which they began is 1933, compared with a mean date of 1922 for noninerrant denominations. The Christian Reformed Church, a denomination that shifted its official position away from inerrancy only in 1972, permitted congregations to ordain women elders only in the 1990s. Overall, the odds against an inerrantist denomination's beginning to ordain women in 1950 are about 180 to 1, two and a half times the odds (about 70 to 1) against a noninerrantist denomination's beginning to ordain women in that year. Both sacramentalism and biblical inerrancy represent substantial pockets of resistance to formal gender equality in American religion.[4]

Furthermore, resistance to women's ordination in these denominations is often justified in terms of their sacramentalist or inerrantist identities. Most arguments against women's ordination appear across virtually all denominations: the Bible prohibits female clergy, women are not suitable for the role, congregations will not accept female clergy, women's ordination will threaten ecumenical relations, tradition requires an all-male clergy, and so on. When a denomination is officially inerrantist, however, the ubiquitous biblical argument against female clergy is far more salient than other arguments. When a denomination is sacramentalist, a peculiarly sacramentalist argument emerges to justify resistance to women's ordination. In both types of denominations, resistance to female clergy is understood as part of a denominational identity that encompasses, but is broader than, the issue of gender equality.

Among sacramental denominations, opponents of female clergy use a type of argument, sometimes called the iconic argument, that does not occur within less sacramental denominations. Its essence is the claim that the efficacy of the sacramental act of changing bread and wine into the body and blood of Christ requires an agent who resembles Christ, and maleness is an essential component of that representation. By this logic, it is literally impossible for a woman to be a priest; the sacrament, if performed by a female, would not be valid. The Roman Catholic 1976 *Declaration on the Question of the Admission of Women to the Ministerial Priesthood* contains the argument:

The Christian priesthood is therefore of a sacramental nature: the priest is a sign, the supernatural effectiveness of which comes from the ordination received, but a sign that must be perceptible and which the faithful must be able to recognize with ease. . . When Christ's role in the Eucharist is to be expressed sacramentally, there would not be this "natural resemblance" which must exist between Christ and his minister if the role of Christ were not taken by a man.

It is opportune to recall that problems of sacramental theology . . . cannot be solved except in the light of Revelation . . . Thus one must note the extent to which the Church is a society different from other societies, original in her nature and in her structures . . . For this reason one cannot see how it is possible to propose the admission of women to the priesthood in virtue of the equality of rights of the human person. (Sacred Congregation for the Doctrine of the Faith [1976] 1991:6, 8)

This argument is repeated in the two most recent papal statements on the question. In his June 1994 "Letter on Ordination and Women," Pope John Paul II essentially endorsed the 1976 declaration. His July 1995 "Letter to Women," a letter prompted by the United Nations World Conference of Women in Beijing, contains a particularly clear statement of the argument:

One can also appreciate that the presence of a certain diversity of roles is in no way prejudicial to women, provided that this diversity is not the result of an arbitrary imposition, but is rather an expression of what is specific to being male and female.

This issue also has a particular application within the church. If Christ—by his free and sovereign choice, clearly attested to by the Gospel and by the church's constant tradition—entrusted only to men the task of being an "icon" of his countenance as "shepherd" and "bridegroom" of the church through the exercise of the ministerial priesthood, this in no way detracts from the role of women . . . These role distinctions should not be viewed in accordance with the criteria of functionality typical in human societies. Rather they must be understood according to the particular criteria of the sacramental economy, i.e., the economy of "signs" which God freely chooses in order to become present in the midst of humanity. (John Paul II 1995)

Women cannot be priests, so the argument goes, not because of any lack of appropriate skill or ability, but because their femaleness makes it impossible for them to resemble Christ in the Eucharistic sacrament.

This argument also occurs in other sacramental denominations, and it occurs in less subtle forms. The 1988 "Conclusions of the Interorthodox Consultation on The Place of the Woman in the Orthodox Church and the Question of the Ordination of Women," for example, bases "the impossibility of the ordination of women" on, among other things, "the typological and iconic experience of worship [in which] Christ as the High Priest is presented to us appropriately and fittingly only by a male in the High Priestly image" ("Conclusions" [1988] 1989:396–397). Presiding Bishop John Maury Allin in 1977 announced his opposition to women's ordination in the Episcopal Church by saying:

> I have prayed to be open to any new understanding of either priesthood or human sexuality which may be given to me. Thus far my understanding of Christian priesthood, of the inter-relatedness of the Christian ministry, of New Testament imagery and symbolism, of the roles and interrelations of human sexuality prevent my believing that women can be priests *any more than they can become fathers or husbands* . . . I remain unconvinced that women can be priests. (Ward 1991:xxvii, emphasis added)

And at the November 1992 meeting of the National Conference of Catholic Bishops, Auxiliary Bishop Austin B. Vaughan of New York City said: "In the year 2000, 20,000, or 2,000,000 there will still be a Catholic church and it will still have an all-male clergy. *A woman priest is as impossible as for me to have a baby*" (Steinfels 1992:A13, emphasis added). Within sacramental denominations, then, resistance to women's ordination is often expressed in terms of that sacramentalism. An all-male clergy is not just a contingent fact about these denominations; it is bound up with their core sacramentalist identity.

An analogous point can be made about biblically inerrant denominations. Here the standard biblical argument against female clergy is not just one among several kinds of "evidence" offered by women's ordination opponents. It is the central argument, often to the exclusion of all other arguments. To illustrate, consider again the 1984 Southern Baptist resolution prohibiting female clergy. Chapter 2 reproduced the resolution's final paragraph in order to emphasize Southern Baptists' awareness of external pressure towards gender equality, pressure they felt called to resist. Here I reproduce more of the justification offered for forbidding female clergy:

> WHEREAS, We, the messengers to the Southern Baptist Convention . . . recognize the authority of Scripture in all matters of faith and practice . . . and
> . . .
> WHEREAS, The Scriptures attest to God's delegated order of authority (God the head of Christ, Christ the head of man, man the head of woman, man and woman dependent one upon the other to the glory of God) distinguishing the roles of men and women in public prayer and prophecy (I Cor. 11:2–5); and
> WHEREAS, The Scriptures teach that women are not in public worship to assume a role of authority over men lest confusion reign in the local church (I Cor. 14:33–36); and
> WHEREAS, While Paul commends women and men alike in other roles of ministry and service (Titus 2:1–10), he excludes women from pastoral leadership (I Tim. 2:12) to preserve a submission God requires because the man was first in creation and the woman was first in the Edenic fall (I Tim. 2:13ff.);
> . . .
> Therefore, be it *Resolved,* That we not decide concerns of Christian doctrine and practice by modern cultural, sociological, and ecclesiastical trends or by emotional factors; that we remind ourselves of the dearly bought Baptist principle of the final authority of Scripture in matters of faith and conduct; and that we en-

courage the service of women in all aspects of church life and work other than pastoral functions and leadership roles entailing ordination. (Melton 1991:236)

This resolution is a typical argument from the premise of biblical inerrancy to the conclusion "no female clergy." The intervening step is not the inability of women to represent Christ, as it is in sacramental denominations, but rather the biblically mandated submission of women to men. Such a justification relies on a logic of interpretation, in which biblical citations are an essential part, that is itself the core feature of denominations that self-identify as biblically inerrant. Resistance to women's ordination is here expressed in a way that makes it seem the inevitable implication of a core commitment to inerrancy.

That both sacramentalism and inerrancy are today strongly associated with resistance to women's ordination is beyond dispute. Less obvious than the fact of this association, however, are the reasons for it. Why are inerrancy and sacramentalism so deeply and so tightly connected to resistance to female clergy? My answer to this question extends the argument developed in the preceding three chapters concerning the symbolic significance of rules about women's ordination and the crucial importance of interactions between denominations and their environments. I will argue that, contrary to both the official ideology of these denominations and the popular understanding of them, resistance to women's ordination is not a necessary outcome of either biblical inerrancy or sacramentalism. The fusion of inerrancy and sacramentalism with resistance to women's ordination is more cultural achievement than logical necessity. The persuasiveness of the argument that inerrancy or sacramentalism implies "no women clergy" has been greatly enhanced by the construction of institutional environments within which that inference, which could easily go the other way, is taken to be not merely valid, but obvious. I will argue that this connection—between inerrancy and sacramentalism on the one hand and gender inequality on the other hand—has been forged, and continues to be renewed, in the effort to carve out and sustain religious worlds that are not liberal. To say this another way, a denomination's commitment to biblical inerrancy or to sacramentalism should be understood in the context of its commitment to a religious subculture defined largely by resistance to certain features of the liberal world, including the liberal commitment to gender equality. These denominations' strong resistance to women's ordination is part of their broader antiliberal identity.

This thesis—that official resistance to women's ordination is part of a broader resistance to liberal modernity—applies to both the inerrancy and the sacramentalist denominational subcultures. The details of the connection between denominational identity and women's ordination are different, however, for these two subgroups. For this reason, this chapter is divided into two sections, the first about inerrantist denominations and the second about sacramentalist denominations. The structure of the argument within each of these sections is the same. First, I will argue against the idea that resistance to female clergy is required by the internal logic of either inerrancy or sacramentalism. Both the Bible and sacramentalist ritual are in fact fundamentally ambiguous when it comes to issues of gender equality, and individuals committed to inerrancy or sacramentalism can be found on either side of the women's ordination issue. Second, I will argue for the idea that resistance to women's ordination within these two theological subcultures symbolizes a broader resistance to the liberal world, a resistance that is central to the collective identity of both inerrantist and sacramentalist denominations.

Women's Ordination and Inerrancy

THE AMBIGUITY OF THE BIBLE

A striking feature of women's ordination debates is the ease with which either proponents or opponents of gender equality are able to use the Bible to support their position. Equally striking is that the Bible-based pro and con arguments of 1990 are virtually identical to the Bible-based pro and con arguments of 1890 and before. It is very difficult for an observer of this sort of intellectual stalemate to avoid the conclusion that the biblical text simply is not definitive on the issue of women's ordination. The theoretical significance of this hermeneutical stalemate is this: the strong association that we observe today between a denomination's commitment to biblical inerrancy and its official resistance to women's ordination cannot be explained entirely as a matter of intellectual consistency. Biblical inerrancy does not cause resistance to women's ordination as a matter of logical deduction. The association is very much a cultural association, and therefore it begs for a sociological explanation.

The fundamental ambiguity of the Bible on the matter of female clergy stems from the fact that the text contains some passages that clearly imply a commitment to gender inequality and others that clearly imply a commitment to gender equality. Among the passages frequently cited as definitive by opponents of women's ordination are these:

> Let a woman learn in silence with all submissiveness. I permit no woman to teach or to have authority over men; she is to keep silent. (I Timothy 2:11–12)

> As in all the churches of the saints, the women should keep silence in the churches. For they are not permitted to speak, but should be subordinate, as even the law says. If there is anything they desire to know, let them ask their husbands at home. For it is shameful for a woman to speak in church. (I Corinthians 14:33b–35)

Among the passages cited as definitive by proponents of women's ordination are these:

> There is neither Jew nor Greek, there is neither slave nor free, there is neither male nor female; for you are all one in Christ Jesus. (Galatians 3:28)

> Any man who prays or prophesies with his head covered dishonors his head, but any woman who prays or prophesies with

her head unveiled dishonors her head. (I Corinthians 11:4–5)

But this is what was spoken by the prophet Joel: And in the last days it shall be, God declares, that I will pour out my Spirit upon all flesh, and your sons and your daughters shall prophesy . . . yea, and on my menservants and my maidservants in those days I will pour out my Spirit; and they shall prophesy. (Acts 2:16–18)

The first two passages seem to proscribe female clergy while the last three seem to prescribe, or at least allow, them.

For the noninerrantist Christian, to whom a variety of interpretive options are available, the presence of such apparently contradictory biblical texts poses no serious problem. Once one accepts the conclusion of higher biblical criticism, for example, that different texts included in the Bible were written by various people in various contexts for various purposes, inconsistency is be expected. Indeed, to impose consistency on such a collection of texts seems foolish. Similarly, if one's regard for the authoritative status of the Bible is lowered, justifying practice by finding biblical mandate or, at least, allowance for the practice seems less important. Many noninerrantist Christian supporters of gender equality in general and women's ordination in particular have taken these interpretive paths.

Elizabeth Cady Stanton's *Woman's Bible* represents a prominent early example of a noninerrantist approach, one that avoids wrestling with biblical ambiguity by rejecting biblical authority altogether. The hostile reception of the *Woman's Bible,* however, even by prominent advocates of gender equality in religion, shows that Stanton's rejection of biblical authority was not considered a necessary condition for wholehearted support of women's ordination at the turn of the twentieth century.

Stanton explicitly distinguished herself from those who, "having made a fetish of these books and believing them to be the veritable 'Word of God,' with liberal translations, interpretation, allegories and symbols, glossed over the most objectionable features of the various books and clung to them as divinely inspired" (Stanton [1895] 1972:8). Instead of the more usual tack of maintaining the Bible's authority and interpreting it to support gender equality, Stanton rejected inerrancy altogether:

> The only points in which I differ from all ecclesiastical teaching is that I do not believe that any man ever saw or talked with God, I do not believe that God inspired the Mosaic code, or told the historians what they say he did about woman . . . The canon law, the Scriptures, the creeds and codes and church discipline of the leading religions bear the impress of fallible man, and not of our ideal great first cause. (Stanton [1895] 1972:12–13)

The women who produced the *Woman's Bible* "do not regard the Bible as the 'Word of God,' but like any other book, to be judged by its merits" (Stanton [1895] 1972:9).

In the closing decades of the nineteenth century, however, most of those who supported gender equality both in society and in the churches, unlike Stanton, attempted to do so within the bounds of biblical authority and even of full-blown inerrancy. Work on the *Woman's Bible* was delayed, for example, because, in her first (1886) attempt to mobilize female biblical scholars, Stanton was "disappointed to find that most of the learned women she tried to enlist in the project still considered her claim that the Bible was not divinely inspired to be suspect" (Fitzgerald 1993:xxv). And when the *Woman's Bible* was published in 1895, the National American Woman Suffrage Association "passed a resolution disavowing any connection to its publication or intent" (Fitzgerald 1993:xxvi). Before the turn of the twentieth century, then, for reasons of both religious commitment and political expediency, it did not seem necessary to most supporters of gender equality to reject biblical authority. Although inerrancy was interpreted by some late nineteenth-century people to imply gender inequality in church and society, to many others it implied no such thing. Stanton's complete rejection of inerrancy was unusual.[5]

Those, unlike Stanton, who remained within the inerrancy framework faced a serious interpretive problem, whatever their position on women's ordination. To appreciate the problem, consider that biblical inerrancy, to oversimplify, can be characterized by two axioms: the Bible is the authoritative source for every aspect of social and organizational life, and it can contain no internal contradictions. Given these axioms, the problem faced by an inerrantist is how to understand the set of biblical passages relevant to gender equality so that the texts' apparent contradictions disappear into a coherent interpretive whole that sends an unambiguous message about the acceptability or unacceptability of female clergy. The solution, hit upon by virtually every commentator, is to make either the first or second set of biblical passages reproduced above the definitive statement of principle, and then to interpret the other set of passages as somehow of secondary importance.

If you are opposed to women's ordination, the first set of passages becomes definitive and the second set is secondary. From this perspective, Galatians 3 implies equality in access to salvation, but not with respect to positions of religious authority. I Corinthians 11 and Acts 2 imply approval of women *prophesying,* but "prophecy" is not the same as "preaching" or "teaching," or the approval is limited to the last days, or it is limited to apostolic times. From this perspective, the several examples of women in the Bible exercising religious leadership are exceptions to the general principle of subordination.

If you are in favor of women's ordination, the second set of passages is given interpretive priority. From this perspective, I Timothy 2 and I Corinthians 14 are seen as Paul's historically contingent accommodation to the sexist cultural norms of his day. Or they are seen as admonitions directed at particularly disruptive women in the specific churches to which these letters were directed. In the authoritative light of the second set of passages, it is not difficult to conclude that the first set does not contain definitive rules of Christian living valid for all time. From this perspective, female leaders in biblical stories are precedent setting.

Concrete examples will illustrate the basic interpretive options in practice. In 1868, an opponent of female clergy interpreted the relevant texts in the following way:

Now these passages [I Timothy 2 and I Corinthians 14] most evidently do not forbid females to take any part in religious meeting, for it is evident that they did exercise their spiritual gifts in the early churches. They prayed and prophesied, and exercised perhaps the gifts of faith, and sacred song, and unknown tongues. But we may judge from the instructions of the Apostle that the more manly and assuming spiritual gifts of teaching, government, miracles, healing, were rarely, if ever, bestowed upon them, or exercised by them . . . [Therefore, a] woman should not take such a part in religious meeting, as shall seem to be assuming authority; she should not be a public religious teacher; she should not put herself forward and make herself conspicuous. She is then forbidden to lead in any of the exercises of public worship . . . She is debarred certainly, by the rule of the Apostle, from the ministry, the duties of which belong to men.

Moreover, the writer goes on, biblical examples of female leadership are special exceptions to the general rule, since "some special mission may at times be given to woman, as to Deborah and Huldah of old" (reprinted in Ruether and Keller 1981:224–225, 227).

An 1889 opponent illustrates the standard way of interpreting Galatians 3 so that it does not imply equal access to religious positions:

There [in Galatians 3] woman is seen in the kingdom of grace as man's equal and companion, entitled to all the blessings of the New Dispensation. Every privilege purchased by atoning blood is open to her. She equally and as fully as man can "put on Christ" . . . But while proclaiming woman's equality with man, the Scriptures just as plainly affirm her subordination to him.

Later, this same Presbyterian writer says that Galatians 3:

sets forth the great fundamental principle of the New Dispensation, that there is no distinction of persons in it. The artificial or natural distinctions that prevail in the world do not disqualify any from participating in the benefits and blessings of a common salvation. All become sons and daughters of God, and joint heirs with Christ Jesus.

However, notwithstanding this equality with respect to salvation,

[Another] fact clearly seen on the whole face of the narrative is that woman's work was subordinate to that of man. In accordance with the great principles already referred to, man has the leadership . . . [The] gift of prophecy [in Acts 2] must not be confounded with the preaching and teaching of the Gospel. (reprinted in Ruether and Keller 1981: 230, 233–234)

Galatians 3 implies equality in Christ, not equal access to positions of authority.

A century later, the standard biblical argument against women's ordination remains unchanged. In a 1981 *Christianity Today* debate about the ordination of women, the "no" argument was summarized in this way: "I believe the New Testament makes a two-fold declaration: first, men and women stand equal in Christ (Gal. 3:28), and second, women are not to lead and teach either the church corporate or men in the church" (I Tim. 2:11–14; I Cor. 14:35ff.). In I Timothy 2, "the present tense does not mean [Paul] limits the prohibition to that time only. Rather it indicates the kind of action, so he means, 'I am continually not permitting' " (Knight 1981:16).

Perhaps more surprising, and more directly relevant to the argument here, are examples of inerrantists who adopt the alternative interpretive strategy and use the Bible to support female clergy. An 1862 defender of female preaching, for example, answered "some of the frivolous objections to woman's rights in the church." I Timothy 2, she argues, is far from decisive:

Who was she [the woman referred to in I Timothy], the man's wife? Who was she forbidden to teach? The man, not the church. Now if this teaching means preaching, it would read thus: "I suffer not a woman to teach in the church." But this has no reference to that; for Paul never silenced them, only when he silenced the men, and then he assigns a reason. But some men are so willing to silence them, they take this Scripture that proves she should be in subjection to her husband to silence them in church, when it is not mentioned in this chapter. (reprinted in Ruether and Keller 1981:219–220)

According to this Disciples of Christ author, the passage forbids only wives teaching husbands; it does not say that women cannot teach the church.

Janette Hassey has uncovered several prominent examples of nineteenth- and twentieth-century inerrantists "who saw their support of women preachers as consistent with their biblical literalism" (Hassey 1986:xiii). Phoebe Palmer, for example, a nineteenth-century Holiness leader and lay revivalist, followed a "God said it, I believe it" approach in which "the scriptural way of arriving at right Bible conclusions is by comparing scripture with scripture" (quoted in Hassey 1986:97–98). Palmer's inerrancy was not in doubt, yet she had no trouble using the Bible to defend female preaching. She "asserted that the gift of the Spirit promised by the Father arrived at Pentecost and was received by both men and women . . . Palmer explained I Corinthians 14:34 . . . in the context of disorderly debates—only disruptive women must not speak" (Hassey 1986:98).[6]

Catherine Booth, cofounder of the Salvation Army, provides another example. She thought it "backwards" to use two passages—I Timothy 2 and I Corinthians 14—as the key to all Scripture. For her, "only a false translation of the Bible prohibits women's preaching." In I Timothy, for example, "Paul was simply prohibiting a woman's right to preach when one's own husband imposes silence" (Hassey 1986:99–100). The Salvation Army granted full formal equality to women from its beginnings.

The Baptist leader A. J. Gordon, as described by a contemporary, "was not among those who doubt either the inspiration or infallibility of the divine Word. He believed that it was essentially inerrant." At the same time, Gordon believed "that Joel's prophecy . . . was fulfilled at Pentecost and brought equal privileges to women." Although Gordon found it difficult to decide whether or not I Timothy 2 forbids women's ordination, "public prayer and prophecy . . . imply no exercise of authority and therefore are undebatable issues" (Hassey 1986:106–107).

The German revivalist Fredrik Franson "concluded that Scripture overwhelmingly supports women's public evangelization and found it remarkable that two passages (I Tim. 2:12 and I Cor. 14:34) could be made to contradict the rest." Elizabeth Bushnell, a missionary to China, "regarded Scripture as God's infallible Word, rejecting higher critical theories such as the documentary hypothesis in Genesis." But her inerrancy did not prevent her from arguing, in 1919, "Not only may woman preach, she must preach and teach" (Hassey 1986:108, 111, 113).

Hassey's final example, John Roach Straton, was a militant Fundamentalist leader in the 1920s who supported female preaching. Straton's "critics charged that allowing a female to preach constituted a denial of biblical authority and a 'flagrant violation of the clear teaching of the Scriptures' " (Hassey 1986:118). Straton wrote his 1926 pamphlet "Does the Bible Forbid Women to Preach and Pray in Public?" to answer that criticism. He saw "Joel 2 and Acts 2 as 'absolutely determinative in connection with the question of women speaking in public.' " He believed that "Galatians 3:28 declared the abolition of sex distinctions for the born-again." 1 Corinthians 14:34, in his view, reflected a local rather than a universal proscription, with "Paul regulating women's speaking in view of the shameful, degenerate Corinthian setting." I Timothy 2:12 only forbade female teaching "which usurped authority" (Hassey 1986:118–119). To Straton, inerrancy and female preaching did not seem contradictory.

Individuals prominent in the nineteenth-century women's movement also commonly experienced their commitment to biblical authority as wholly consistent with their support for gender equality. For Antoinette Brown, in 1853, "the God of the Bible, is the God everywhere; . . . the revelations of his will do not conflict . . . and I have no hesitation in planting my feet upon the Bible." Sarah Grimké, in her 1837 *Letters on the Equality of the Sexes,* says that she "shall depend solely on the Bible to designate the sphere of woman."[7] Nancy Hardesty (1991: chap. 4) reported that women's rights conventions throughout the nineteenth century presented speakers and reports that grounded gender equality in biblical authority. The usual move was to reject certain interpretations of the Bible, not biblical authority itself.

This combination—a firm sense of biblical authority and support for at least female preaching and, less often, full women's ordination—becomes more rare as the twentieth century moves on. But it is not extinguished. In 1981, *Christianity Today* did not have to move outside the inerrantist world to find someone to argue the "yes" side of the women's ordination question:

> As one firmly committed to the Bible as the inerrant Word of God and who turns to it as the only infallible rule of faith and practice, I must ultimately settle all such issues on the basis of "What saith the Lord?" in Holy Scripture. When our conclusions on this issue are drawn from the Bible rather than church tradition . . . we discover that women have full equality with men in church functions. (Stouffer 1981:12)

As in the "no" side of the debate, contemporary arguments parallel the arguments of one hundred years ago. In I Corinthians 11:3–12, "women are permitted to pray or prophesy as long as they meet the cultural expectation of covering, showing that they have the authority to [pray or prophesy]." In this light, since Paul cannot contradict himself, in I Corinthians 14 "he directs his remark ad hoc to the specific situation in Corinth." The author paraphrases I Timothy 2:11–12 like this:

> I command that women learn (be taught) in quietness and full submission (to the teaching authority). I am (presently) not permitting a woman to teach and she is not to exert evil influence over a man.

The "quietness and full submission" is not a gendered requirement, but "is what any teacher would ask of his pupils" (Stouffer 1981:13, 14).

These examples are meant to illustrate the basic point that a commitment to biblical inerrancy does not require, either logically or historically, opposition to women's ordination. Although some inerrantists, especially within the Holiness and Pentecostal traditions, draw a sharp distinction between female preaching and full ordination, supporting the former while reserving judgment about or even opposing the latter, that distinction should not be taken as "given" by the text any more than prohibition of female public speaking is a given. Some inerrantists stopped short of supporting full ordination for women; others did not.

The key point, then, is that the biblical text is ambiguous enough to make it intellectually possible, even easy, to support women's ordination without giving up biblical inerrancy. One does not need the "liberal" interpretive strategies of Stanton's *Woman's Bible* or higher criticism in order to support women's ordination. A century of stalemate on the issue strongly suggests that there is no compelling reason internal to the Bible to grant interpretive primacy either to the texts opposing gender equality or to the texts supporting gender equality.[8] This is why the strong empirical connection between inerrancy and resistance to women's ordination requires sociological interpretation. An all-male clergy is not logically required by a commitment to inerrancy. If it is not logically or intellectually difficult to combine inerrantism with full gender equality, why has it become so culturally difficult to do so?

WOMEN'S ORDINATION AND THE CONSTRUCTION OF AN INERRANTIST INSTITUTIONAL FIELD

The answer to this question lies in the construction of an inerrantist institutional world defining itself in opposition to the world of liberal religion. Support for women's ordination became increasingly difficult to harmonize with biblical inerrancy within Protestantism because the fundamentalist movement took on antimodernity as its central defining identity, and made inerrancy and opposition to women's ordination, among other issues, symbols of that antimodern stance. Because gender equality is such a defining core of the modern liberal agenda, resisting women's ordination became a way to symbolize antiliberalism within the religious world. Only as biblical inerrancy took on the symbolic weight of defining an antiliberal Protestant religious subculture did it become very difficult to combine inerrancy with support for women's ordination.

Three points are key. First, antiliberalism was, and remains, a central identifying feature of the fundamentalist movement and its progeny, including contemporary evangelicalism. Second, opposition to full gender equality was, and remains, one part of that antiliberal identity. Third, fundamentalism, and the biblical inerrancy at its core, was, and remains, more than a set of theological ideas; inerrancy is carried and sustained via an institutional world that is a major legacy of the fundamentalist movement. Opposing women's ordination is one way that denominations signal commitment to that institutional world.

Fundamentalism as Antimodernism. Interpreters of both Protestant liberalism and Protestant fundamentalism agree that what was centrally at stake in the nineteenth- and twentieth-century cultural conflicts between modernists and fundamentalists was, and is, the relationship between religion and "modernity." William Hutchison (1976:2) defined modernism as "first and most visibly . . . the conscious, intended adaptation of religious ideas to modern culture."[9] Whatever its initial sources, "liberalism under the modernist impulse had declared openly that the church is and must be in the world" (Hutchison 1976:310). "Modernism," according to George Marsden (1980:146), "meant first of all the adaptation of religious ideas to modern culture." From this liberal perspective, "the progress of the Kingdom of God is identified with the progress of civilization, especially in science and morality" (Marsden 1980:24).

Organized opposition to liberal religion, when it came, focused on this adaptationism. Marsden (1980:4) has defined fundamentalism as "militantly antimodernist Protestant evangelicalism." In its early days it was "a loose, diverse, and changing federation of co-belligerents united by their fierce opposition to modernist attempts to bring Christianity into line with modern thought." Summarizing the content of antiliberal book reviews appearing in Princeton Seminary's theological journal between 1890 and 1910, Hutchison (1976:200) observed that, for the writers of these reviews, people were faced with "a choice between Christianity and a well-intended, quite inadequate humanism." One could accept "scriptural revelation" or the "Christian consciousness of the age." Liberals chose the latter and, for antiliberal reviewers, "the result, whatever else it might be, was not a Christian theology." Fundamentalism emerged in response to a liberal religion that embraced key features of the modern world, and fundamentalism consequently defined itself in opposition to that world.

A key feature of that oppositional identity would be to insist on the supernatural basis of revealed religion, and this meant insisting on the superhistorical status of the Bible as the main conduit of that revelation. J. Gresham Machen was a fundamentalist leader within the northern Presbyterian church. According to Hutchison (1976:265), Machen viewed liberalism as "another religion" because it disbelieved "the supernatural Christ-events . . . denied the unique authority of the scriptures . . . viewed Christ as an example rather than as a supernatural person and the Savior of mankind . . . [and] made man rather than God the author of salvation." Biblical inerrancy thus became attached to antimodernity in the context of a fundamentalist social movement that emerged in response to the religious liberalism of the late nineteenth century.

This basic antimodern identity remains central to the biblically inerrant world, and it lies behind inerrantists' construction of women's ordination as part of a larger accommodation to the modern world. When the Southern Baptist Convention opposed female clergy in 1984 by saying that "we not decide concerns of Christian doctrine and practice by modern cultural, sociological, and ecclesiastical trends" (Melton 1991:236); when the Lutheran Church–Missouri Synod expressed its opposition by saying that, even though "the political and social milieu of a culture influences the church and always will . . . a specific sociological 'mindset' must never be allowed to be decisive for expressing theological judgments" (Commission on Theology 1985:39); when the Christian Reformed Church expressed its opposition by saying that "the ideological underpinnings of much of the movement [for women's rights] grows out of the radical individualism of modern western thought which stands opposed to a Christian covenantal understanding of church and family" (Godfrey 1994:1), these biblically inerrant denominations are displaying the same antimodern core identity that has defined fundamentalism from its beginnings.

Antimodernism and Gender Inequality. "Modernity," of course, is many-faceted, and it is clear that fundamentalism has never opposed every aspect of the modern world or every sort of social innovation. Resisting full gender equality, however, became a key feature of fundamentalism's broader antimodern identity. Although scholars have long noted that higher criticism of the Bible and Darwinian evolution were of central concern to the developing world of biblical inerrancy, recent work has suggested that gender equality is among the aspects of modern culture identified with liberalism (if not fully embraced by actual liberals) and therefore rejected by fundamentalism.

Betty DeBerg (1990:7) studied twenty fundamentalist periodicals publishing between 1880 and 1930, and she found that gender and family issues "dominated much of the rhetoric in the popular fundamentalist and proto-fundamentalist media." Fundamentalists emphasized "completely distinct spheres of activity for men and women" (43), the "exaltation of motherhood" (46), and the "subjection of wife to husband" (49). Even though women's suffrage was becoming an increasingly respectable idea during this period, DeBerg (1990:51) found that "antisuffrage statements in popular fundamentalist periodicals outnumbered prosuffrage statements by a ratio of more than ten to one." Also, their deep anti-Catholicism notwithstanding, at least some prominent early fundamentalists explicitly allied with Roman Catholics on gender issues: divorce, female dress, and birth control (DeBerg 1990:70, 107, 115). The point here is not that fundamentalists were alone either in their opposition to various aspects of the women's movement or in the arguments they used to oppose it; they certainly were not alone in either sense. The point is rather that antifeminism emerged as one of the defining features of fundamentalist antimodernism.

Margaret Lamberts Bendroth (1993:2) adds further support to this point. She found that "gender issues stood at the heart of fundamentalist desire to be different." Placing the fundamentalist movement in the context of the growth and prominence of women's missionary societies, a development that coincided with the fundamentalists' loss of institutional control over several major denominations, Bendroth argues that the "apparent alliance between women and the liberal enemies of fundamentalism verified rising doubts about feminine morality" (56). Among both northern Presbyterians and Baptists, women's mission societies became associated with women's ordination, and both of these were seen by fundamentalists as part of a "liberal conspiracy" to realize the modernist agenda. Bendroth (1993:58) reports that the fundamentalist pastor Mark Matthews considered 1929 Presbyterian efforts to ordain women as the " 'well-laid plans, schemes and designs' of an elite few." Ethelbert Warfield, president of Wilson College in Chambersburg, Pennsylvania, called it " 'only one manifestation of a world-wide movement' in revolt against historical Christianity" (Bendroth 1993:58). The key role of women's mission societies in conflicts over women's ordination will be explored more fully in the next chapter. Here, the point is that, as Bendroth (1993:63) argues, female mission executives' participation in the intradenominational controversies of the 1920s "gradually discredited women in fundamentalist eyes" and helped to solidify the anti-gender-equality component of the fundamentalist cultural program.

Opposition to full gender equality implied opposition to women's ordination. DeBerg (1990:79) found that "no matter what the position expressed concerning women speaking in church or in any other mixed assembly, all writers and editors of these [fundamentalist] magazines opposed ordaining women to traditional parish ministry." Understanding the meaning of this opposition requires placing it next to two other facts: first, as emphasized in Chapter 2, such formal opposition and even formal rules prohibiting female clergy are only loosely coupled with actual practice. Women in fact served as ministers and other sorts of religious leaders within fundamentalism. Given the high level of resistance to female clergy among even "liberal" congregations, the congregation-level resistance to female clergy probably was no greater among fundamentalist congregations than it was among congregations in general. Second, as I argued earlier, an intellectual commitment to inerrancy does not itself lead to resisting women's ordination. The militant opposition to women's ordination—opposition that is greater in rule and in rhetoric than it is in practice—was so prominent in the biblically inerrant world of fundamentalism because it partook of that movement's broader antiliberalism.

It still does. A large body of social research consistently finds strong associations between resistance to gender equality and biblical inerrancy measured either as personal belief or as affiliation with a denomination that espouses inerrancy (Peek, Lowe, and Williams 1991; but compare Himmelstein 1986). The prevalence of inerrantists and other religious conservatives on the traditional side of recent and contemporary conflicts over gender equality (for example, conflict over the Equal Rights Amendment) represents another manifestation of the successful fusion of biblical inerrancy with opposition to gender equality.

The liberal side also helped to construct this connection. Although many within the nineteenth-century women's movement maintained a commitment to biblical authority, the issue of how much deference was due the Bible was contested within this movement. A resolution "that the Bible recognizes the rights, duties, and privileges of Woman as a public teacher as every way equal with those of man" was tabled at an 1852 national woman's rights convention after several prominent women, including Ernestine Rose and Lucretia Mott, argued against the need to ground their goals in any written authority (Hardesty 1991:75–76). The 1890s dispute over the *Woman's Bible* was a similar instance of conflict. The position taken by Stanton, Rose, and Mott became more typical as the women's movement entered the twentieth century. Antiliberal fundamentalists, then, were not alone in connecting inerrancy to gender inequality. At least some segments of the women's movement shared the position that commitment to biblical authority was inimical, or at least not necessary, to working for gender equality. The symbolic connection between gender inequality and inerrancy was thus mutually constructed by those on both sides of the conflict between liberalism and antiliberalism.

Inerrancy as an Institutional Field. Although antimodernism has been a defining feature of the biblically inerrant world from the beginnings of the fundamentalist movement, and although opposition to gender equality was present as part of that broader identity from early on, this package of identifying features has become more firm over time. As the biblically inerrant world has become increasingly organized, its identifying features—including resistance to gender equality—have become more deeply institutionalized. Biblically inerrantist denominations today are embedded in a concrete institutional field that sustains their organizational identities. This institutional field is constituted by denominations, mission societies, publishing companies, seminaries, television and radio operations, and it is represented by such interdenominational organizations as the National Association of Evangelicals and the Council of Bible Believing Churches. The historical development of this institutional sphere corresponds to the increasingly tight connection between biblical inerrancy and resistance to women's ordination, a correspondence that is not a coincidence.

Marsden (1980:141) places the key organizational shift within fundamentalism at World War I. Before this, fundamentalism consisted of a loose interdenominational coalition of antimodernists, organizationally manifest in urban revivals, Bible and prophecy conferences, Bible institutes, and various publications

(Ammerman 1991:17–22). Even *The Fundamentals,* twelve vol-
umes published between 1910 and 1915 from which the movement would eventually take its name, were characterized by a
certain moderation (with respect to evolution, for example) that
"was clearly transitional in a movement that had not yet found
any firm identity" (Marsden 1980:123). After 1920, however, a
pervading sense of cultural crisis, accompanied by more aggressive liberalism within several major denominations, prompted
interdenominational organizing around antimodernist themes
and a concomitant firming of the ideological boundaries surrounding the movement.

The "first explicitly fundamentalist organization," the
World's Christian Fundamentals Association, was formed in
1918 and 1919, and the term "fundamentalist" was coined in
1920 (Marsden 1980:157–159). The movement climaxed during
the next half-decade with major attempts to gain control of several denominations as well as with vigorous efforts to combat
the teaching of evolution in schools. These efforts were famously
unsuccessful, but these well-publicized losses did not in any way
represent a rout of the movement's organizational resources. On
the contrary, the decades since 1925 have seen an increasingly
organized subculture of biblical inerrancy. "The effort to purge
the leading denominations having failed," Marsden (1980:193–
194) observed, "the leadership now re-emphasized working
through local congregations and independent agencies." The institutional results were impressive:

> Radio, peculiarly suited to the revivalist style, gave new impetus
> to the movement. Bible schools flourished, with twenty-six new
> schools founded during the depression years of the 1930s . . .
> Other important new institutions of learning, such as Dallas
> Theological Seminary and Bob Jones University, became signifi-
> cant centers for branches of the movement. Wheaton College
> was for several years during the 1930s the fastest growing liberal
> arts college in the nation. A network of similar colleges grew in
> size and influence. Fundamentalist publications increased in cir-

culation; summer Bible conferences and other youth movements attracted the young; mission agencies continued to grow.

In addition to the educational, publishing, and broadcasting institutions emphasized by Marsden, Nancy Ammerman (1991: 29–34) calls attention to the formation of new fundamentalist denominations and interdenominational associations with which dissident congregations could affiliate. The Independent Fundamental Churches of America took that name in 1930; the American Council of Christian Churches was founded in 1941; the National Association of Evangelicals began in 1942.[10] This organizational and cultural world formed the basis of today's newly resurgent fundamentalism, with Christian day schools and explicitly political groups adding to the institutional world of biblical inerrancy (Ammerman 1991:42–44; Liebman and Wuthnow 1983).

As the biblically inerrant world became increasingly institutionalized, the empirical connection between inerrancy and resistance to women's ordination became increasingly tight. Observers of the developing world of biblical inerrancy are unanimous in pointing to the fact that gender policies become increasingly strict from the 1930s onward. Moreover, this historical movement of biblically inerrant denominations toward more visible displays of gender inequality can be connected in various ways to the increasingly organized pandenominational fundamentalist movement.

Bible institutes, for example, formed one important site of interdenominational fundamentalism. As already noted in Chapter 2, policies regarding women at these schools became more restrictive as fundamentalism became more organized. Examining the Moody Bible Institute (MBI), for example, Janette Hassey demonstrates that "at the turn of the century, Moody women openly served as pastors, evangelists, pulpit supply preachers, Bible teachers, and even in the ordained ministry." Women graduated from MBI's "Pastor's Course" as late as 1929. This activity, furthermore, was promoted in official MBI publications during this period, as were explicit defenses of female clergy (Hassey 1986:31, 44). But the situation began to change in the 1920s and 1930s. The extent and durability of the change can be seen in a 1979 official publication from the Moody Bible Institute, which states that "our policy has been and is that we do not endorse or encourage the ordination of women nor do we admit women to our Pastoral Training Major" (quoted in Hassey 1986:31).

Such increasing gender restrictiveness was not atypical in the developing fundamentalist world. As mentioned in Chapter 2, four of the six most significant turn-of-the-century fundamentalist Bible institutes began by supporting female clergy, only to become more restrictive as time went on. Hassey (1986:13–14) describes how the World's Christian Fundamentals Association and the Baptist Bible Union began in the 1920s to pressure Bible institutes to symbolize their commitment to the developing movement. The Baptist Bible Union, for example, would "approve, patronize, and support" only schools that "unequivocally show themselves to be loyal to the inspiration and authority of the Bible and all the consequent fundamentals of our Confession" (reprinted in Hassey 1986:13). One specific indicator of this unequivocal loyalty was the formal exclusion of women from some official positions, and consequently Bible institutes oriented to this broader fundamentalist environment instituted more gender-exclusive policies during the 1920s and 1930s. An increasingly self-conscious fundamentalist organizational subculture constructed its collective identity, in part, around maintaining resistance to female clergy.

Newly organized fundamentalist denominations and associations also helped disseminate this collective identity. A Baptist congregation in Lynn, Massachusetts, for example, had a female pastor in the 1920s. This congregation joined the fundamentalist Conservative Baptist Association in 1952 and, consequently, "only males can serve today as pastor, elder, or deacon" (Hassey 1986:69). The Independent Fundamental Churches of America, to offer another example, began its organizational life in 1923 as an association of congregations opposed to modernism in their home denominations. Initially called the American Conference of Undenominational Churches (ACUC), its constitution used "his or her," female clergy were welcomed as full members, and women chaired its committees and spoke at its conventions. "By 1930, 13 of 174 members were ordained women with the title 'Reverend' and were serving as pastors or pastors' assistants." In 1930, however, the ACUC changed its name to the Independent Fundamental Churches of America, and in the same year "eliminated women from membership." After 1930, "only male delegates could represent affiliated churches and vote; female leadership at the national level came to an abrupt halt" (Hassey 1986:79–80). In this way, an increasingly organized fundamentalist world, which had to demarcate itself from the world of liberal religion that it opposed, produced the tight association between biblical inerrancy and resistance to women's ordination. The symbolic connection between inerrancy and resistance to female clergy should be seen as part of the construction of an antiliberal identity for this developing institutional world.

The argument I am offering here is similar to the argument that Marsden (1980) offers with respect to fundamentalist resistance to the Social Gospel. Although pre-1920 fundamentalism is characterized by "the lack of a distinctive social or political stance" (141), and although the precursor movements that would coalesce into fundamentalism were characterized by a variety of social efforts into the first decade of the twentieth century, social concerns virtually disappear from fundamentalism by the 1920s (85). Marsden's (1980:91–92) explanation of this development parallels my explanation of the relationship between biblical inerrancy and female clergy:

> By the time of World War I, "social Christianity" was becoming thoroughly identified with liberalism and was viewed with great suspicion by many conservative evangelicals ... When fundamentalists began using their heavy artillery against liberal theology, the Social Gospel was among the prime targets. In the bar-

rage against the Social Gospel it was perhaps inevitable that the vestiges of their own progressive social attitudes would also become casualties . . . By the 1920s the one really unifying factor in fundamentalist political and social thought was the overwhelming predominance of political conservatism. Whether they spoke as pietists who would use government merely to restrain evil, or as Calvinists preserving Christian civilization, or even when they sounded like radical Anabaptists opposing all Christian involvement in politics, they were (with few exceptions) antiliberal . . . But among fundamentalists these tendencies were reinforced by the close relationship between the Social Gospel and the progressive movement in politics. Rejecting the one seemed to demand rejecting the other.

Likewise, I am arguing, once women's ordination became identified with liberalism and a broader principle of gender equality, it became a target for fundamentalist attack. In the process, an earlier tradition, in which commitment to biblical authority was perfectly consistent with female clergy, was lost.

Another Perspective. It may be helpful to view the connection between opposition to women's ordination and the construction of a fundamentalist institutional field from a different perspective. I am arguing that the construction of a fundamentalist, biblically inerrant, institutional world has helped to produce the tight connection between inerrancy and gender inequality that we observe today. The other side of this argument is that gender policy is less driven by these symbolic, boundary-marking concerns in denominations that are less caught up in the basic conflict between fundamentalism and liberal modernism, and therefore less oriented to one or the other of these institutional worlds. Empirically this means that, among such denominations, the connection between inerrancy and opposition to women's ordination should be less tight.

Pentecostal and Holiness denominations constitute a relevant test case. Uniformly committed to biblical authority, these denominations nevertheless have had ambivalent relationships with organized fundamentalism. Early Pentecostal groups were institutionally connected neither to one another nor to the broader world of fundamentalism (Blumhofer 1989b:13–14). Marsden (1980:94) observes that "Pentecostals were only tangentially part of the fundamentalism of the 1920s." Even though Pentecostals "often identified themselves as 'fundamentalists,' read fundamentalist literature, and adopted anti-Modernist and anti-evolution rhetoric . . . other fundamentalists seldom welcomed them as allies or called them into their councils." Indeed, in 1928, Pentecostalism was explicitly attacked by the World's Christian Fundamentals Association, which declared itself "unreservedly opposed to Modern Pentecostalism" (Blumhofer 1989b:17).

Holiness groups were similarly ambivalent about fundamentalism, influenced by it but never fully aligned with it. Paul Bassett describes the way in which the Church of the Nazarene shifted its orientation from the Methodism of its origins to fundamentalism. In the 1920s, this denomination "adopted as her own heroes the principal soldiers in the ever more clearly defined Fundamentalist camp." By 1928, "a fundamentalist orthodoxy with respect to the inspiration and authority of Scripture had become a *de facto* mark of the 'good Nazarene' " (Bassett 1978:75, 81). At the same time, "fundamentalism could not leaven the whole lump" (Bassett 1978:85), and Susie Stanley (1997:25) argues that "Wesleyan/Holiness fundamentalism is an oxymoron."

Over time, Pentecostal and Holiness denominations have become more identified with the broader fundamentalist and evangelical world. The qualification quoted above notwithstanding, Bassett emphasizes the ways in which the Church of the Nazarene became more oriented to fundamentalism over time. Representatives from the largest Pentecostal denomination, the Assemblies of God, helped to organize the National Association of Evangelicals, and the denomination officially affiliated with that group in 1943 (Blumhofer 1989b:13, 32). Still, it is important to emphasize that these denominations have constructed their own institutional world that is distinct both from organized inerrancy and from liberal Protestantism. The Pentecostal Fellow-ship of North America was formed in 1948 and the World Pentecostal Conference began in 1947 (Blumhofer 1989b:47–48).

Pentecostal and Holiness denominations, in short, are not fully embedded in the dominant Protestant antiliberal subworld, and we should therefore expect their gender policies to be less completely responsive to that world. This is indeed the case, and can be seen in three ways. First, Holiness and Pentecostal denominations are well known for their much greater acceptance of female preaching than in other denominations professing inerrancy, an openness that itself differentiates them from the broader world of organized inerrancy.

This greater openness toward female preaching, however, has often misled observers to overstate the extent of full gender equality within these groups. Acceptance of female preachers should not be taken as greater acceptance of gender equality with respect to all religious positions. Pentecostal and Holiness denominations in fact vary in the extent to which they have granted full leadership rights to women, and this variation—much greater than among other inerrantist denominations—is the second way to see that these denominations, less fully integrated into organized fundamentalism, are consequently less oriented to that world when they make gender policy.

On the one hand, women were not granted full ordination within the Assemblies of God, for example, until 1935. At their 1914 founding, the Assemblies of God granted women the right to preach, though only men could be ordained elders (Barfoot and Sheppard 1980:8). Women could be evangelists or missionaries, but not pastors. Nor could they vote at national meetings (Blumhofer 1989a:364, 368). Women also are formally restricted from at least some positions of authority in the Church of God (Cleveland), the Church of God (Huntsville), the Pentecostal Church of Christ, the Church of God of Prophecy, and the Church of God in Christ (Barfoot and Sheppard 1980; Gilkes 1986).

On the other hand, formal gender equality has existed within the Church of the Nazarene, the Church of God (Anderson), and the Salvation Army from the founding of these denominations. The Pillar of Fire, a smaller Holiness group, also granted women full equality from its beginnings (Stanley 1997:6). This variation among Pentecostal and Holiness denominations regarding women's ordination further illustrates the basic point that inerrancy alone does not produce resistance to women's ordination. Denominations committed to inerrancy as an interpretive principle but not fully integrated into the (fundamentalist) institutional world of inerrancy are not as likely to oppose women's ordination. Because they are not primarily oriented to the institutional world symbolized, in part, by gender inequality, these denominations do not need to fly the flag of that world.[11]

A third way to see that women's ordination policy within these denominations is driven by something other than orientation to the wider world of organized inerrancy is to note that, much like support for women's ordination typical of earlier nineteenth-century rhetoric, pragmatic concerns are very salient. A 1915 editorial written by the chairman of the founding convention of the Assemblies of God is illustrative:

> There are some things under normal circumstances that God does not require of women . . . and one of these is to be a Ruling Elder in the Church of Christ. Even here we allow such liberty as not to interferre [sic] with special calls God in His sovereignty may give to women under exceptional circumstances, nor do we prohibit her from a scriptural use of any special gift bestowed upon her by the Holy Ghost. She may, with profit and blessing, when so fitted and called and need so require, feed a flock as a Pastor, in the glory of God. She may run a Rescue Home, Faith Home, or anything else which God has beyond doubt called, endowed and commanded her to do, and it is a foolish man who will break up any good work God has called a woman to do and which she is doing to the glory of God and the good of mankind. (quoted in Barfoot and Sheppard 1980:8–9)

The stance of the early Assemblies of God toward female clergy thus exhibits a certain practical ambiguity and flexibility, indicating that the symbolic weight of these policies is less than for other denominations, at least at this early point in their history. This sort of focus on practical need is typical of Pentecostal and Holiness support for female clergy in much the same way, as we saw in Chapter 4, that it was typical of antebellum discussions of the issue in many denominations. Organizational policy is more responsive to practical need when and where women's ordination carries less symbolic weight.[12]

Examining these denominations thus strengthens the overall argument about the influence of an institutional field—an organizational subculture larger than any one denomination—on rules about women's ordination. If the argument is correct, organizational distance from a larger institutional world that maintains gender inequality as a key identifying principle should mean that gender policy is more flexible. This indeed seems to be the case with respect to Holiness and Pentecostal denominations.[13]

This section has described the development of a cultural connection between inerrancy and resistance to women's ordination. Before women's ordination became symbolically tied to the broader theme of liberal modernism, those committed to biblical authority commonly went both ways on the question. But as the issue took on the symbolic weight of liberalism and modernity, and as strict inerrancy became firmly institutionalized as a symbol of resistance to the modern world, it became more and more difficult to be both an inerrantist and a supporter of women's ordination. The difficulty is mainly cultural. The text has not become less ambiguous over this period; rather, the loyalties signified by inerrancy have become less ambiguous. One of those loyalties is to be against the modern liberal world and the gender equality it supports.

Women's Ordination and Sacramentalism

THE AMBIGUITY OF SACRAMENTALIST THEOLOGY

One of the most important differences between the institutional world of biblical inerrancy and the institutional world of sacramentalism is the dominance of the latter by a single denomination—the Roman Catholic Church. In the inerrant world, no single denomination or organization is in a position to define the identity of the entire field. Although it would be an overstatement to say that the Vatican's policies solely define the boundaries of legitimate sacramentalism, the Catholic Church clearly is the most influential player in that world. Other sacramentalist denominations—Episcopalian, Orthodox, and, to a lesser extent, Lutheran—look to the Catholic Church for signals about how to be good sacramentalist denominations more than the Catholic Church looks to them. Because of this, I will concentrate in this section on women's ordination and antimodernism in the Catholic Church.

Earlier in this chapter I pointed out that, in addition to the usual arguments opposing women's ordination, sacramentalist denominations like the Catholic Church connect their official opposition to female clergy to their core sacramental identity. As with biblical inerrancy, an all-male clergy is thought to follow inexorably from sacramentalism's internal logic, especially from the need for the sacrament to be performed by an individual who represents Christ qua biological man. Daniel Trapp (1989:369) summarizes the argument about "sacramental symbolism":

> From the point of view of the eucharistic celebration as a memorial of the Last Supper, this symbolism is important. The memorial is not a sacred drama requiring photographic likeness, but the event symbolized does require fitting, congruent signs . . . The sign of the maleness . . . functions as a congruent sign of Christ Incarnate and Risen.

The "high" nature of the sacramental ritual in these denominations, its real efficacy in transmitting salvation, is said to require a male priesthood because of the necessity for the priest to resemble Christ. This argument has its origins in Aquinas and scholastic theology (Hannon 1967:35–36).

Upon close inspection of both the argument's logic and the relevant empirical realities, it is difficult to avoid the conclusion that an all-male clergy is no more inherent in sacramentalism than in the Bible. As many Catholic theologians point out, the sacramental requirement for a priest that "resembles" Christ does not in and of itself require that such resemblance rests on gender.[14] Commitment to a truly efficacious sacrament does not logically imply that that sacrament be performed only by males, any more, it would seem, than it would imply that it be performed by Jewish males, or by males with beards, or any other dimension of resemblance among persons one might choose to emphasize. Insisting that gender is the primary dimension of literal resemblance between the priest and Christ seems an arbitrary addition to the requirements of the sacrament rather than a straightforward outcome of them. Mary Douglas (1992:275–276) puts the point nicely when she adopts the persona of a "questioner" of sacramental rejection of female clergy:

> Among the famous Nuer of the Sudan a cucumber can substitute for an ox in a sacrifice . . . and among the Mandari a ritual that requires a red ox to be sacrificed can be performed with a white ox if the right words are uttered. . . So why cannot a woman be transformed by an agreed incantation into a man?

Literal maleness thus seems less than necessary to maintain the sacramental focus on the priest as representative of Christ.

It may seem that the standard justification for emphasizing gender as the key dimension of resemblance for the sacrament's efficacy receives some support from contemporary social scientific arguments about the fundamental nature of gender as a cross-cutting "master role" that shapes every human encounter, however subtly (see, for example, West and Zimmerman 1987). If no human interaction is gender-neutral, if individuals in every social context always are perceived as female or male individuals, then perhaps the maleness of the priest is indeed a necessary part of a theological commitment to a sacrament that claims to represent, in a stronger way than a Protestant communion service, the original event. Here, however, recent research on the way that individuals respond to female clergy undermines this argument. The standard result found in Protestant congregations—that resistance to female clergy is significantly reduced after individuals have some experience with them—is also evident among Catholics exposed to female "pastors" in priestless parishes (Wallace 1992:171; Lehman 1987:324; Dudley 1995:2–3). Moreover, surveys of Roman Catholics in the United States routinely have found a majority supporting women's ordination, and the percentage who approve of the change has been increasing (Goldman 1992:A8). A 1996 poll found that 65 percent of Roman Catholics in the United States favored women's ordination (Hout and Greeley 1997).

Many committed Catholic lay people, theologians, and biblical scholars have actively supported women's ordination in recent decades, further weakening the argument that opposition to women's ordination is built in to sacramentalist ritual. In addition to the Women's Ordination Conference, the primary group advocating women's ordination within the Catholic Church, support for women's ordination has also been prominently expressed through other Catholic organizations. The 1974 annual meeting of the Leadership Conference of Women Religious passed "two important resolutions, one supporting the principle that all ministries in the church be open to women and men as the Spirit calls them, and one affirming women's rights to active participation in all decision-making bodies in the church" (Weaver [1985] 1995:112). In 1978 a Catholic Theological Society of America task force produced a report on the subject, followed the next year by a report from a Catholic Biblical Association task force. "Both reports suggested that the evidence pointed towards the admission of women to the priesthood" (Trapp 1989:227).

It is difficult to make the case, therefore, on the basis of the internal logic of sacramentalism, the experience of the ritual by congregants, or consensus among Catholics, that sacramental practice and theology require male priests. We are faced with a question analogous to the one that emerged in the previous section: if it is not logically or intellectually difficult to combine sacramentalism with support for full gender equality in the church, why are sacramentalist denominations, the Roman Catholic church being the prime example, especially resistant to women's ordination? The answer is this: the cultural connection between sacramentalism and resistance to women's ordination, like the connection between inerrancy and women's ordination, emerged as part of the antiliberal identity of the sacramentalist world, a world in which the Roman Catholic Church is the dominant, though not the only, actor.

SACRAMENTALISM AND ANTIMODERNISM

Antimodernism has been a central feature of official Roman Catholic identity at least since the French Revolution.[15] The eightieth, and final, of the "errors" condemned in Pius IX's infamous 1864 Syllabus of Errors was "That the Roman Pontiff can and ought to reconcile and harmonize himself with progress, with liberalism, and with modern civilization." Although opposition to progress, liberalism, and modernity have been constant themes of official Catholic organizational identity in recent centuries, the specific signifiers of that identity change substantially over time. It is possible to discern three major phases in the changing content of Catholic antimodernist identity.

From the French Revolution until the end of the nineteenth century, the primary content of Catholic antimodernism was opposition to the separation of church and state implied by political liberalism. In 1832 Pope Gregory "condemned the principles of separation of church and state, freedom of the press, and freedom of religion" (Burns 1992:27). Approximately half of the eighty "principal errors of our time" contained in the 1864 Syllabus concern issues of church autonomy from state or civil authority. In 1870, after the Italian republic annexed Rome, further dismantling the Vatican's political authority, Pius IX prohibited Catholics from voting in Italian republican elections, a prohibition that remained in force, if increasingly disregarded, until 1919 (Burns 1992:28). Pope Leo XIII's 1899 condemnation of "Americanism" was targeted at the presumed acceptance among American Catholic leaders of church–state separation as the most desirable political arrangement.

Fighting political liberalism, however, was to prove a losing battle, and Catholic antimodernism found other targets. Although "the papacy did not fully accept [that the alliance of throne and altar had gone forever] until Vatican II" (Burns 1992: 31), theological and intellectual liberalism became more salient targets in the second, turn-of-the-century, phase of Catholic antimodernism. Opposed to these modern intellectual movements was a renewed commitment and fidelity to Thomistic theology. Just as in Protestant antimodernism of the time, higher biblical criticism and biological evolution emerge in this period as major symbols of the liberal world. Just as for Protestants, these were prominent symbols of a liberalism that seemed to threaten the supernatural basis of religious authority claimed by the Catholic Church.

Comparing the condemnations of 1864 with Pius X's condemnations of 1907 reveals the shifting content of Catholic antimodernism. In 1864, as noted, about half of the errors officially condemned concerned the separation of church and state; only one was directed at higher biblical criticism. This emphasis was reversed in the 1907 *Syllabus Condemning the Errors of the Modernists*. Here, biblical criticism received much more attention, as in the following condemned propositions:

9. They display excessive simplicity or ignorance who believe that God is really the author of the Sacred Scriptures.

. . .

11. Divine inspiration does not extend to all of Sacred Scriptures so that it renders its parts, each and every one, free from every error.

12. If he wishes to apply himself usefully to Biblical studies, the exegete must first put aside all preconceived opinions about the supernatural origin of Sacred Scripture and interpret it the same way as any other merely human document. (Pius X [1907] 1954a:224)

Approximately 40 percent of the sixty-five propositions "condemned and proscribed" by Pius X in 1907 concerned biblical criticism; only one clearly concerned political liberalism.

This 1907 syllabus was followed two months later by Pius X's broadside against modernism as the "synthesis of all heresies" (Pius X [1907] 1954b:117). This encyclical reiterated nineteenth-century condemnation of the liberal political idea that "the State must, therefore, be separated from the Church, and the Catholic from the citizen" (Pius X [1907] 1954b:105), but philosophical and theological liberalism and humanism now bore the brunt of the attack. The fundamental conflict was between Thomistic scholasticism and a modernist Catholicism "that would not appeal exclusively, as did the neo-scholastic system, to a supernatural, 'extrinsic,' once-and-for-all 'deposit of faith,' " but would instead recognize "that all dogmas and practices were viewed as products of particular historical periods and in need of periodic revision" (Dinges and Hitchcock 1991: 79). Biblical criticism was a symbol, par excellence, of this divide.

During this period Catholic modernists "refused . . . to exempt the Bible from the standard operating procedures and questions of historical and literary criticism." They "concerned themselves with the foundational question of the proper limits of ecclesiastical and Scriptural inerrancy [and] raised objections to the received teaching on inerrancy" (Appleby 1992:70). Biblical scholars who did not conform their conclusions to the decisions of the Pontifical Biblical Commission about such issues as the Mosaic authorship of the Pentateuch could, and did, lose their professorships.[16]

Although modern science, of course, had occupied the Vatican's attention for centuries, biological evolution emerged during this period as another important symbol of the boundary between the Catholic Church and the modern world. While only four of the sixty-five condemned propositions promulgated in 1907 concerned science (a slight increase from two of the eighty 1864 condemnations),[17] the experience of John

Zahm—priest, Notre Dame professor, and popularizer of Darwinian evolutionary theory among Catholics—illustrates evolution's true salience for official Catholic identity of the period.

Zahm's major work, *Evolution and Dogma,* published in 1896, was an "attempt to reconcile post-Darwinian theories of evolution with Catholic theism" (Appleby 1992:3), an effort that "his neo-scholastic detractors adamantly rejected" (Appleby 1992:6). Scott Appleby describes the environment in which Zahm operated:

> Because the heresies of modernity appeared to infect culture in all of its diverse expressions, traditionalists perceived the presence of the disease everywhere: in the application of the higher criticism to sacred texts; in the separation of church and state; in the attempt to assimilate Catholicism to the local and national communities to which the churches belonged; and, invariably, in the advances of the natural sciences. (Appleby 1992:44)

Darwinian evolutionary theory symbolized modernity and liberalism to Catholic conservatives just as it did to Protestant conservatives of this period. *Evolution and Dogma* was banned by the Roman Congregation of the Index in 1898 (Appleby 1992:49).

The turn-of-the-century similarities between Protestant and Catholic antimodernism are quite striking, a fact often overlooked both because of Protestant anti-Catholicism and because Catholic creationism and biblical inerrancy fade over the course of the twentieth century.[18] The Catholic Church, however, has continued to make efforts to demarcate itself from liberal modernity. The specific symbols of that demarcation change over time; the struggle to construct the symbolic boundary is constant. Liberals thought they saw "the success which inevitably must crown the progressive efforts of the modern world," and they wanted to accommodate the church to that world (Tyrrell 1908:136). Official Catholic organizational identity was constructed in opposition to that vision.

The third period of Catholic antimodernism centers around the great moment of liberal success within the Catholic Church, the Second Vatican Council, occurring between 1962 and 1965. Here the church officially affirmed much of the modern world that it had resisted for the previous century: religious pluralism, political democracy, the separation of church and state, freedom of religious conscience, and human rights. It "legitimated a view that doctrine can develop, or evolve, according to the 'signs of the times' " (Burns 1992:70). Contemporary Catholic antimodernism—both official and popular—is best understood as a reaction to the broad acceptance of modernity underlying the documents of Vatican II. This is the context in which women's ordination has emerged as a central symbolic issue within the sacramentalist world dominated by the Roman Catholic Church.[19]

Gene Burns (1992) argues persuasively that the eventual acceptance by the Church of liberal democratic states forced Vatican elites to demarcate the Catholic Church from the world by emphasizing other facets of liberal ideology to which it remained opposed. Burns calls attention to the Church's enhanced emphasis on the morality of individual behavior, especially regarding abortion and sexual mores, as one aspect of the Church's continuing boundary-drawing activity. My argument is that the Church's resistance to full gender equality, and its expression of that resistance in terms of its core sacramentalist identity, should also be understood in the context of constructing a boundary between the Church and the world.

The sacramentalist world is different from the nonsacramentalist religious world in that the issue of women's ordination did not emerge in a serious way in these denominations until the second wave of the feminist movement. This is partly because of sacramentalism's "higher" view of the clergy, partly because of the organizational centralization that characterizes these denominations, and partly because (with the exception of Episcopalians) their social base in ethnic enclaves made these denominations relatively isolated from the liberal women's movement of the nineteenth century. When the issue did arise, however, it arose with the same symbolic resonance that it had in other denominations. Women's ordination was seen as a symbol of the secular modernism against which the sacramentalist world defined itself even, perhaps especially, after Vatican II.

Agitation on the issue of women's ordination first arose in the Catholic Church in the 1960s and grew in the 1970s. A petition concerning women priests was submitted to the preparatory commission of the Vatican Council in 1962; the first doctoral dissertation on the question was written in the same year; and the group that would become the Women's Ordination Conference began meeting in 1974 (Weaver [1985] 1995:111–112). It is significant that the very first Vatican statement specifically opposing women's ordination, and offering justification for that opposition, came only in 1976. The issue was perceived on both sides as an indicator of a broader struggle between openness and resistance to the modern world, now symbolized by full gender equality rather than by church-state separation, higher biblical criticism, or evolution.

The 1976 *Declaration on the Question of the Admission of Women to the Ministerial Priesthood* begins and ends by placing the issue in the context of a broader movement for gender equality, a movement that was strongly endorsed by the Second Vatican Council. "Among the characteristics that mark our present age," the document begins, "[is] the part that women are now taking in public life." And, near its end, the statement again recognizes the broader context: "It is not surprising that, at a time when [women] are becoming more aware of the discriminations to which they have been subject, they should desire the ministerial priesthood itself." This issue, however, is not subject to the same principles of gender equality that govern secular matters: "But it must not be forgotten that the priesthood does not form part of the rights of the individual, but stems from the economy of the mystery of Christ and the Church. The priestly office cannot become the goal of social advancement; no merely human progress of society or of the individual can of itself give access to it; it is of another order" (reproduced in Melton 1991:1, 8). By this logic, the Vatican's commitment to the principle of gender equality in the secular world does not imply full gender equality in the church. This sacramental justification for resisting women's ordination—tying an all-male clergy to the very identity of the organization—represents the use of this issue as a marker of core Catholic organizational identity. Why this issue? Because it continues the long-term effort to mark a boundary between the sacramental world and the liberal world. Full gender equality is not the only issue that does this work, of course, but today it is one of the most prominent.

In the case of the Catholic Church, the antimodern symbolic content of women's ordination can be seen even more clearly in the rhetoric of organized traditionalist movements than in the careful language of official documents. The conservative group, Women for Faith and Family, organized in 1984, for example, circulated an "Affirmation for Catholic Women." The fifty thousand signers of this affirmation "reject all ideologies which seek to eradicate the natural and essential distinction between the sexes." The affirmation's fifth statement illustrates the fusion of antiliberalism and sacramentalism that the issue of women's ordination has come to represent:

> We therefore also reject as an aberrant innovation peculiar to our times and our society the notion that priesthood is the "right" of any human being, male or female. Furthermore, we recognize that the specific role of ordained priesthood is intrinsically connected with and representative of the begetting creativity of God in which only human males can participate. Human females, who by nature share in the creativity of God by their capacity to bring forth new life, and, reflective of this essential distinction, have a different and distinct role within the Church and in society from that accorded to men, can no more be priests than men can be mothers. (Hitchcock 1995:177–178)

This sort of opposition to women's ordination is not limited to explicitly antifeminist Catholic groups such as Women for Faith and Family. Antifeminism, and therefore opposition to women's ordination, is evident in virtually every conservative Catholic organization, whatever the group's primary focus.[20]

Thus, although the most prominent symbols of Catholic antimodernism have changed over time, the Church's effort to find some way to demarcate itself from the liberal world in which it exists is constant. The specific content of that antimodernism at any particular moment should be seen as a response to that day's chief symbol of modern liberalism. Women's ordination, today, functions in this way for the Catholic Church. Denominations looking to Rome for clues about how to be a legitimate sacramentalist religious organization receive the clear message that refusing to ordain women is one of the requirements. In Chapter 3, I described one example of such a message, delivered by a cardinal. An even clearer example is Pope John Paul II's 1984 letter to the Archbishop of Canterbury, in which the Pope reminded the archbishop that Paul VI had, in 1975, considered the possible ordination of women by the Anglican Church "an element of grave difficulty," even "a threat" to their ecumenical dialogue. He went on to say that, although "we have celebrated together the progress towards reconciliation between our two Communions ... the increase in the number of Anglican Churches which admit, or are preparing to admit, women to priestly ordination constitutes, in the eyes of the Catholic Church, an increasingly serious obstacle to that progress" (John Paul II [1984] 1986). The particularly strong resistance of sacramentalist denominations to women's ordination is partly the result of the antimodernism of the dominant actor within the sacramentalist institutional world.[21]

Conclusion

Earlier chapters documented the strong external pressure felt by denominations to institutionalize full gender equality. It is clear, however, that not all denominations responded to this pressure by ordaining women. I have argued that denominational policy on gender equality is influenced by the expectations of relevant actors in the religious environment as well as the expectations coming to denominations from the secular environment. Consequently, understanding formal rules about female clergy requires an understanding of the relevant environments in which denominations are embedded. In the previous chapter, I showed that denominations with organizational ties to prior ordainers of women are more likely to themselves ordain women.

This chapter has established that sacramentalism and biblical inerrancy represent cultural boundaries within the denominational population that strongly influence rules about women's ordination. More precisely, rules about women's ordination partly constitute the boundaries drawn around biblical inerrancy and sacramentalism. The deep connections between gender inequality and sacramentalism, on the one hand, and between gender inequality and biblical literalism, on the other hand, have a similar source. Both were forged in self-conscious response to a modern and liberal agenda that included gender equality as one of its main goals. Because gender equality became identified with "modernity," religious organizations that resisted modernity took on gender inequality as one of the primary symbols of that resistance. Rules about women's ordination, then, often have less to do with women clergy than with symbolizing cooperation with or resistance to a much broader social project. The tight connection between resistance to women's ordination and both inerrancy and sacramentalism should be seen as part of the construction of an antiliberal collective identity for the institutional fields defined by inerrancy and by sacramentalism. Women's ordination symbolizes liberal modernity, and that is why it is so deeply resisted by religious organizations defined most centrally by their antiliberal spirit.[22]

The phenomenon examined in this chapter—gender inequality as a symbol of resistance to liberal modernity—is not limited to Christian antimodernism in the United States. Opposition to gender equality is a central feature of antimodernist religious movements, now generically referred to as fundamentalist movements, throughout the world (Lazarus-Yafeh 1988; Riese-brodt 1993a; Marty and Appleby 1993; Hawley 1994). Islamic fundamentalists insist that women be covered in public and often oppose female suffrage and equal access to various occupations; Hindu fundamentalists insist that women wear saris; Jewish fundamentalists prohibit women from carrying the Torah; and even conservative "new religions" of Japan call for women to leave the workplace (Hawley and Proudfoot 1994:5; Riesebrodt 1993a:127). Most recently, when the fundamentalist Taliban militia captured the Afghanistan capital, the militia's "first move," after hanging the ex-president, was "to set curbs on women" (*New York Times,* Sept. 28, 1996:1). Martin Riesebrodt (1993a: 206, 202), in his comparative study of U.S. Protestant fundamentalism of the 1920s and Iranian Islamic fundamentalism of the 1970s, was impressed enough with the anti-gender-equality content of both movements to conclude that "fundamentalism is therefore most appropriately characterized as a patriarchal protest movement." It should be interpreted "primarily as a protest against the assault on patriarchal structural principles in the family, economy, and politics."

The ubiquity of opposition to gender equality in self-consciously antiliberal and antimodern movements in different countries and within different religious traditions further belies the claim that opposition to women's ordination is simply and straightforwardly an internal requirement of either biblical inerrancy or sacramentalism. It stretches credibility too far to imagine that the internal requirements of movements in such different contexts all lead independently to gender inequality in one form or another. Far more likely is that these movements share a patriarchal content because they define themselves against a common enemy—a liberal modernity for which gender equality is a key symbol. Rules prohibiting women's ordination function primarily as signals of loyalty to this broader antimodernism.

⊷ 6 ⊷

INTERNAL
ORGANIZATIONAL
FACTORS

The previous chapters have emphasized the political, normative, network, and cultural pressures on denominations. I have argued that these factors, all of which concern the ways in which denominations negotiate with various parts of the environment in which they sit, take us far in our effort to understand historical and cross-sectional variation in denominations' formal policies on women's ordination. But it is important to recognize that these largely external factors, as significant as they are, do not constitute the whole story. Policies on women's ordination are not wholly produced by interactions between denominations and their environments. Features that are largely internal to denominations have also played a role in producing the variation that we observe across these organizations in their gender policies. In this chapter and the next, I focus on denominations' internal affairs. This chapter describes internal features of denominations that have influenced policy on women's ordination, and it describes internal features that we might expect to influence such policy, yet do not. The next chapter describes the changing nature of conflicts over women's ordination.

There are of course many ways to describe the internal characteristics of denominations. I will consider two types of internal organizational features. First, there are features representing internally generated organizational problems for which women's ordination—or resistance to it—might be a "rational" or pragmatic solution. Second, there are features representing structural characteristics of denominations that can be expected to influence the likelihood that a denomination will incorporate gender equality at an early date. Two structural features in particular—centralization and autonomous women's organizations—can be expected to influence formal rules about women's ordination because they alter the political dynamics of denominational policy formation.

Internal Organizational Problems

I begin by discussing organizational problems for which women's ordination might constitute a solution.

CLERGY SHORTAGES

It is certainly the case that clergy shortages influence the extent to which women do the work of clergy. This phenomenon—women filling slots that men do not want—is widely observed across occupations and historical periods (Reskin and Padavic 1994). Religious work is no exception. Even Martin Luther apparently believed "that women should preach if there were ever a shortage of men" (Todd 1996:257). The phenomenon, described in Chapter 2, of women "pastors" administering priestless Roman Catholic parishes is the most obvious contemporary instance.

It is also the case that the pragmatic concern to employ as many as are willing in the religious work that needs doing is present in denominational debates about women's ordination, even after the rise of the women's movement. For example, when Church of God officials noticed, in 1907, "that membership rolls contained more females than males [they] realized that women workers could be a valuable factor in the church's growth and concluded that this source of strength had to be utilized" (Crews 1990:93).

Given these facts, it is plausible to suppose that denominational rules about women's ordination are driven largely by pragmatic concerns about staffing congregations, missions, chaplaincies, and other slots traditionally filled by ordained clergy. If denominations grant equality to women to meet pragmatic needs of the organization, then we might expect the existence of a clergy shortage to hasten the advent of women's ordination. Clergy shortages come and go, and not necessarily on the same schedule for all denominations. The 1950s, for example, was a time of clergy shortage for several major Protestant denominations, and observers (Brereton and Klein 1980:187; Carroll, Hargrove, and Lummis 1983:42) have suggested that those shortages were responsible for the fact that some denominations granted full clergy rights to women during that decade. In more recent decades, some Protestant denominations have experienced clergy surpluses (Carroll and Wilson 1980) at the same time that the Roman Catholic church is famously and increasingly short of clergy (Schoenherr and Young 1993). In light of this sort of historical and cross-denominational variation, it is plausible to hypothesize that a denomination finding it difficult to fill its key positions will be pressured to change its criteria of office to create a larger pool of eligible individuals. This logic of organizational rationality implies that denominations will be more likely to begin to ordain women when they are in the midst of a clergy shortage.

The argument of this book, however, while not denying the market forces that lead congregations faced with a shortage of male clergy to draft women to do the work, emphasizes the likelihood that such market forces will not directly translate into formal rules that enshrine gender equality. Indeed, recall the 1970 Lutheran report, which advocated ordaining women even though only an occasional "lone woman appears ready to make a test case after she graduates from a theological seminary" (Melton 1991:93). We also have seen, more generally, how organizational rules are largely uncoupled from the numbers of women doing the work of clergy in denominations. From this perspective, we would counterintuitively expect that a clergy shortage will *not* raise the likelihood that a denomination will begin to officially permit women's ordination.

Indeed, that is the case. Table 6.1 shows, for selected denominations, the noncorrelation between periods of clergy shortage and the beginnings of full clergy rights for women. The table gives the ratio of the number of clergy to the number of congregations between 1919 and 1989. If this ratio is less than 1.0 the denomination has fewer clergy than congregations—a personnel shortage. If this ratio is greater than 1.0 the denomination is experiencing a surplus of clergy. The asterisks in each column indicate the date at which each of these denominations began to officially ordain women.

This table indicates that, at least for these denominations, women's ordination seems as likely to begin during times of clergy surplus as during times of clergy shortage. Furthermore, there is no relationship between longer-term trends toward declining clergy supply and women's ordination. Women's ordination is as likely to begin during a period of overall increase in clergy supply within a denomination as during a period of overall decline in clergy supply.

Quantitative analysis of the larger denominational population reveals that the nonrelationship evident in Table 6.1 is more general. Denominations experiencing a clergy shortage are neither more nor less likely to grant full clergy rights to women than are denominations without a clergy shortage. Although denominations with a clergy shortage are more likely to draft women to do the necessary work of the church, these results show that such drafting of women does not necessarily translate into granting them official status and recognition. The loose coupling of rule and practice means that on-the-ground personnel supply problems are not necessarily reflected in formal policies.

Table 6.1 Trends in clergy-to-congregation ratios for selected denominations

Year	Lutheran			Anglican	Baptist/Free Church		Reformed			Methodist
	ALC	LCA	Mo. Synod	EC	ABC	Breth.	UPUSA	PCUS	RCA	MC
1919	—	.73	.68	.75	1.06 ★	3.06	.96	.54	1.06	.64
1931	—	.85	.83	.77	1.07	2.66	1.06	.67	1.14	.71
1939	.84	.88	.73	.81	1.22	2.97	1.12	.70	1.15	.65
1949	.92	1.01	1.14	.95	.86	2.91	1.08	.76	1.19	.61
1959	1.01	1.05	1.04	1.13	1.11	2.11 ★	1.22 ★	.88	1.27	.68 ★
1969	1.20 ★	1.21 ★	1.15	1.48	1.23	1.97	1.46	1.08 ★	1.38	.77
1979	1.38	1.35	1.26	1.74 ★	1.23	1.85	1.61	1.29	1.66 ★	.92
1989	1.53	1.53	1.38	1.94	1.35	1.87	1.72	1.72	1.75	1.01
Year granting full clergy rights to women	1970	1970		1976	1907	1958	1956	1964	1981	1956

Key: ALC = American Lutheran Church; LCA = Lutheran Church in America (merged with ALC in 1987 to form the Evangelical Lutheran Church in America); Mo. Synod = Lutheran Church–Missouri Synod; EC = Episcopal Church; ABC = American Baptist Churches; Breth. = Church of the Brethren; PCUS = Presbyterian Church, US; UPUSA = United Presbyterian Church in the USA (merged with PCUS in 1983 to form the Presbyterian Church (USA)); RCA = Reformed Church in America; MC = Methodist Church.

Denominations are quasi-political organizations, by which I mean that, with only a very few exceptions, they contain more or less democratic mechanisms meant to ensure that national policy represents the wishes of the constituency. Thus another way that denominational policy concerning gender equality might be a rational or pragmatic solution to an internal "problem" would be if that policy reflected the wishes of the membership on the matter. Gender equality, as a goal, does not enjoy equal levels of support in all corners of our society. Survey data show, for example, that individuals living in the South and living in more rural areas are significantly less likely to endorse principles of gender equality, whether they apply to family and work in general or to clergy in particular. In Table 6.2, while approximately 37 percent of nonsouthern and nonrural respondents opposed female clergy in 1986, approximately 43 percent of southern and rural respondents did so. The differences are not large but they are notable, especially given the crudity of the operationalizations of "south" and "rural." Moreover, they apparently represent long-standing social differences in attitudes toward gender equality (Flexner 1974:229–230).

The distinctive resistance of the southeastern United States to institutionalized equal opportunity in general and to gender equality in particular is evident in other ways besides survey data. John Beggs developed a composite measure of state-level institutional support for equal opportunity from the 1960s through the 1980s. The five components of this measure are (1) state action on passage of the Equal Rights Amendment; (2) state actions on a variety of civil rights and fair employment practice laws; (3) percentage of a state's House of Representative delegation voting positively on a variety of equal opportunity bills; (4) ratio of state residents subscribing to liberal versus conservative magazines; and (5) extent to which women held statewide elected offices. Southeastern states made up nine of the ten states scoring lowest on this composite measure of state-level support

Table 6.2 Southern and rural antifeminism

	Percentage		
	South	Non–South	Difference
Agree that it is more important for wife to help husband's career than have one herself.	39.3	34.3	5.0*
Disapprove of married woman working if husband can support her.	23.9	21.2	2.7
Agree that it is better for everyone if woman takes care of the home and family.	52.4	45.4	7.0**
Against female clergy.	43.0	36.8	6.2**
	Rural	Nonrural	Difference
Agree that it is more important for wife to help husband's career than have one herself.	41.9	33.7	8.2***
Disapprove of married woman working if husband can support her.	29.9	19.3	10.6***
Agree that it is better for everyone if woman takes care of the home and family.	57.7	44.0	13.7***
Against female clergy.	42.9	37.4	5.5*

*$p < .10$.   **$p < .05$.   ***$p < .01$.

Source: General Social Survey, 1986 (Davis and Smith 1994).

Note: "South" means living in the south atlantic, east south central, or west south central census regions. "Rural" means living in an area that is not within a standard metropolitan statistical area, as defined by the 1970 U.S. census.

for equal opportunity, a measure that specifically included several direct indicators of support for gender equality (Beggs 1995).[1]

Denominations, of course, vary in their cultural contexts. Some are based in certain geographical regions, some are more rural in their social base, some are more middle class than others, and so on. To the extent that these social/cultural variations are associated with feminism or antifeminism, they should influence the likelihood that a denomination grants full equality to women *if* official policy represents an aggregation of members' wishes. More specifically, from this perspective we would expect denominations that are more rural and more southern to adopt the innovation of female equality later than denominations that are more urban and nonsouthern.[2]

We also would expect a correlation between organizational rules and preferences of members if individuals' preferences are themselves influenced by the institutional context in which they are embedded. From this perspective, members of denominations not ordaining women would be expected to be less in favor of gender equality, but not because organizational policy reflects members' independently held prior preferences. Rather, the correlation would be produced because denominations that do not ordain women themselves help to shape the preferences of their members. It is very difficult to distinguish between these two mechanisms.

Another complication involves the extent to which a denomination's social basis is rural. This factor might "rationally" influence organizational policy both via a clergy-shortage mechanism and via an aggregation-of-preferences mechanism. On the one hand, as described above, individuals living in rural areas are less supportive of gender equality as a goal; as a result, rural denominations might be expected to be *more* resistant to ordaining women. On the other hand, it is rural congregations that are most likely to be unable to find male clergy willing to work for the lower salaries characteristic of these congregations. Consequently, it is in rural congregations that women are most likely to function as clergy both in denominations that ordain them and in denominations that do not (Carroll, Hargrove, and Lummis 1983; Wallace 1992). By this mechanism, if women's ordination is partly a solution to an internal labor shortage, rural denominations might be expected to be *less* resistant to women's ordination. Thus, positing that rules about women clergy are a response to internally generated organizational problems—for example, matching rules to members' preferences or needing to staff rural congregations—does not yield a clear expectation regarding the effect of a more rural constituency on such rules.

There is similar ambiguity regarding how the racial composition of a denomination will influence its propensity to grant full clergy rights to women. On the one hand, both waves of the women's movement have involved mainly white women, and there is a long-standing competitive tension between the goal of expanding women's opportunities and the goal of expanding opportunities for African Americans. In the years immediately following the Civil War, for example, prominent feminists agitated against the Fourteenth Amendment because it gave the vote to black males ahead of white women (Flexner 1974:145). For obvious reasons, African-American organizations, including religious organizations, may be more focused on issues of race than on issues of internal gender equality (Gilkes 1985:698). From this perspective, it is reasonable to expect that black denominations will be less likely to ordain women, simply because the issue is of lower priority to their constituents. On the other hand, official rules concerning women's access to formal positions vary considerably among African-American denominations (Lincoln and Mamiya 1990). Recent work documenting the salience of gender inequality as an issue within African-American religion (Higginbotham 1993; Gilkes 1985) also suggests the possibility that black denominations are not systematically different from predominantly white denominations when it comes to the likelihood of ordaining women.

As it happens, quantitative analysis shows that neither having a rural constituency nor having an African American constituency influences the rate of adopting female ordination. The likelihood that a denomination will begin to ordain women in a given year is neither higher nor lower for rural than for nonrural denominations, and it is neither higher nor lower for predominantly black than for predominantly white denominations.

These results, coupled with the similar noneffect of a clergy shortage on the likelihood of ordaining women, add weight to one of the basic arguments of this book. Formal rules about women's ordination are driven much more strongly by the ways in which denominations interact with their environments than by the ways in which denominations respond to internal pragmatic organizational needs. Rules about female clergy are symbolic display more than "rational" solution to pragmatic organizational problems.

Denominations with largely southern constituencies, however, are less likely to officially ordain women than are denominations with nonsouthern constituencies. For example, the odds against a nonsouthern denomination's beginning to ordain women in 1950 were about 105 to 1. For southern denominations, however, the odds against beginning to ordain women in that year were one and a half times greater, at about 155 to 1.[3] This result is the only support for the view that denominational rules reflect a rational organizational response either to internally generated problems or to constituent preferences. As noted earlier, however, the meaning of this result is ambiguous: it is unclear whether it is produced by the aggregation of member preferences into formal rules or by the influence of denominations (and other institutions) on members' preferences. Whatever the exact causal mechanism, it does appear that denominations with largely southern constituencies are more resistant to formal gender equality than are denominations with largely nonsouthern constituencies.[4]

Internal Organizational Structure

Labor supplies and member preferences are not the only internal features of denominations plausibly connected to policies about women's ordination. Indeed, another set of factors having to do with organizational structure proves to be much more strongly connected than clergy shortage or member preferences to rules about women's ordination. Specifically, a denomination's level of centralization and the presence or absence of an autonomous women's mission society are key organizational variables distinguishing between early and late ordainers of women. These variables structure denominational politics in significant ways. For different reasons, advocates of women's ordination are more likely to successfully achieve formal gender equality in decentralized denominations and in denominations in which there is a strong and autonomous women's organization.

CENTRALIZATION

Barbara Brown Zikmund (1986:34) has emphasized the importance of the centralization of religious authority in conflicts over women's ordination. In decentralized denominations, congregations have the authority to ordain whomever they like and otherwise run their own affairs; in more centralized denominations, congregations are subject to the policies of regional or national bodies. There are several reasons to expect that decentralized denominations will ordain women earlier than centralized denominations. Most important, decentralization means that there will be fewer denominationwide rules of any sort governing the behavior of congregations. Decentralization also means that the denominational administrative infrastructure will be less well developed, making enforcement of whatever national rules might exist more problematic. Either way, a low level of denominational centralization leaves congregations with greater freedom of action. In such denominations, the presence of only a very few women wanting to be clergy can be enough to force the issue, as long as such women find even one sympathetic congregation or local association. Such denominations would be expected to begin to ordain women almost as soon as there were any women who wanted to be ordained.

Compare, for example, the experience of Clara Celeste Babcock within the decentralized Disciples of Christ to the experience of Louisa Woosley within the more centralized Cumberland Presbyterian Church. Babcock began preaching in 1888. A gifted speaker, she was hired by a congregation in Erie, Illinois, after they heard her deliver a sermon, and she remained pastor there for twelve years, becoming the first officially recognized female minister in this denomination (Riley 1989).

In 1887 Louisa Woosley was asked to preach at a Cumberland Presbyterian church in Kentucky. Another fine preacher, she was welcomed into the pulpits of congregations in the area, and the presbytery (the local governing body) ordained her in 1889. In 1890 the Kentucky Synod (the regional governing body) revoked the ordination, an action that was ratified by the 1894 General Assembly (the national governing body). Woosley continued to function as a minister despite being stripped of her formal status, but it was not until 1921 that the denomination officially declared that religious offices were equally open to males and females (Hudson 1990; F. Smith 1989:58).

This example illustrates the importance of organizational decentralization to the early granting of full clergy rights to women. Small numbers of women were attempting to preach and be ordained throughout American religion in the last decades of the nineteenth century. Often such women could find congregations who would hire them and support their quest for formal status within the denomination. In a relatively decentralized denomination like the Disciples of Christ, a sympathetic congregation was all that was needed to break the formal gender barrier within the denomination. In more centralized denominations, by contrast, higher-level judicatories stood in the way. The result was that small numbers of women seeking ordination could succeed in decentralized denominations, but not in centralized denominations. In the latter the formal change would require more pressure, and the pressure would need to be of a different sort.

Not incidentally, in the 1880s and 1890s, there appears to have been as much debate over the issue of women's ordination in the Disciples of Christ as in the Cumberland Presbyterian Church. Thus it seems likely that early adoption of formal gender equality is generally attributable neither to the absence of opponents nor to intradenominational theological consensus concerning proper roles for men and women. Relevant theological differences and debates existed, and still exist, but they occur *within* virtually all denominations. The key factor producing differences in organizational policy is that, in more highly centralized denominations, opponents to women's ordination have had at their disposal an organizational infrastructure that could be used to block the adoption of such a change.

Quantitative results also suggest that decentralization was especially important in the earliest cases of legitimate female ordination. Five of the six denominations granting full formal equality to women before 1880 had decentralized religious authority.[5] More generally, denominations with centralized religious authority are about one and a half times less likely to begin ordaining women in a given year than are denominations with less centralized religious authority. In 1950, for example, the odds against a decentralized denomination's beginning to ordain women were about 100 to 1 while the odds against a centralized denomination's ordaining women were about 140 to 1. When other variables are controlled, the effect of decentralization is even stronger. Holding constant other differences between denominations, the odds against centralized denominations ordaining women are about two and a half times the odds against decentralized denominations doing so. Decentralized organization is highly predictive of women's ordination, and it is especially highly predictive of very early female ordination.

AUTONOMOUS WOMEN'S MISSIONS

The likely importance of a second internal organizational factor is suggested by recent work on nineteenth-century women's voluntary organizations and their social and political influence (for example, Freedman 1979; Scott 1991; Clemens 1993). Theda Skocpol (1992), for example, has found that women's groups were key to explaining state-level variation in the enactment of "mother's pensions" in the early part of the twentieth century. Within American religion, women's organizing was most evident in the form of women's mission societies. Virtually every denomination formed a women's mission society in the decades surrounding the turn of the century (Beaver 1980; Gilkes 1985; Hill 1985; Higginbotham 1993). A 1902 Centennial Survey of Foreign Missions (Dennis 1902:9–13) lists ninety societies directly engaged in foreign missions. Of these, forty-two were women's mission societies and most were affiliated with particular denominations.

However, although many denominations formed women's mission societies, and although these societies almost always raised a substantial proportion of a denomination's missions budget, denominations varied substantially in the extent to which their female mission societies and boards were organizationally autonomous. Women's boards in some denominations were completely independent, raising their own money, sponsoring their own missionaries, and completely controlling their organizational lives. In other denominations, women's societies were merely "auxiliary" to the denominational agencies, providing another avenue for fund raising but granted little say over the disbursement of funds (Beaver 1980:95).

This variation in the extent to which women's organizations were autonomous connects to women's ordination in two ways. On the one hand, women in autonomous organizations appear to have been more likely to develop a consciousness about gender inequality that led them to advocate women's ordination more strongly. On the other hand, autonomy also provided women with enhanced power within denominations. Via these two mutually reinforcing mechanisms, the intradenominational organizational position of women's mission boards affected the likelihood that a denomination would grant full clergy rights to women. Autonomous women's societies were more likely to take on the cause of women's ordination and, more generally, women's access to religious positions. When they pursued this cause, they wielded more intradenominational power and consequently were often effective activists.[6]

The paths by which women's mission societies helped to achieve greater equality within denominations are several. In one way or another, however, female executives of these organizations often used both their personal influence and the organizational infrastructure at their disposal to bring pressure to bear on denominational political processes. An initial comparison between the United Brethren in Christ and the Evangelical Association introduces the basic themes of this section.

Both of these denominations formed women's mission organizations in the 1870s or 1880s. The Brethren's women's organization was autonomous but the Evangelical Association's organization was not. When women "petitioned the Board of Missions of the Evangelical Association in 1878, they were refused permission to organize." The idea was revived two years later, but with a shift: "The propriety of organizing an independent Woman's Missionary Society is questionable, . . . but we find no reason whatever why Woman's Missionary Auxiliaries should not be formed." Women's Auxiliaries were approved, "but their enabling action stipulated that women's groups could exist only on the local level and must be 'under the supervision of the preacher' " (Gorrell 1981:235). A national society was organized in 1883, but still was subordinate. In contrast, "when the United Brethren women met in October 1875, they decided that it was necessary to be related only to the General Conference and that they could be otherwise independent in structure and function" (Gorrell 1981:236).

Donald Gorrell (1981:237) makes it clear that autonomy had real consequences for the functioning of these organizations. Even after their organization was approved, "Evangelical women were forced to wait a year to begin to function, because the board, which needed to approve the constitution and officers of the woman's society, did not meet officially until October 1884." And when the women "wanted to publish a periodical [or] support a 'special field' of work, it was necessary for them to petition the board, which repeatedly rejected their requests." By contrast, United Brethren women "were able to do as much mission work as they could afford to support. When they felt the need of a periodical . . . they solicited subscriptions [and] began publication of their own monthly, the *Woman's Evangel,* in January 1882" (Gorrell 1981:237).

This autonomy, and the activities it permitted, gave organized Brethren women more intradenominational power than their Evangelical Association counterparts. When, in 1909, the Brethren Woman's Missionary Association combined its resources with the other mission boards, "the women would constitute one-third of the membership of the boards and their executive committees," thereby securing "a new status and power for women, described by one officer as 'epoch-making.' " The Evangelical Woman's Missionary Society, by contrast, had "far less power and influence" (Gorrell 1981:238–239). This contrast is also reflected in greater formal gender equality in the Church of the United Brethren in Christ than in the Evangelical Association. Women were permitted to be delegates to the Brethren national governing body in 1889. In the Evangelical Association, no women delegates were seated until the 1940s.

Although it is difficult to assess definitively causal direction, autonomous women's boards are associated with increased access of women to religious positions. This difference, it is important to note, is not produced by any difference in the propensity of women to organize. Gorrell (1981:245) comments, "Women in both the Evangelical Association and the United Brethren in Christ felt similar impulses to organize, to assume leadership, and to engage in more visible and recognized service during the years from 1870 to 1910." The important difference arose in how these impulses were organized, and especially in how autonomous the women's organizations would be relative to the rest of the male-controlled denomination. Greater organizational autonomy translated, in a number of ways, into greater influence over denominational policymaking on women's issues.

The ways in which autonomous women's organizations promoted women's ordination depended in part on how centralized or decentralized was denominational authority. In more decentralized denominations, female mission executives could be effective activists through their publishing and individual lecturing or preaching. Within the Christian Church, Disciples of Christ, the Christian Women's Board of Missions (CWBM) began its organizational life by emphasizing "the conventional concepts of true womanhood" (Bailey 1979:96). In a speech marking the founding of the CWBM in 1874, Marcia Goodwin, a prominent organizer of the board, "assured her brothers that few sisters desired to stand behind the 'sacred desk' and to preach. Instead, mission women would set pious examples for their husbands, their children, and their neighbors" (Bailey 1979:94).

This cautious stance changed, however, during the 1880s. "In 1881, [Marcia Goodwin] published in the *Christian Standard* a series of articles strongly advocating woman's right to the pulpit." Through the CWBM, "numerous Christian Church women gained the experience of participating in church polity, speaking before audiences, and in a few cases even laboring in foreign and domestic mission fields." Moreover, "liberal Disciples allowed their missionary sisters to 'lecture' before mixed audiences" (Bailey 1979:97–98). Persis L. Christian, a "charter member of the national CWBM" and president of the Illinois CWBM in the 1880s, "was one of the Disciples' most popular female speakers . . . Her lectures expounded upon the importance of church missions, but she also encouraged temperance, advocated woman suffrage, and hinted that women ought to occupy the pulpit" (Bailey 1979:100–102).

This advocacy of female clergy by women associated with the CWBM brought down the wrath of conservative Disciples on the organization. Even the wife of the denomination's founder "was horrified to hear a sister suggest that the CWBM would bring 'women before the public in such a way that they would become preachers' " (Bailey 1979:47). The significance of the CWBM for women's ordination within this denomination was evident both to proponents and to opponents of that development.

In more centralized denominations, female mission executives were able to use their organizational position to influence the official actions of denominations' regional and national governing bodies. The Woman's Foreign Missionary Society (WFMS) of the Methodist Protestant Church, for example, was founded in 1879 as an independent agency in which "the women retained the right to make their own decisions and to control and manage their own funds" (Noll 1981:222). When the 1884 General Conference brought the society under the control of a denominational missions board, the WFMS leaders resisted, and their autonomy was restored in 1888. The leaders of this autonomous organization were crucial to furthering formal gender equality in this denomination. "With the memory of 1884 uppermost in their minds, [WFMS leaders] planned how they might obtain even more influence on the floor of the General Conference to protect their work and authority" (Noll 1981: 226).

Four women, all WFMS leaders, were elected delegates to the General Conference in 1892, the first time female delegates had been so elected. One of these four, Eugenia St. John, "also had been ordained an elder . . . in 1889, although clergywomen had not yet been officially recognized in the Methodist Protestant Church" (Noll 1981:226–227). The General Conference debated the legitimacy of these female delegates, eventually seating all four. As a by-product of this debate over seating women delegates, a resolution was passed "which permitted annual [regional] conferences to forbid women to be ordained or to serve as delegates to the General Conference" (Noll 1981:230). By shifting the authority to elect and ordain women to the regions, and by forcing regions to explicitly forbid women access to clergy status or to the General Conference, this resolution removed denomination-level barriers to women's ordination, albeit in a backhanded sort of way. Still, at the national level, women were granted the right to ordination at the same time that they were granted full laity rights, and both occurred via the direct action of women mission society leaders.

Female mission executives, as well as leaders of the largely Methodist Woman's Christian Temperance Union, also were instrumental in winning greater gender equality within the

Methodist Episcopal Church (MEC). Carolyn Gifford reports that "by the 1870s and 1880s some Methodist women, very often those who participated in the Women's Home and Foreign Missionary Societies (WFMS and WHMS) and the Woman's Christian Temperance Union (WCTU), were demanding access to [the governing bodies of the denomination]." Five women were elected as General Conference delegates in 1888, at least three of whom were women's society leaders: "Angie Newman . . . was a state officer of the WCTU as well as an organizer of both the WFMS and the WHMS in her annual conference. Mary Clark Nind was the president of a regional branch of the WFMS. Frances E. Willard was the national president of the WCTU, the largest and most powerful women's organization in the country" (Gifford 1987b:2, 7).

These women were not seated in 1888, but that General Conference (GC) agreed "to submit the question of women's eligibility as lay delegates to GC to a referendum by the entire church membership. . . Once again both sides geared up for the fight, producing more editorials, pamphlets, articles, etc. on the issue." The main "pro" pamphlet, written by a St. Louis Conference clergyman, George W. Hughey, "was published by the Woman's Temperance Publishing Association, the publishing arm of the WCTU. The pamphlet was merely one of many ways the WCTU attempted to influence the membership of the MEC on the issue of women's laity rights." This activity paid off in 1904, when the first female delegates were seated at a General Conference of the Methodist Episcopal Church (Gifford 1987b:9, 12).

Female missions executives similarly pressured the Christian Methodist Episcopal Church (CME) to grant full laity rights to women. After an effort to allow female delegates to the General Conference failed in 1922 by a vote of 435 to 85, "The Women's Connectional Missionary Society presented a resolution to the 1926 General Conference asking the conference 'to grant the women of the CME Church laity rights, as have been accorded to our sister churches and our Mother Church, the

M.E. Church, South' " (Lakey 1985:418). These women's efforts were noticed by the bishops. Whereas in 1922 the bishops opposed seating female delegates, in 1926 the bishops, as part of their address to the Conference, said, "The women of the CME Church have striven many years to get recognition of the General Conference, but completely failed. They are very much discouraged and have about decided that the CME Church will never accord them equal rights with their brothers . . . Give them the right to vote in all conferences and to hold office" (quoted in Lakey 1985:418). The 1926 conference did just that.

Female executives could also influence denominational politics by mobilizing support for change from lower levels of the denomination. The Woman's Division of Christian Service of the Methodist Church was instrumental in mobilizing support in this way for women's full clergy status during the 1950s conflict within that denomination. The 1952 General Conference saw an "impressive" number of memorials supporting full clergy rights for women, many of which came from local women's societies (Bucke 1962:525). After women's full clergy rights lost narrowly at this General Conference, women church leaders mobilized additional support:

> The Woman's Division of Christian Service, through its section on the status of women, took an interest in the question, stimulating what later turned out to be an uncontrollable flood of memorials to General Conference—a large number of them from Women's Societies in churches from all over the country. In all, more than 2,000 memorials on the subject were received. More memorials (petitions) came to General Conference on this one subject than have come on all subjects to any previous Conference. (*Christian Advocate,* May 24, 1956:15)

The April 21, 1955, edition of the *Christian Advocate* provided a glimpse of the way this mobilization worked at the local level. It reported that, in the New England Conference, approximately one hundred churches supported a petition to grant full rights to women ministers. This local endorsement occurred because a Mrs. Kennedy, Conference secretary of the Woman's Society of Christian Service (WSCS) in the area of the status of women, "enlisted the aid of four district secretaries in the matter of women's rights. She also communicated with local WSCS presidents. Together they saw to it that the memorial went before the official boards [of the congregations]. With the endorsement of the boards, it will be presented to the 1956 General Conference" (*Christian Advocate,* April 21, 1955:14). In this way, substantial support for formal gender equality was generated. After losing in 1952, the 1956 motion to institute full clergy rights for women passed "by an overwhelming show of hands" (*Christian Advocate,* May 24, 1956:15).

When the Lutheran Church in America (LCA) began considering the question of women's ordination in the late 1960s, it was partly because of the activity of Lutheran Church Women (LCW). The LCW had conducted a study of the issue, and in 1970 it "adopted a position paper calling upon [the LCA] to allow the ordination of women and 'to implement these changes creatively and vigorously.' The LCW vigorously supported women's ordination and the development of materials that would be persuasive to the church" (Grindal 1990:170–171; see also Reumann 1987:121).

Even in the absence of vigorous mobilizing and politicking, women's mission boards often supported women's ordination in less visible, but still important, ways. Within the (southern) Presbyterian Church, United States, for example, when a denominational ad interim committee raised the issue of women's ordination in 1962, the Board of Women's Work strongly supported the change (Carson and Price 1981:256). Women's ordination was subsequently won at the 1963 General Assembly of this denomination.

An important variation on this theme of female mission executives influencing denominational policy in the direction of greater gender equality concerns the relationship between conflicts over the autonomy of women's mission societies themselves and conflict over female access to positions of denominational authority in general. In virtually every denomination that had an autonomous women's organization, these societies were incorporated into denominational agency structures by the end of the first quarter of this century. These incorporations were conflict-ridden: the men running the other denominational agencies dearly wanted the resource-rich women's societies more completely under the denominational umbrella, and the women running their own mission societies often resisted those efforts to centralize control (Beaver 1980; Hill 1985). These conflicts often brought to the fore broader issues of women's participation in denominational life, and the still powerful female executives of these organizations were often key players in the resulting conflicts. Virginia Brereton and Christa Klein (1980:182) note that conflicts surrounding the women's organizations themselves may have "conferred an indirect and unexpected side benefit." As a result of these conflicts, "some women (and men) of the church were jolted into greater awareness of the issue of women's place in the church." The following examples illustrate that this dynamic did indeed occur in at least several denominations.

In the Methodist Episcopal Church, South, for example, the Woman's Home Missionary Society (WHMS) was organized in 1886 with a large degree of autonomy. The WHMS lost this organizational independence when all missionary activity was centralized under one Board of Missions in 1910. Women's work was directed by a Woman's Missionary Council, subservient to the board. In the process of fighting their (losing) battle for organizational autonomy, however, a larger battle for greater gender equality was joined. Upset by the impending loss of organizational autonomy, Belle Harris Bennett, president of the WHMS, mobilized support for full laity rights for women. Under her leadership, the WHMS requested that the 1910 General Conference grant "full lay rights and privileges for women." The WHMS mobilized their district and local societies to support this resolution, producing "148 memorials, 637 petitions, and hundreds of telegrams in support of women's laity rights" to the 1910 General Conference. In this way, "the controversy over the unification of mission work . . . served as the mainspring for the women's suffrage movement within the southern Methodist church" (Shadron 1981:266–267).

The resolution lost by a vote of 74 to 188, but women's mission leaders mobilized again in preparation for the 1914 General Conference. "They continued to distribute leaflets and petitions and agitated in the church press . . . In 1912, they asked each annual conference to appoint a special committee to evaluate conference opinion on the women's rights memorial." Leaders also "decentralized their efforts still further by sponsoring discussions in local missionary societies on the relationship between woman's suffrage and world evangelization. Local women then formulated their own methods for promoting laity rights . . . In one Texas conference, women resolved to work to elect to church office only men known to favor laity rights for women." They even formed what appears to have been a special purpose group, the Woman's Laity Rights League, "a separate organization of missionary-society women" (Shadron 1981:268, 270, 272). These efforts bore fruit in 1918, when the resolution passed, 270 to 50.[7] The Women's Missionary Council continued to call for greater equality between men and women throughout the following decades.

This same connection between conflict over autonomy for women's organizations and broader issues of gender equality is evident within the Presbyterian Church, U.S.A. In 1923, "by a sweeping act of the General Assembly, the semi-independent missionary groups Presbyterian women had formed and led for nearly fifty years were merged into two new denominational boards" (Bendroth 1987:49). This action generated anger among missionary society women which developed into discontent over women's position in general:

Instigator of the public discontent [over the reorganization] was Louise Blinn, an outspoken advocate of sexual equality and energetic President of the Women's Missionary Society of Cincinnati, Ohio . . . Blinn drew up a petition which she circulated for endorsement and forwarded to the General Assembly in May, 1924. The petition asked for the removal of sexual discrimination in all ordination standards, the organization of a Women's Missionary Society which would have the power to appoint women who sit on General Assembly boards, and the right of such an organization to receive and disburse funds from women's organizations designated for the work of the boards. (Brackenridge 1980:144)

Although this petition did not succeed, the general perception of discontent was strong enough for the 1925 General Assembly to appoint a "Commission of Fifteen to investigate the causes of unrest in the Presbyterian Church" (Brackenridge 1980:145). This commission's report cited the status of women as one factor contributing to overall denominational unrest. This, in turn, led the 1926 General Assembly to ask M. Katherine Bennett and Margaret Hodge, presidents of the Woman's Board of Home Missions and the Woman's Board of Foreign Missions, respectively, to write a report on the causes of unrest among Presbyterian women. This report "decried the persistence of 'artificial inhibitions that savor of another century,' and asked that woman's role in the church be 'considered in the light of her ability and not of her sex' " (Bendroth 1987:56).

The denomination's General Council referred this report to a Committee of Four (Hodge, Bennett, and two male leaders) for recommendations. The committee invited fifteen women, almost all of whom were leaders in women's mission work within the denomination, to a conference. Committee correspondence after this meeting shows that issues of ordination and representation were now fully entwined, mainly because the overarching theme was now equality. Although the women's initial focus was on representation in bodies making decisions affecting their work, this concern mushroomed into calls for full equality. Bennett wrote: "If it is right that women have equal place with men in the church, then it should be given to them;

if it is not right, then let them not be given the eldership . . . [The] fundamental rightness or wrongness of the matter must be faced, and action taken accordingly. Let the Church deny further 'rights,' or remove restrictions and inhibitions that are based on sex" (quoted in Brackenridge 1980:153). The work and mobilizing efforts of this Committee of Four, prompted by "unrest" over the takeover of the women's mission boards, led directly to three 1929 overtures to ordain women as ministers and elders, to ordain them as ruling elders only, and to license them as evangelists. The General Assembly sent these overtures to the presbyteries, where only the second passed.

These last two cases illustrate the complex relationship between conflicts over the organizational autonomy of women's mission societies and conflict over broader issues of gender equality. They represent a particularly important variation on the general pattern. We should be careful, however, not to allow the interestingly different details to obscure the features of that general pattern: in one way or another, organizationally autonomous women's mission societies often were able to influence denominations in the direction of greater gender equality. That influence was made possible by the political advantages produced by organizational autonomy. Like decentralization, autonomous women's mission organizations represent a feature of denominational structure that has had major consequences for the institutionalization of formal gender equality within American religion.

The quantitative analyses of the larger population of denominations strongly supports this claim. For denominations that never had an autonomous women's mission society, the odds against ordaining women are more than three times what they are for denominations that have had an autonomous women's organization. In 1950, for example, the odds against ordaining women for a denomination that had never had an autonomous women's organization were about 150 to 1. For denominations that had had an autonomous women's organization, these odds drop to about 45 to 1. The magnitude of this effect is not greatly reduced when other variables are controlled.

The presence or absence of autonomous women's organizations inside denominations is also connected to the sacramentalism and inerrancy discussed in Chapter 5. Both sacramentalism and inerrancy inhibit the development of autonomous women's institutions. None of the sacramentalist denominations and only 9 percent of the inerrantist denominations examined in this study ever had autonomous women's organizations. By contrast, 57 percent of denominations that are neither inerrantist nor sacramentalist had an autonomous women's organization at some point in their history. Thus, in addition to the symbolic weight women's ordination came to carry as a marker of sacramentalist and inerrantist identity, it appears that these denominations' organizational traditions also decreased the likelihood that they would ordain women. In sacramentalist and inerrantist denominations, the relative absence of autonomous women's organizations inside the denominational sphere meant that one very important agent of change in the direction of gender equality did not emerge before the second wave of the women's movement.[8] Beyond shedding light on the way internal organizational structure has influenced women's ordination policies, attending to women's organizations thus reveals another mechanism by which sacramentalist and inerrantist denominations lower their chances of ordaining women at an early date.

Conclusion

This chapter has argued, negatively, that neither the presence of a clergy shortage nor the racial composition nor the urban/rural composition of a denomination influences how quickly or slowly a denomination has institutionalized formal gender equality. These results suggest that rules about female clergy are not particularly responsive to relevant pragmatic concerns about personnel supply. The rules do show some consistency with constituency preferences—southern denominations are more resistant to women's ordination than are nonsouthern denominations—but this correlation has an ambiguous meaning in this context: how much do organizational rules reflect an aggregation of constituent preference and how much do the rules help to shape those preferences? It is impossible to answer this question definitively.

This chapter has also argued, positively, that both the level of centralization and the presence or absence of an autonomous women's mission society strongly influence how early or late a denomination formally begins to ordain women. Thus internal organizational structure clearly influences the rate at which even externally driven organizational change occurs. This is because new organizational ideas, such as gender equality, will often be contested, and the outcome of those contests will be shaped by intraorganizational political dynamics. Some aspects of organizational structure will give the political advantage to proponents of change; others will give the advantage to those who resist change. In the case at hand, decentralization sometimes permitted small numbers of women and congregations to break the gender barrier very early.

Women in autonomous organizations were also more likely to come to believe that gender restrictive rules are undesirable. Moreover, the same autonomy that promoted this consciousness gave extra organizational influence to female leaders inside denominations. Women were ordained earlier when theological and organizational traditions, however unintentionally, encouraged the emergence of actors who both wanted the change and possessed the organizational wherewithal to promote it effectively.

By focusing in this chapter on some of the internal organizational actors who promoted gender equality, I have tried to correct the impression sometimes created by analysis of organizational change that emphasizes environmental pressures toward change. Such analysis tends to depict organizational change as the inevitable result of homogenizing pressure. Organizational change seems to occur inexorably as faceless organizations helplessly succumb to unyielding environmental pressures. A consequence of this focus is that human agency tends to drop out of the picture (DiMaggio 1988). Yet agents, or carriers, of institutional change do exist, and fully understanding even externally driven organizational change requires closely attending to the intraorganizational politics practiced by these agents.

There is much more to say about what happens inside denominations. In particular, the social location of those who advocate women's ordination has shifted over time in nonrandom ways that have important consequences for how conflicts over this issue develop. Women's mission executives, for example, were key players especially in early and mid-twentieth-century conflicts over this issue, but they are much less visible in more recent conflicts over women's ordination. The "action" in intradenominational conflicts over gender equality has shifted from the realm of ordinary politics conducted mainly by denominational elites to the realm of more extraordinary politics conducted via special purpose groups and social movement organizations. The following chapter describes this and other changes characterizing conflicts about women's ordination over the past 150 years.

·· 7 ··

THE CHANGING NATURE OF CONFLICTS OVER WOMEN'S ORDINATION

To this point I have focused on the cultural, organizational, and environmental forces that influence denominations' formal rules concerning women's ordination. But organizations are not just passive structures buffeted by these forces. They are made up of people who advocate—or resist—changes of various sorts. Organizational policies are often the product of internal struggles between those who want one policy and those who want a different policy. The process of institutionalization, in other words, is often contested. This is especially true of rules about women's ordination, and this chapter focuses on the changing nature of conflicts over those rules.

There has been conflict over women's ordination within virtually every U.S. denomination. Formal policies concerning female clergy are the result of those conflicts. But, interestingly, those conflicts have changed over time in certain systematic ways. Five such changes are especially apparent. First, and most obviously, conflicts over female clergy vary in the frequency with which they occur; some periods see many more such conflicts than other periods. Second, the meaning of conflicts over female clergy has changed over time, becoming more commonly understood in terms of gender equality. These changes, especially the second, were discussed in Chapter 4. The present chapter describes three additional changes in these conflicts: the organizational location of individuals advocating women's ordination, the tactics and strategies pursued by those actors, and the extent of organized opposition to women's ordination. In addition to describing these changes, this chapter also argues that, like the shift of meaning explored in Chapter 4, these changes can be connected to developments in the larger women's movement.

The Changing Environment

We have seen, especially in Chapters 3 and 4, that the women's movement influenced formal policies about women's ordination. Here I want to argue that the women's movement has also influenced the nature of organizational conflict over women's ordination. It is helpful to distinguish, as in Chapter 3, two distinct paths by which the women's movement has influenced denominations. On the one hand, denominations have been targets of this movement during its two waves of high mobilization and activity. On the other hand, the opinions and beliefs associated with the women's movement—especially the idea of gender equality—have become increasingly accepted over this century. Another way in which the women's movement has influenced denominations, then, is by virtue of the diffusion of gender equality as a value among organizational elites and other important constituencies.

Table 7.1 cross-tabulates these two aspects of the broader movement for gender equality—whether or not there is active mobilization and whether or not there is normative pressure stemming from what relevant constituencies believe to be the correct way to run a denomination. The body of the table gives the approximate dates for which the U.S. women's movement can be characterized by the situation represented by one or the other of the table's cells. Before 1848, there was neither an or-

Table 7.1 Two dimensions of the women's movement

| | | Societal Acceptance of Principle of Gender Equality | |
		Low	Medium to high
Level of Mobilization	Low	earlier than 1848	1920–1969
	Medium to high	1848–1919	1970 and later

ganized women's movement nor any normative pressure on organizations to institutionalize gender equality. From 1848 until the ratification of the Nineteenth Amendment in 1920, there was an active women's movement (albeit with some waxing and waning within these years) attempting to influence both state and nonstate organizations. At the same time, there began to be normative pressure stemming from the internalization among educated women and men of the desirability of formal gender equality, but that pressure remained slight. From the 1920s through the middle of the 1960s, the organized woman's movement was relatively inactive. As described in Chapter 3, however, the idea of formally equal access for women to professional positions continued to gain a foothold within the society such that, when the second wave of the women's movement mobilized in earnest, this mobilization occurred in the context of a more widespread acceptance of the principle, if not the practice, of gender equality.

This table greatly oversimplifies the historical picture, but it illustrates basic features of the context in which conflicts over women's ordination have occurred. Previous chapters have argued that this context influenced denominational policies about women's ordination. This chapter argues that this context has influenced the nature of conflicts over the issue, whatever the formal policy outcome of those conflicts. That is, religious denominations experienced conflict over gender equality throughout this period, but the nature of that conflict changes as normative pressure to institutionalize gender equality increases, and it changes depending on the presence or absence of an active women's movement.

The Changing Conflicts

The evidence on which this chapter is based comes from thirty-nine intradenominational conflicts occurring since the 1830s in twenty-nine different denominations.[1] These conflicts are listed in Table 7.2. Most of these conflicts were about clergy rights, but some were about increasing gender equality in ways short of granting women full clergy status, such as conflicts over seating women at General Conferences or conflicts over allowing women to be deacons or elders. Some of these conflicts continue at this writing. Although this is not a random sample of all conflicts, these thirty-nine represent all the conflicts I was able to identify through searching a variety of primary and secondary sources. The primary bias in these data is that larger conflicts from larger denominations are overrepresented, because these are the conflicts most likely to be documented in the written sources on which I mainly relied.

Conflicts over women's ordination look very different at different points in time, and these differences are largely produced by variation in the cultural and political context in which these conflicts occurred. Table 7.3 summarizes the changes in conflicts over women's ordination across the four major periods defined by phases of the women's movement. The rest of this chapter elaborates the patterns outlined in this table.

FREQUENCY AND MEANING OF CONFLICTS OVER WOMEN'S ORDINATION

Social movements punctuate historical time with periods of extensive activity. These movements group together during certain

Table 7.2   Conflicts over formal female access to religious positions

Denomination	Approximate dates of conflict
1. African Methodist Episcopal Church	1840s–1850s
2. African Methodist Episcopal Church	1880s
3. African Methodist Episcopal Zion Church	1890s
4. American Lutheran Church	1960s
5. Brethren Church	1890s
6. Christian Church, Disciples of Christ	1880s–1890s
7. Christian Methodist Episcopal Church	1880s–1890s
8. Christian Reformed Church	1980s–present
9. Church of the Brethren	1830s
10. Church of the Brethren	1880s–1920s
11. Church of the Brethren	1940s–1950s
12. Congregationalists	1830s
13. Cumberland Presbyterian Church	1890s
14. Episcopal Church	1940s–1950s
15. Episcopal Church	1970s
16. Evangelical Association	1880s
17. Freewill Baptists	1830s
18. General Conference Mennonite Church	1900s
19. Lutheran Church in America	1960s
20. Lutheran Church–Missouri Synod	1970s–present
21. Mennonite Church	1880s–1920s
22. Mennonite Church	1970s
23. Methodist Episcopal Church	1880s
24. Methodist Episcopal/Methodist Church	1920s–1950s
25. Methodist Episcopal Church, South	1900s–1920s
26. Methodist Protestant Church	1880s–1890s
27. Presbyterian Church, US (South)	1950s–1960s

Table 7.2   (continued)

Denomination	Approximate dates of conflict
28. Presbyterian Church in the U.S.A.	1830s
29. Presbyterian Church in the U.S.A. (North)	1880s–1890s
30. Presbyterian Church in the U.S.A. (North)	1920s–1950s
31. Reformed Church in America	1950s–1970s
32. Reformed Presbyterian Church	1880s
33. Roman Catholic Church	1970s–present
34. Seventh-day Adventist Church	1970s–present
35. Southern Baptist Convention	1880s
36. Southern Baptist Convention	1970s–1980s
37. Unitarians	1870s–1880s
38. United Brethren in Christ	1840s–1850s
39. United Brethren in Christ	1880s

periods, making those periods times of particularly extensive collective action (Tarrow 1994). Any specific movement is thus likely to experience moments of intense activity bracketed by moments of relative inactivity. This has been the case with the women's movement, which has enjoyed two "waves" of mass mobilization, the first occurring approximately between 1880 and 1914 and the second approximately between 1963 and 1980. Figure 4.1 indicated that periods of high women's movement activity in the society at large also are times of greater conflict over women's ordination. Two groups of women's ordination conflicts—one in the 1880s and the other in the 1970s—align temporally with the two waves of intense activity connected to the women's movement. Furthermore, if I included conflicts over gender equality that have occurred in denominations already granting full clergy rights to women, the heightened level of intradenominational mobilization over gender equality in the post-1970 period would be even more apparent.

Chapter 4 also described the changed meaning of these con-

Table 7.3 Characteristics of conflicts over women's ordination in four periods

Period	Context				Characteristics of conflicts					Outcome
	Mobilized women's movement	Normative pressure	Framed as equality	Pragmatic vs. symbolic	Beneficiaries as actors	Adherents as actors	Extrainstitutional actions	Organized opposition		Leads to formal equality
Before 1848	No	No	No	Pragmatic	Yes (individually)	No	No	No		No
1848–1919	Yes	Somewhat	Yes	Both	Yes (individually)	No	No	No		Somewhat
1920–1969	No	Yes	Yes	Symbolic	No	Yes	No	Some		Yes
1970–present	Yes	Yes	Yes	Symbolic	Yes (collectively)	Yes	Yes	Yes		Somewhat

flicts when they occurred in the context of this secular movement. Social and historical proximity to the secular women's
movement makes it much more likely that conflicts over
women's ordination are understood by participants as conflicts
over the principle of gender equality. I will return to this theme
later, arguing that this change in meaning produces additional
opposition to women's ordination.

THE ORGANIZATIONAL LOCATION OF ACTORS

In addition to changing the meaning of women's ordination
conflicts, the presence of a social movement and a changing
normative context has also changed the organizational location
of actors advocating women's ordination. Specifically, in times
of extensive movement mobilization, intraorganizational conflict over women's ordination was more likely to be generated
by individuals who were "potential beneficiaries" of the changes
encouraged by the movement—by women who themselves
wanted to be ordained. At the same time, as the norm of gender
equality became more widely accepted, women's ordination was
advocated more by individuals who were "adherents" of the
movement—individuals believing in gender equality without
themselves necessarily being women who wished to be ordained
(McCarthy and Zald 1977:1221).

There are two different ways in which potential beneficiaries—women who want to be ordained—have generated conflict
over this issue inside denominations. The first is via the action
of individual women, often already functioning as clergy, peti-
tioning a denomination to grant them formal clergy status. This
occurred even before the women's movement's first period of
mass mobilization. Women in earlier decades were motivated to
seek clergy status through other movements, such as religious
revivalism, temperance, and abolition. But these instances of individual women approaching, or coming to the attention of,
denominations multiplied during the 1870s and 1880s. Women
"in situ"—individual women already functioning as clergy—
were visible actors in 92 percent (twenty-two out of twenty-

four) of the conflicts occurring between 1830 and 1919; they were visible actors in only 20 percent (three out of fifteen) of the conflicts occurring after 1920.

The case of Anna Oliver provides a useful illustration.[2] Anna Oliver received the bachelor of sacred theology degree from Boston University in 1876, and she immediately began to pastor a troubled church in Passaic, New Jersey. After revitalizing this congregation, Oliver moved in 1879 to another troubled congregation in Brooklyn. This congregation, too, grew under her leadership. In 1880 Oliver "launched a Spring offensive on the Methodist Episcopal Church, hoping to press a test case on the ordination of women" (Rowe 1974:64). She mobilized her Boston University classmates, resulting in a pro-ordination resolution from the alumni association of the Boston University School of Theology.

Anna Oliver addressed the New England Annual Conference, giving her reasons for seeking ordination, but the presiding bishop would not allow consideration of her ordination. Still, this Annual Conference passed a resolution calling on delegates to the upcoming General Conference "to use their influence to remove all distinctions of sex in the office and ordination of our ministry" (quoted in Rowe 1974:65).[3] Oliver was not a delegate to the 1880 General Convention, but she "made the long trip from Brooklyn to Cincinnati in May for the Conference, her suitcase filled with copies of a pamphlet she had prepared for distribution at the proper moment" (Rowe 1974:66–67). Oliver distributed copies of this pamphlet, which contained her reasons for wishing ordination, to the delegates. The request for ordination was denied. Oliver continued pastoring the Brooklyn congregation until 1883, but little is known about her ministerial career after that (Rowe 1974:72).

A very similar story was unfolding almost simultaneously in the African Methodist Episcopal Church. Sarah Ann Hughes and Margaret Wilson were, by 1883, both pastoring congregations with the official approval of, respectively, the North Carolina and New Jersey conferences. Along with at least five other preaching women, both attended the 1884 General Conference, where a resolution that women "shall be eligible to any of the offices that are now filled by the male members of our churches" failed to reach the floor. Instead, two motions—one permitting the licensing of women preachers and one forbidding women to pastor churches—were passed. Both Hughes and Wilson lost their pastorates in the two years following this action (Angell 1996, quote from p. 100).

While Oliver's proactive participation in trying to secure her own ordination was perhaps a bit atypical, these examples illustrate a common way in which this issue was raised in the 1880s: a very small number of women, already functioning as clergy, sought full status and thereby generated conflict over the issue of women's ordination.

A second way in which potential beneficiaries of women's ordination have been key actors in these conflicts is via the collective action of women who come together for the purpose of promoting gender equality inside a denomination. This collective action was facilitated by the increased presence of women in seminaries after 1970, an increase that occurred even in denominations that did not yet ordain women. Besides creating a pool of women who had equivalent training to men but were denied access to positions available to men, seminaries also served the crucial function of helping to forge social networks among women with this shared grievance. Seminaries became primary sites of activism in favor of female ordination during and after the 1970s.

The most visible form of this activity was the emergence of social movement organizations (SMOs) to press for greater gender equality within denominations. Such collective actors became more significant within denominations during second-wave feminism.[4] In only 22 percent (seven out of thirty-two) of the pre-1970 conflicts were such organized collectivities important actors, while such groups were present in all of the seven conflicts observed after 1970.[5]

Combining the presence of women in situ and the presence

of SMOs in conflicts over women's ordination makes clear the connection between the presence of a social movement and the extent to which organizational change is promoted by potential beneficiaries of such change. Women who themselves wanted to be ordained were key actors in all but one of the twenty-five conflicts occurring either between 1870 and 1919 or after 1970 (96 percent). By contrast, they were prominent actors in only half (four out of eight) the conflicts occurring between the two waves of the women's movement. Although the form in which women advocated change was very different during the second wave than it was during the first—more organized collective action took the place of more individualized action—the presence of an active social movement made nonelite women more likely to be initiators of organizational conflict over women's ordination.

At the same time that the ebb and flow of feminist mobilization produced rises and falls in the prominence of potential beneficiaries as advocates of gender equality within denominations, the continually increasing legitimacy of formal gender equality in American society prompted steadily increasing activity on the part of movement adherents. Concretely, this means that denominational ad hoc committees, seminary faculties, and, as described in Chapter 6, denominational women's organizations become more prominent actors in conflicts over women's ordination as the twentieth century progressed. If we compare conflicts before and after 1920, we find that denominational committees promoted change in the direction of gender equality in 4 percent (one out of twenty-four) of the earlier conflicts and in 87 percent (thirteen out of fifteen) of the later conflicts. Seminary faculty were important collective actors in 4 percent (one out of twenty-four) of the pre-1920 conflicts but in 67 percent (ten out of fifteen) of the post-1920 conflicts. Denominational women's organizations officially promoted change in 25 percent (six out of twenty-four) of the pre-1920 conflicts and in 80 percent (twelve out of fifteen) of the post-1920 conflicts. Denominational elites have clearly become more likely to push for women's ordination as its legitimacy as an organizational policy has increased.

This last result shows that the denominational women's organizations that are the descendants of the women's mission societies discussed in the previous chapter remain, throughout this period, likely to support women's ordination. By the 1970s, however, these organizations, largely composed of women who do not want to be clergy themselves, became overshadowed in intradenominational conflicts by the social movement organizations composed mainly of seminary-educated women desiring ordination.

Within the Southern Baptist Convention, for example, the organizing of women in ministry began at a 1982 Women in Ministry dinner sponsored by the Women's Missionary Union, "the organization which provides missions education for Southern Baptist churches and which sponsors conventionwide offerings for home and foreign missions" (Groves 1984:202). This dinner led to the formation of a special purpose group, Women in Ministry, organized "to provide support for the woman whose call from God defines her vocation as that of minister, or as that of woman in ministry within the Southern Baptist Convention, and to encourage and affirm her call to be a servant of God" (quoted in Groves 1984:202). The women's missionary organization thus provided the opportunity for initial network building, but then a new organization was formed to carry on the fight for greater gender equality within this denomination.

A similar shift in the organizational location of women's ordination activists can be seen within the Episcopal Church. The nonautonomous Woman's Auxiliary (later called Episcopal Church Women or ECW) supported greater gender equality within the denomination at least since 1946, when it "adopted a resolution requesting the General Convention to interpret the word 'laymen' in the Constitution and Canons of the Church to include women" (*Living Church,* Sept. 29, 1946:21). This change would have made women eligible to be General Convention delegates. Although its requests for gender equality in General Convention representation went largely unheeded, the women's group repeated them from 1946 until women were finally allowed to be delegates in 1967. The first women seated as General Convention delegates, in 1970, came from ECW (Huyck 1981:18). Additionally, the Woman's Auxiliary was "perennially asking for more women to be allowed on church committees or positions" (Huyck 1981:13) and, in 1961, the ECW considered withholding its money from the denomination (Huyck 1981:15). Until the late 1960s, then, the primary, if largely ineffectual, proponent of greater gender equality within the Episcopal Church was the denomination's (nonautonomous) official women's organization.

After 1970, however, the movement in favor of greater gender equality within the Episcopal Church was based elsewhere. Suzanne Hiatt (1983:577) dates the beginning of "women's taking authority in the Episcopal Church" to a 1970 conference that "had grown out of the secular women's movement." "In fact," she writes, "the conference had been organized by women active in the Episcopal Peace Fellowship who simply sent out a call to all women on their mailing list to come together to discuss the church's discrimination against women." This led to the organization of the Episcopal Women's Caucus in 1971, composed mainly of young, seminary-trained women who themselves wanted to be priests. The push for women's ordination to the priesthood thus came from women other than those involved in the ECW. Even the 1970 ECW resolution "that all orders of ministry be opened immediately to women" was the result of the mobilizing done by the women's network that grew out of the 1970 conference (Booty 1988:67; Hiatt 1983:578). Some branches of ECW actually opposed women's ordination, although the leadership supported it (Huyck 1981:45).

Similar developments can be observed in virtually every denomination that did not ordain women by the 1970s. Women's ordination advocacy now is based mainly in social movement organizations for which women who themselves want to be ordained are a prominent constituency. This is very different from the mid-twentieth-century conflicts, in which women's ordination proponents were more likely to be denominational elites, and it is very different from a still earlier period, in which women's ordination proponents, though typically not organizational elites, were more likely to act individually rather than collectively.

TACTICS

Advocates of women's ordination have used a full range of tactics at one point or another in the history of intradenominational conflicts over this issue. Individuals have petitioned national governing bodies, mobilized congregations and/or regional bodies to exert pressure on national governing bodies, argued in the denominational press, published and distributed pamphlets and books on the subject, and organized conferences, networks, and special purpose groups for mutual support, communication, lobbying, and so on. In addition to these activities, all of which may be understood as "normal" politics, there have also been instances of extrainstitutional tactics. Probably the best-known extrainstitutional action in conflicts over women's ordination remains the 1974 "irregular ordination" of women to the Episcopal priesthood. In this event, eleven women were ordained by retired bishops even though the Episcopal Church did not yet permit female clergy. "Illegitimate" ordinations also have occurred in the Christian Reformed Church, in the Reformed Church in America, and in the Southern Baptist Convention (Bratt 1992:808; Mulder 1989:233; Stancil 1988:45).[6]

Other sorts of extrainstitutional action have also occurred. Protesting a vote that continued to deny women full clergy status, some two hundred women occupied the delegates' chamber during the 1992 Synod of the Christian Reformed Church (*Christian Century,* July 1–8, 1992:642). "Illegitimate" celebrations of the Eucharist by Roman Catholic women are not uncommon (Weaver [1985] 1995:114).

Activists do not choose randomly from the extensive repertoire of available tactics. Rather, there is a clear patterning of tactical choice over time. One pattern, in particular, stands out. According to social movement theorists, the shift in the social location of women's ordination activists, described in the previous section, is likely to produce a shift in the tactics used by proponents of women's ordination to achieve their goals. This can be understood as a special case of a more general phenomenon by which the social location of activists shapes the type of movement activity pursued. Carol Mueller (1992:18) notes that "social location helps determine the nature of grievances, resources, and levels of organization." In particular, "it plays a crucial role in whether movement tactics and strategies encompass violence and conflict and, thus, the level and type of mobilization that develops."

From this perspective, it seems likely that as the nature of intradenominational conflicts moves from being top-down to bottom-up (that is, from being elite-driven to nonelite-driven), the tactics used become more extrainstitutional. Social movement organizations composed of women, many of whom themselves want to be ordained, face a different calculus of costs and benefits than do denominational elites. The former, on the one hand, have much less stake in the current organizational arrangements and much more to gain from a policy change in the direction of gender equality. Because these women, unlike denominational elites, are risking neither established careers nor long-term standing in the denomination, they are much more willing to engage in extrainstitutional tactics. Organizational elites, on the other hand, have much more stake in the current organizational arrangements, and so are much less likely to use extrainstitutional tactics; they tend to limit their activity to more "normal" politics. It was no accident, in this regard, that despite the fact that many Episcopal bishops favored ordaining women by 1974, only retired bishops actually ordained the eleven women participating in the "illegitimate" ordination of that year.

There is, in fact, a clear correlation between the active presence of potential beneficiaries organized into special purpose groups and the use of extrainstitutional tactics. Although women's ordination advocates have always used a variety of institutional and extrainstitutional tactics to advance their position, extraordinary tactics become more common after 1970. "Illegitimate" tactics (sit-ins, unauthorized ordinations, and so on) were used in only two of the thirty-two pre-1970 conflicts (6 percent); they were used in five of the seven post-1970 conflicts (71 percent). In all five cases of extrainstitutional tactics, the relevant actors included women who wanted to be ordained. In four of these cases, these women were organized into social movement organizations; the other case (the Reformed Church in America) involved unauthorized ordinations of individual women. When the proponents of women's ordination are individual, unorganized, women who want to be ordained, and when they are organizational elites (such as female missions executives or seminary professors) who are adherents but not potential direct beneficiaries of the movement for gender equality, extrainstitutional tactics are used far less commonly.[7]

LEVEL OF OPPOSITION

In addition to the increased use of illegitimate tactics, more recent conflicts have also involved more organized opposition and countermovement. Organized opposition was observed in none of the twenty-four pre-1920 conflicts, in one-quarter (two out of eight) of the conflicts between 1920 and 1970, and in all but one (six out of seven) of the post-1970 conflicts. Especially when combined with the previous finding that the use of extrainstitutional tactics increased over time, it is clear that conflicts over women's ordination have become more contentious over time.

This increased contentiousness is somewhat surprising. After all, by later in the century, as described in Chapter 3, women have achieved formally equal status in virtually every other profession, there is greater overall cultural acceptance of women in positions of power and authority, and there are decades of accumulated knowledge and experience specifically with female clergy. We might expect these factors to make later considerations of women's ordination less problematic than earlier instances. Instead, the reality seems just the opposite. Contrary to a commonsensical assumption that organizational innovators will be the ones to experience the harshest conflict over proposed change, it is actually the laggards in the diffusion process who experience the most wrenching controversy. Why?[8]

This increased contentiousness has several causes. First, as described above, the different cost/benefit calculus faced by non-elite women who themselves want to be ordained compared with that faced by denominational elites makes contentious tactics a more "rational" choice for the former than for the latter. Organizational elites, on the one hand, are more likely to write articles in the denominational press, serve on committees that make recommendations, and try to mobilize votes at national conferences. Women who have paid to educate and otherwise prepare themselves for a job that a denomination's gender-exclusive policies prevent them from obtaining, on the other hand, are more likely to sit-in, to demonstrate, and to participate in "illegitimate" actions. In this way, the changing organizational location of women's ordination activists produced more contentious conflicts.

Second, denominations still not ordaining women by the 1970s are, by definition, the denominations most resistant to such a policy. Advocates in these denominations are likely to perceive accurately that normal, insider politics will not win the day. It is likely that those routes have been tried to no avail. In such a situation there is little reason to refrain from extraordinary tactics in favor of normal politics, and so the strategic calculus shifts further in the direction of more extraordinary tactics that make conflicts more contentious.

These two routes to greater contentiousness invoke an image of rational political actors calculating the potential costs and rewards associated with various tactical options. The basic idea is that one reason that conflicts over women's ordination have become more antagonistic over time is that the structure of tactical choices has changed in ways that make extraordinary and illegitimate tactics more attractive. A third cause of increased contentiousness around women's ordination is more cultural. That is, increased opposition to women's ordination seems to be generated when women's ordination is understood in terms of gender equality. Chapter 4 described the ways in which proponents increasingly connected women's ordination to the principle of gender equality. But opponents of women's ordination also made this connection, and whenever participants on either side of the debate saw the prospect of female clergy as part of a broader trend toward gender equality, it appears that additional opposition was generated.

In 1879, for example, a Presbyterian opponent to female preaching wrote: "This common movement for 'women's rights,' and women's preaching, must be regarded then, as simply infidel. It cannot be candidly upheld without attacking the inspiration and authority of the Scriptures" (quoted in Zikmund 1981:205). Such examples can be multiplied throughout the period and across the denominational spectrum. At the 1906 Southern Methodist General Conference, George R. Stuart "maintained that the woman's emancipation movement in all its dimensions aimed at the destruction of the home." This movement "included, in Stuart's estimation, four deadly 'ambitions'—deadly, that is, when envisioned by women: financial, social, political, and finally, ecclesiastical" (Shadron 1981:268). It is not just women's preaching that is contrary to the Bible; it is the whole movement for women's rights that must be resisted.

Even conflicts over issues concerning less than full clergy rights generated this same sort of connection to the principle of gender equality and opposition to that principle. During the 1920s the Mennonite church debated the appropriateness of a devotional covering worn by women. One defender of the covering noted that "creation principles . . . will not change despite the rantings of feminists or the laws of nations." Another noted: "In these days, when woman is usurping man's position and power . . . it is peculiarly significant that she is unwilling to wear anything that shows, in any way, that she is second to man in God's order" (quoted in Klingelsmith 1980:179).

Closer to the present, the 1984 Southern Baptist statement against women's ordination resolves "That we not decide concerns of Christian doctrine and practice by modern cultural, sociological, and ecclesiastical trends or by emotional factors" (reprinted in Melton 1991:236). Most recently, a 1994 report from a Christian Reformed Church committee that recommended repealing an earlier change that had permitted women's ordination begins:

> The movement for women's rights has addressed a number of areas of injustice and has had a variety of positive results. But as the Committee on Headship in the Bible . . . pointed out, the ideological underpinnings of much of the movement grows out of the radical individualism of modern western thought which stands opposed to a Christian covenantal understanding of church and family. (Godfrey 1994:1)

To the authors of this report, women's ordination is part of a women's movement that in turn is part of a movement for "radical individualism." The connection to *this* movement, I am suggesting, generates additional resistance to women's ordination.

Not incidentally, although the vast majority of women's ordination advocates over this period embraced the connection to gender equality once it emerged, some, perhaps out of a strategic awareness of the extra adversity that comes with identifying this organizational issue with a movement for gender equality, explicitly differentiated themselves, and their call for women's ordination, from the women's movement or the principle of gender equality. Marie Wiens, of the Mennonite Brethren, for example, "made it clear that her viewpoint was not due to 'any women's lib tendencies, but because of a deepening awareness of the church's meaning in our lives' " (Redekop 1990:268). This also was true of some late nineteenth-century proponents of women's ordination (see, for example, Bailey 1979:201).

Notwithstanding these relatively uncommon instances in which proponents of women's ordination have backed away from the general principle of gender equality, the point here is that the increasingly tight connection among women's ordination, gender equality, and individual rights generates a layer of opposition that is not present when this symbolic connection is avoided. Denominations that have begun by now to ordain women are denominations in which the extra opposition generated by this symbolic connection was outweighed by the support it also produced. Denominations proud to be "liberal" ordained women earlier. Denominations still not ordaining women today, however, are denominations in which symbolic opposition to "liberalism" and its manifestations is fundamental to organizational identity. For such denominations in such a context, it seems that connecting women's ordination to the secular principle of gender equality is likely to lower rather than raise the likelihood of gaining female access to positions of religious authority. As observed in Chapter 4, the symbolic connection between women's ordination and "women's rights" or "gender equality" means that denominations not yet ordaining women by the 1970s are resisting something more than actual females in pulpits and at altars. They are resisting a part of modernity.

A final point about opposition to women's ordination: the increasing legitimacy of the principle of gender equality—indeed, its almost hegemonic status by the second half of the twentieth century—has produced a notable rhetorical shift in opponents' arguments. As the twentieth century progresses, even opponents of women's ordination become more and more likely to endorse some version of gender equality in principle. Support for an abstract principle of gender equality is then rendered consistent with opposition to women's ordination via a "complementary but equal" argument. Archbishop Buechlein's reaction to John Paul II's 1994 reaffirmation of the Catholic Church's official opposition to female clergy is typical: "In an egalitarian climate of society it is difficult for many to understand that the distinction of roles for women and men does not contradict the social doctrine of equal rights among women and men" (Buechlein 1994:56–57).

This argument is not new, as these nineteenth-century examples illustrate:

> We find at the present time the "strong-minded" leaving the teachings of Scripture, and trying to reason out the duty and mission of woman; and they are quite confused by the acknowledged fact that she is the equal of man, and the unquestioned fact also that she is differently organized . . . She is the equal of man, and his help; in some qualities she is his inferior, in other qualities his superior . . . They are not equal, in the sense that they have both equal rule and authority, but equal in their respective spheres. (1868, reprinted in Ruether and Keller 1981:224)

> In unequivocal terms, it [Christianity] teaches the equality of the sexes . . . But while proclaiming woman's equality with man, the Scriptures just as plainly affirm her subordination to him. (1889, reprinted in Ruether and Keller 1981:230)

Though not new, such arguments from complementarity have become increasingly dominant as time goes on and the increasingly legitimate principle of gender equality requires at least some acknowledgment.

Contemporary Vatican opposition to women's ordination presents an interesting variation on this theme. We saw in Chapter 5 that pressure for women's ordination within Roman Catholicism is indeed understood as part of a broader movement for gender equality, as it is in the Protestant and Jewish worlds. The Vatican's official response to that connection, however, is different from that of Archbishop Buechlein, which is more like the typical Protestant response. Protestant opponents to women's ordination are likely to make their opposition to women's ordination part of their explicit and active resistance to a modern movement attempting to expand individual rights. Official Catholic opposition, by contrast, at least since Vatican II, supports the movement for individual rights and gender equality in the secular world, but declares the Church immune from that movement, at least with respect to the priesthood.

Recall that the 1976 *Declaration on the Question of the Admission of Women to the Ministerial Priesthood* does not oppose the principle of full gender equality. Rather, it says that the Catholic Church is itself not subject to that principle because "the priesthood does not form part of the rights of the individual, but stems from the economy of the mystery of Christ and the Church." As such, "the priestly office cannot become the goal of social advancement; no merely human progress of society or of the individual can of itself give access to it: it is of another order" (reproduced in Melton 1991:8). Pope John Paul II's 1994 and 1995 statements on the subject contain the same combination: endorsing gender equality while asserting the priesthood's exemption from that principle (John Paul II 1994, 1995). Official Catholic opposition to gender equality is today one of limiting its scope rather than resisting it altogether.

The women's movement, it seems, has by now almost completely won the framing battle—outright disavowal of some version of a principle of gender equality is very rare today, even in the most conservative religious circles. It is unclear, however, that this victory in the realm of meaning will help women's ordination proponents in the denominations that still do not ordain women. There the rhetorical availability of "complementary but equal" arguments drains the liberal content from the principle of gender equality. Moreover, to the extent that any liberal content remains, it is actively resisted by denominational elites proud to be counted countercultural on this score.

Conclusion

Have changing women's ordination conflicts produced changes in the likely outcomes of these conflicts? Are conflicts over this issue more or less likely to result in greater gender equality as time goes on? Of the thirty-nine conflicts studied in this chapter, fourteen (36 percent) led to full formal equality for women. But the likelihood of a successful outcome for proponents of women's ordination has varied greatly over time. None of the six pre–Civil War conflicts led to the establishment of gender equality. About one-quarter of the conflicts occurring during the first wave of the women's movement led to women's ordination (five out of eighteen) and about one-quarter of the post-1970 conflicts led to women's ordination (two out of seven). Only during the period from 1920 until 1970 did the majority of conflicts produce success for proponents of women's ordination. During that period, almost 90 percent (seven out of eight) of the observed conflicts led to full clergy rights for women. Thus the likelihood of an intradenominational conflict over this issue resulting in women's ordination increased from the 1830s until the 1960s and then decreased again after 1970.

Most striking in this pattern is that conflicts in the period between 1920 and 1970 show such a high rate of "liberal" success. This finding suggests that normative pressure felt and carried by organizational elites is a very important mechanism by which social movements effect organizational change, even in the absence of mass mobilization or grass-roots support. The increasing advocacy of women's ordination by organizational elites—seminary faculty, denominational committees, and especially women's mission executives—seems associated with an increased likelihood of successful institutionalization of formal gender equality.

The decreased likelihood of a "liberal" outcome for post-1970s conflicts is attributable to several factors. First, I have already pointed out that denominations still not ordaining women by these decades are, by definition, more resistant to this change and so are less likely to succumb even in the presence of severe internal conflict on the issue. Second, the observation time for these conflicts is truncated. Some intradenominational conflicts over this issue began in the 1920s and continued, with ebbs and flows, until the 1950s, taking more than thirty years to produce an outcome in favor of women's ordination. Several of the conflicts beginning in earnest in the 1970s continue at this writing and may yet lead to women's ordination in their denominations. Third, we have seen that these more recent efforts to win women's ordination face higher levels of opposition than did earlier efforts. The presence of organized countermovements is likely to further reduce chances of success.

It would be incorrect to conclude that the collective action of women wanting to be ordained, the most prominent form in which women's ordination is pursued after 1970, is responsible for lower chances of winning the desired organizational change. In addition to the issues described in the previous paragraph, there is also evidence that this form of agitating within denominations positively influences the outcomes of these conflicts. Multivariate analysis of the likelihood that denominations will begin to ordain women shows that, when one statistically controls for the fact that denominations not yet ordaining women by 1970 are a group of organizations more resistant to this change, denominations are more than twice as likely to begin to ordain women during the second wave of the feminist movement than they were during other decades. It seems reasonable to attribute this increased success rate partially to the collective action characterizing this most recent period. The appropriate general conclusion about the relationship between type of action and organizational outcome therefore seems to be that both collective action from the "bottom" and elite action nearer the "top" of denominations increase the likelihood that conflicts over women's ordination in fact lead to greater formal gender equality within denominations.

⌣· 8 ·⌣

CONCLUSION

In this book I have argued that formal gender equality—or inequality—is the result of a complex politics of organizational identity construction and maintenance in the presence of a broad social movement for gender equality. I have developed this argument by emphasizing four major themes in the story of women's ordination in the nineteenth and twentieth centuries: rules about women's ordination possess symbolic significance; they are constructed via denominational interactions with various institutional environments; their adoption is influenced by organizational characteristics that shape intradenominational politics; and they generate conflict inside denominations, conflict that changes over time in systematic ways. Understanding the historical and cross-sectional variation in women's ordination requires attending to all four of these aspects of the phenomenon.

The symbolic significance of women's ordination rules suggests both their connection to external forces impinging on denominations and their disconnection from denominations' internal pragmatic affairs. A denomination's formal rules about women's ordination respond to political action from a mobilized women's movement. They also respond to normative pressure—from the increasing legitimacy of gender equality, from the expectations of other denominations in interdenominational networks, and from the expectations of theological subcultures in which denominations are embedded, a factor related but not reducible to network ties. Denominations embedded in sacramentalist and biblically inerrant subcultures are particularly resistant to women's ordination. By contrast, women's ordination is not at all influenced by the presence or absence of a clergy shortage. Denominations' pragmatic staffing needs surely influence the extent to which women do the work of churches, but allowing women to do the work—even the work of congregational leadership—is not the same as granting them full formal equality.

Formal rules about female clergy thus respond to pressures different from those that drive the presence or absence of actual, functioning female clergy. As in other organizations, when environmental pressure is not fully aligned with internal pragmatic needs, rule and practice diverge. John Meyer and Brian Rowan ([1978] 1991:58) note that "decoupling enables organizations to maintain standardized, legitimating, formal structures while their activities vary in response to practical considerations." We have seen that this applies to women's ordination.

We have also seen the way in which the very meaning of women's ordination varies both historically and cross-sectionally. Women's ordination is not always and everywhere understood as an issue of gender equality. Supporting women's ordination comes to mean supporting a principle of gender equality only in the context of a broader women's movement that, whatever else it does, represents an effort "to extend to women the individualistic premises of the political theory of liberalism" (Cott 1987:6).

Still, since even organizational change that is largely symbolic and externally driven is often contested, intraorganizational politics have to be part of the story. Hence how early or late a denomination adopts full gender equality as official policy is influenced by its level of centralization, by the presence or absence of an autonomous women's mission organization, and by the extent to which the denomination's social base is in the South. Centralization and autonomous women's organizations matter because of their consequences for the emergence and efficacy of agents promoting change in denominations. Throughout the denominational world, women in their own autonomous organizations were more likely to advocate full gender equality. Moreover, organizational autonomy often translated into intradenominational influence on this issue. Decentralization, in different ways, also generated organizational openings for proponents of women's ordination.

The key point here is that organizational change often occurs because those who want it win political battles against those who oppose it. In decentralized denominations, and in denominations with autonomous women's organizations, agents of change have been more likely to be present and, when present, they have been more likely to be effective. This is true throughout the denominational population. In particular, however, part of the tardiness of biblically inerrant and sacramentalist denominations when it comes to women's ordination is that these denominations discouraged the formation of autonomous women's organizations. Effective agents of change in the direction of gender equality thus were less likely to emerge. In these denominations, in this way, organizational structure worked together with organizational identity to reinforce resistance to women's ordination.

Whatever the outcome of women's ordination conflicts, the conflicts themselves look different at different times. The earliest challengers to restrictive gender policies in denominations were individual women, many of whom were already functioning as clergy. After the first wave of the women's movement, these individual, nonelite challengers gave way to organizational elites—seminary faculty, denominational committees, and women's mission executives—as the main carriers of gender equality within American religion. Then, after 1970, potential beneficiaries—women who themselves want to be ordained—

again became the primary actors, now acting collectively rather than individually. Recent advocates are more likely to use extrainstitutional tactics, and they are more likely to confront organized opposition. All in all, conflicts over women's ordination have become more harsh and contentious over time.

This book's findings and arguments should prompt rethinking about the complex ways in which gender, organizations, social movements, and religion intersect. Three themes seem particularly worthy of emphasis or reemphasis: the manner in which social movements effect organizational change in the absence of legal mandates backed by the state; the relationship between gender inequality and religious authority; and the symbolic significance of organizational rules.

The State, Social Movements, and Organizational Change

For most organizations in contemporary Western societies, the state is a key component of the environment, especially with respect to issues of persons' equal access to positions. Formal gender equality—rules prohibiting discrimination with respect to gender—is, by the last quarter of the twentieth century, ubiquitous in certain populations of nonreligious organizations because those organizations are more susceptible to state influence. Government action has also been important for institutionalizing gender equality in religious organizations within societies, especially Scandinavian societies, where churches are an institutional arm of the state.

In the United States, of course, religious organizations are institutionally more distant from the state, and this distance makes the story of gender equality in American religion more complex. Less directly regulated by the state with respect to gender equality, American denominations have been slow, as a population, to formally permit women's ordination. Still today, only about half of U.S. denominations grant full clergy rights to women. As with other organizations, denominations' formal rules are the result of interactions with institutional environments, but the state is a less dominant actor for denominations than often is the case in stories of organizational change.

The diminished role of the state in denominational change means that additional factors take on more importance than they might have for change in other organizational populations. When it comes to formal rules about women's ordination, for example, the broader social movement for gender equality and various denominational subcultures are the most salient parts of denominations' environments. By the same token, the relative absence of state coercion with respect to gender equality in religion increases the importance of internal organizational characteristics affecting the outcome of conflicts over that issue. More centralized denominations are slower to institutionalize formal gender equality, for example, because of the political advantages centralization gives to upholders of the status quo.

We might say that the contested diffusion of women's ordination across the denominational population provides a glimpse of what certain sorts of organizational change would look like more generally were such change *not* mediated by the state. To say this another way, the story of women's ordination is partly the story of what happens when a social movement, in this case the women's movement, "hits" an organizational population directly, rather than indirectly via the state.[1] Without the state, organizational change of this sort diffuses more slowly, intraorganizational conflicts over the relevant issues change as the driving social movement changes in character, organizational features influencing internal politics are key determinants of policy outcomes, and the diffusion of organizational change is structured more strongly by subcultural divisions within the organizational population.

Religious Authority and Gender Inequality

There is much more that could be said about denominational subcultures, the primary ones being those centered on biblical inerrancy and sacramentalism. In Chapter 5, I argued that formal gender inequality has become so deeply entrenched within those two worlds partly because it helps denominations to symbolize—to themselves and to others—an antiliberal organizational identity. Here I want to suggest that it is not coincidental that these are the denominations in which religious authority is most obviously legitimated by reference to privileged access to a supernatural realm. In an era and a culture in which formal gender equality enjoys widespread legitimacy—one indicator of which is the fact that even contemporary opponents of women's ordination do not often oppose the fundamental justice of gender equality—it hardly would be possible to sustain formal gender *in*equality without drawing on a source of authority that is alternative to Enlightenment principles of basic human rights.

Biblical inerrancy and sacramentalism provide just such alternative sources of authority. The first rests on the suprahistorical status of the biblical text. The second rests on the power to consecrate the host, a power that is passed through the apostolic succession represented by ordination into priesthood. It is commonly observed that the classic assertion of individual charismatic authority—"It is written . . . but I say unto you"—provides a new basis for legitimate action. My point here is that these two institutional worlds do the same by asserting, essentially, "It is written in liberal modernity . . . but the Bible/the Magisterium says unto you. . ." In a world in which formal, if not actual, gender equality is by now so deeply legitimate, it would be difficult for any one denomination to sustain formal gender inequality were it not for the support of a wider institutional framework grounding its legitimacy on something other than Enlightenment humanism. Chapter 5 argued that formal gender inequality helps to symbolize orientation to these alternative sources of authority. Here I am suggesting something stronger: that formal gender inequality in the West could not be sustained on a large scale in the late twentieth century *except* by an institutional subworld organized around religious authority. Gender inequality and supernaturally derived religious authority are mutually reinforcing elements of a broader antiliberal organizational identity.

The only sustained sociological examination of the connection between gender inequality and religious authority in either the biblically inerrant or sacramentalist worlds is Nancy Jay's (1992) *Throughout Your Generations Forever.* Contrasting my argument with hers will clarify further the cultural connection I am trying to draw between gender (in)equality and religious authority. In her discussion of Roman Catholicism, Jay emphasized the mutual interdependence between priestly authority via apostolic succession and the sacramental notion of the Eucharist as a literal sacrifice of Christ's body and blood. The power to perform the sacrifice comes from one's place in the apostolic succession of priests, and apostolic succession has meaning only if it conveys the power to perform this and other sacramental acts. Jay provocatively placed this interdependence in the context of what seems to be a cross-cultural correlation between expiatory sacrifice and patrilineal descent, and she argued that women often are excluded from such rituals because expiatory sacrifice largely functions to constitute the all-male descent system. Sacrifice, she wrote, "remedies having-been-born-of-woman, establishing bonds of intergenerational continuity between males that transcend their absolute dependence on childbearing women" (Jay 1992:147).

It seems plausible to argue that protecting apostolic succession's "descent system" requires celibacy. Legitimate biological heirs, after all, might compete with religious heirs for the benefits and powers conveyed through the lineage. It is difficult to see, however, why protecting apostolic succession should require excluding celibate women from places in the descent system. To say this another way, it seems correct that the sacrament constitutes and legitimates the religious descent system—apostolic succession and priestly power to perform a literal sacrifice make sense only in terms of each other. It is not clear, however, even from this angle, why performance of the literal sacrament should require an exclusively male descent system.

Why Roman Catholicism continues an all-male priesthood in the contemporary world thus remains mysterious in Jay's account. Indeed, that connection remains mysterious unless we see both sacramental religious authority and gender inequality as markers of opposition to liberal modernity. Before gender equality became fully identified with liberalism, sacramental denominations were no more exclusive of women than nonsacramental denominations. After gender equality became identified with liberal modernity, sacramental, particularly Roman Catholic, opposition to female priests became part of a more general, long-standing effort to resist liberalism. Emphasizing the supernatural basis of sacramental authority is itself part of that effort, and it is telling to recall here that papal infallibility was instituted as part of the 1870 antiliberal agenda of Vatican I. Jay's argument for an intrinsic connection between sacramental religion and opposition to female clergy therefore seems somewhat overdrawn, just as other attempts to find intrinsic connections between biblical inerrancy, sacramentalism, and gender inequality miss the explanatory mark.[2] The connections are culturally and historically contingent, forged in the context of conflict between liberalism and supernaturally based religious authority.

The Symbolic Significance of Organizational Rules

Conflicts about women's ordination are about gender, not women. That is, they are not, in general, conflicts between women on the one side and men on the other side, and they are not, in general, conflicts about wresting institutional power and resources from men and giving them to women. On the contrary, women's ordination conflicts invariably include women and men on both sides, and very little actual power or resources are transferred from men to women, whatever the outcome of such conflicts. Stated positively, these are conflicts between individuals—both women and men—who want their denomination to display one sort of organizational identity, and other individuals—again including both women and men—who want the denomination to display another sort of organizational identity. Martin Reisebrodt's (1993b:243) observation concerning Iranian Islamic fundamentalism applies as well to women's ordination in the Unites States: "These conflicts are not conflicts between sexes but about the structures of gender relations."

In a way, to say that women's ordination is about gender, not women, is another formulation of one of this book's major themes: women's ordination has a symbolic significance over and above whatever practical consequences it may bring for actual women and men. Rules about women's ordination, I want to suggest here, are not the only denominational policies carrying symbolic significance. Perhaps the contemporary issue most directly analogous to women's ordination is the ordination of sexually active homosexuals. It seems clear that a denomination's policy on this issue carries great symbolic weight. Most telling, the very small number of openly homosexual clergy in Protestant denominations debating the issue means that the vast majority of congregations would never realistically be faced with the prospect of an actual gay pastor. At the same time, I speculate that there are churches in many denominations pastored by more or less openly gay individuals who are well loved by congregations which, nevertheless, would balk at supporting a formal rule officially endorsing full clergy rights for homosexuals. Rules about gay clergy, like rules about female clergy, thus appear to reflect the construction of denominational collective identity as much as, and perhaps more than, the regulation of day-to-day lives of real people in real congregations. Furthermore, it would appear that rules about ordaining gay men and lesbians also share the liberal versus nonliberal meaning that characterizes rules about ordaining women.

It would be a mistake, however, to infer from these points of similarity between women's ordination and homosexual ordination that rules permitting gay clergy will, in time, diffuse as widely as have rules permitting women's ordination. Among the differences between the two cases is the fact that there is nothing comparable to autonomous women's mission organizations in the case of ordaining homosexuals. That is, within denominations, there are no established organizations, created for other purposes, that are likely to advocate this organizational change after the current wave of mobilization via social movement organizations subsides. This difference, among others, makes it unlikely that full clergy rights for homosexuals will diffuse as widely in the coming one hundred years as women's ordination did in the previous one hundred years.

This is not the place for a full analysis and discussion of intradenominational conflicts over ordaining gay men and lesbians. I call attention to such conflicts here in order to illustrate the point that denominational policies other than women's ordination carry substantial symbolic significance. Formal rules carrying symbolic significance are ubiquitous in American religion, as they are in organizations of all sorts. Interpreters of intradenominational conflicts therefore would do well to investigate the extent to which any particular conflict involves competing efforts to construct a denominational identity conforming to expectations of one or another part of the world outside that denomination.

Returning, again, to the symbolic significance of gender equality, consider the 1869 words of John Stuart Mill from his classic essay *The Subjection of Women:*

> But I may go farther, and maintain that the course of history, and the tendencies of progressive human society, afford not only no presumption in favor of this system of inequality of rights [between women and men], but a strong one against it; and that, so far as the whole course of human improvement up to this time, the whole stream of modern tendencies, warrants any inference on the subject, it is, that this relic of the past is discordant with the future, and must necessarily disappear.

In a sense, and with proper qualifications, the main point of this book is that the connections Mill saw between gender equality and "progressive human society," "human improvement," and "modern tendencies" constitute the cultural and ideological context in which formal rules about women's ordination should be understood. If these connections remain as culturally salient as I believe them still to be, then to resist gender equality is to resist a modernizing, liberal agenda within which individuals have distinctive moral standing qua individuals, and not as members of "natural" groups—families, races, genders—possessing certain "natural" rights and functions. To support gender equality was, and remains, to support the larger project of modernity; to resist gender equality was, and remains, to resist that project.

From this perspective, rules about women's ordination largely serve as symbolic display to the outside world, and they point to (or away from) a broader liberal agenda associated with modernity and religious accommodation to the spirit of the age. From this perspective, a denomination's formal policy about women's ordination is less an indicator of women's literal status within the denomination and more an enactment of its position vis-à-vis the liberal and modern agenda of institutionalizing individual rights.

Women's ordination, then, is about something more than females in religious leadership. This book has tried to say what that "more" is.

NOTES
REFERENCES
INDEX

NOTES

1. Introduction

1. Historical research, for example, tends to highlight the experiences of early female preachers and the struggles to achieve greater opportunity for women within American religion (see, for example, Ruether and Keller 1981, 1986; Tucker 1990). Sociological research, similarly, has investigated the social backgrounds of women entering the ministry, their experiences in seminary and on the job market, and the ways in which their careers differ systematically from the careers of male clergy (Carroll, Hargrove, and Lummis 1983; Kleinman 1984; Nesbitt 1993, 1997; Charlton 1995; Zikmund, Lummis, and Chang 1997). Other sociological research has examined sources of continuing resistance to female clergy among lay people (Lehman 1980, 1987), among male clergy (Nason-Clark 1987a), and among denominational officials (Lehman 1981). Still other research has focused on the consequences for denominations of growing numbers of female clergy (Nason-Clark 1987b; Royle 1987). Most recently, social scientists have begun to address the question of whether or not female clergy practice ministry styles that are systematically different from the styles practiced by men (Lehman 1993; Guth et al. 1994; Simon and Nadell 1995; Finlay 1996).

2. The first two examples are drawn from Meyer and Rowan ([1977] 1991:50–51).

3. See, for example, Bliss (1952); Lynch (1975); Bednarowski (1980); Brereton and Klein (1980); Barfoot and Sheppard (1980); Boyd and Brackenridge (1983); Carroll, Hargrove, and Lummis (1983); Gilkes (1985); Zikmund (1986); Ward (1991); and Wessinger (1993, 1996).

4. For textbook discussions of event-history analysis, see Allison (1984) and Yamaguchi (1991).

5. See Chaves (1996) for more detail regarding the quantitative analysis and results.

6. The discussion of women's organizations as key actors in internal conflicts over women's ordination also connects and adds additional support to the idea, proposed recently by scholars working in other areas, that nineteenth-century women's voluntary organizations influenced American society in significant, but not yet fully appreciated, ways (Scott 1991; Skocpol 1992; Clemens 1993).

2. The Symbolic Significance of Women's Ordination

1. Table 2.1 and Figure 2.2 are based on the largest one hundred denominations during this period. Figure 2.2 would not look different if smaller denominations were included.

2. This phenomenon is not unique to United States churches. Although the Church of Norway allowed women clergy as of 1938, twenty-three years passed until the first woman was ordained in 1961 (Maher 1984:6).

3. The four schools supportive of female clergy were Moody Bible Institute, Nyack College, Gordon Bible College, and Northwestern Bible and Missionary Training School. Biola and the Philadelphia School of the Bible were unsupportive from the start.

4. "In the EUB Church there was just one order of ordained ministry—that of elder" (Cooney 1988:27).

5. For examples of gaps between rhetoric and practice with respect to women's roles in households, see Ammerman (1987:136), Rose (1987), and Davidman (1991:161). For an additional example of the gap with respect to women's roles in religious organizations, see Brasher (1994).

6. In this regard as well the situation is not so different in Catholic

congregations. Just as in Protestant denominations, female "ministers" in Catholicism are largely segregated into a variety of "assistant minister" positions.

7. It should also be reported, however, that once lay people have direct experience with a woman minister, their resistance is reduced (Lehman 1987:324; Wallace 1992:171; Dudley 1995:2–3).

8. In this same study, Lehman (1981:113) also observed a gap between a more aggressive denominational affirmative action policy and its implementation—another sort of loose coupling. Although formal policy mandated that denominational executives encourage congregations to hire a woman minister, almost two-thirds of congregations that searched for a minister reported that no denominational executive with whom they had contact raised the issue with them.

9. Two main categories of discussion and debate about women's ordination do not seem strongly driven by recognition of normative pressure toward gender equality: those that occur before the Civil War and those that occur within Pentecostal denominations. But these are exceptions that prove a more general rule. Women's ordination is connected to external normative pressure toward gender equality only when participants in these debates are in a cultural context in which such normative pressure exists and is salient. Put simply, the greater the social distance between a denomination and the women's movement, the more the issue of female clergy is understood as an internal, pragmatic matter rather than as an externally oriented, normative matter. I will return to this point in Chapter 4.

3. External Pressures

1. It would be interesting to investigate whether or not this conclusion would be supported if the comparison were expanded beyond U.S. and Scandinavian Lutheran denominations. The earliness of the Norwegian and Danish policy changes, combined with the fact that almost half of Lutheran denominations worldwide still did not ordain women by 1980 (Maher 1984), suggests that an analysis with such an expanded scope would still strongly support the idea that institutional connection to a liberal state leads to women's ordination at an earlier date.

2. The rise of these organizations, which can be thought of either

as social movement organizations (McCarthy and Zald 1977) or as special purpose groups (Wuthnow 1988), has altered the nature of intradenominational conflict over women's ordination, a point to which I will return in Chapter 7.

3. Figure 2.2 obscures the extent to which denominations began to ordain women in the 1970s. Because there were more denominations in the organizational population by then, the percentage increase in denominations ordaining women is not as dramatic.

4. The 1970s results combine General Social Survey responses from 1972, 1973, and 1974, and they are reported in James Davis (1992: 227). I generated the 1990s results by combining the 1992, 1993, and 1994 General Social Surveys (Davis and Smith 1994).

5. Here, and throughout the book, numerical results expressed in terms of odds come from the event-history analysis of women's ordination described in Chapter 1. In general, the odds reported in the text are calculated from equations that include only a year variable in addition to the independent variable of interest. These equations are available from the author. More elaborate equations that include a variety of control variables can be found in Chaves (1996:863). I call attention in the text to the few instances where results from the simpler equations differ substantively from results when relevant controls are included.

4. The Changing Meaning of Women's Ordination

1. See Chapter 7 for more detail about the data underlying Figure 4.1.

2. This claim can be seen as a version of a Zald and Berger hypothesis (1978:849). That is, the women's movement provided ideological support for advocates of women's ordination and thereby changed the way that these advocates understood their goals.

3. Gifford (1987a:5) makes a similar observation about Palmer.

4. Nor is the theme of gender equality present in Sexton's (b. 1799) own autobiographical justifications for her preaching, based on her diaries and published in 1882 (Sexton [1882] 1987:210–217, 224–231, 238–240, 252–255, 400–403).

5. This is also true for conflicts within denominations that already grant formal equality to women. There, contemporary conflicts are over efforts to implement gender equality more deeply, and proponents virtually always use a language of gender equality. To offer just one

example, although the Church of the Brethren had granted full clergy rights to women in 1958, a 1970 resolution on "Equality for Women" asked the denomination "to support action to bring women into full participation in the mainstream of American society exercising all the privileges and responsibilities thereof in truly equal partnership with men" (Brubaker 1986:177).

6. The other dominant theme, according to Weaver ([1985] 1995: 113), was "a motivation for change located in 'the sake of the Gospel itself.' "

7. There is an anomaly here. Although key players in the 1880 debate over women's ordination surrounding the Methodist Episcopal General Conference of that year were connected to the secular women's movement, the language of gender equality is conspicuous by its absence from the pamphlets generated by that conflict (Norwood 1982:446–456). As I will argue further in Chapter 7, opponents of women's ordination often responded with increased hostility when the issue was framed as one of gender equality. Advocates of women's ordination often perceived this and at times explicitly distinguished themselves and their arguments from the secular movement for gender equality. Given this, did savvy activists in this particular case strategically avoid the gender equality frame? It is impossible to know.

8. Recall, for example, the 1922 statement on women's ordination issued by the Central Conference of American Rabbis and the 1970 report prepared by the Commission on the Comprehensive Study of the Doctrine of the Ministry of the Lutheran Church in America. Both of these construe women's ordination as an issue of gender equality raised by the women's movement and changing gender roles.

9. It is interesting to note that eleven of these thirteen "egalitarian" respondents were African American. That means that 41 percent (eleven out of twenty-seven) of the black female preachers were relatively egalitarian in their self-understanding while only 8 percent (two out of twenty-six) of the white female clergy understood themselves in this way.

5. Inerrancy, Sacramentalism, and Women's Ordination

1. The Lutheran doctrine of communion—consubstantiation—is not identical to the Catholic doctrine of transubstantiation. It is, however, a doctrine maintaining a "sacramental realism" that affirms "the

reality of the presence of the body and blood of Christ in contrast to a merely symbolic element." Lutheran doctrine considers the reception of these elements to be of "indispensable importance . . . as a means of communicating salvation and redemption" (Piepkorn 1978:79–80). This view of communion makes the ritual something more than a symbolic remembrance of a meal long ago, which is why I include Lutheran denominations among the sacramental.

2. In the numerical analyses reported here, Catholic, Episcopal, Orthodox, and Lutheran denominations were coded as "sacramentalist" and all others as nonsacramentalist. A denomination's biblical inerrancy was determined via examination of its official position on the Bible. I considered a denomination to be within the inerrant subculture if it explicitly states its position as one of holding the Bible to be "inerrant" or "infallible." Denominations that did not use these key words (usually instead stating that the Bible is "inspired" or "sufficient for salvation" or some other formulation short of "inerrant") were considered to be outside the cultural boundary marking off denominations committed to biblical inerrancy. See Chaves (1996) for further methodological details.

3. The specific numerical odds cited here—100 to 1 for nonsacramental denominations and 410 to 1 for sacramental denominations—apply only for 1950. The *ratio* between those two odds—about four to one—obtains in every year. The specific numerical odds change because all denominations become increasingly likely to ordain women over time. At each point throughout the period under study, however, nonsacramental denominations are about four times as likely as sacramental denominations to begin to ordain women.

4. On their face, these numerical results seem to suggest that sacramentalism in and of itself represents a stronger barrier to women's ordination than does inerrancy. But this is not the case. The effect of sacramentalism seems stronger than the effect of inerrancy primarily because sacramental denominations also tend to be organizationally centralized while inerrant denominations tend to be organizationally decentralized. As we shall see in Chapter 6, organizational decentralization is a key factor leading to women's ordination at an early date. The conjunction between sacramentalism and centralization thus enhances the correlation described here between sacramentalism and re-

sistance to women clergy. Similarly, the conjunction between inerrancy and decentralization renders inerrant denominations not quite as resistant to women's ordination as they might otherwise be. When the effects of centralization are controlled in multivariate analysis, the direct effects of inerrancy and sacramentalism are about equal: denominations of either type are about three and a half times less likely to ordain women than are denominations that are neither sacramentalist nor inerrantist. See Chaves (1996:863) for these results.

5. My use of the term "inerrant" to describe those who accept biblical authority before the great Fundamentalist/Modernist controversies of the 1920s is somewhat anachronistic. What we think of today as full-blown biblical inerrancy came about as a result of these controversies: that is, the term "inerrant" itself took on symbolic weight as a signifier of alliance with Fundamentalism. Paul Bassett (1978:74) describes the word "inerrancy" as, by 1928, one of the "shibboleths of Fundamentalism." I am using the term to refer more broadly to those with an intellectual commitment to the basic internal consistency and authority of the Bible. This definition emphasizes that such an intellectual commitment does not logically entail opposing women's ordination. Only when inerrancy comes to signify an antiliberal fundamentalism does it also seem to entail opposition to gender equality.

6. Recall, however, that Palmer's strong biblical defense of female preaching was not expressed in terms of a principle of gender equality, nor did it extend into a call for female participation in all aspects of ministry. Other inerrantists, however, went further than she did.

7. Both of these examples are from Hardesty (1991:63,65).

8. A full discussion of the detailed arguments used to justify one or another interpretation of biblical passages regarding women is not possible here. Relevant issues range from questions about authorship (did Paul write I Timothy or, for that matter, I Corinthians 14:33b–35?), to questions about cultural practice (exactly what were gender-role expectations in first-century Palestine?), to questions about nuanced meanings of Greek words (when Paul calls Phoebe *diakonos* in Romans 16:1, should that title be translated "servant" or "minister" or "deacon"?). My general claim about the basic interpretive structure of these arguments would not be altered by attending to these nuances. Whatever the details, exegetes looking to the Bible as an authoritative guide

to practice regarding gender roles somehow either raise the "pro" passages above the "con" passages or vice versa.

9. Hutchison (1976:2) saw two additional ideas as part of Protestant modernism: "One was the idea that God is immanent in human cultural development and revealed through it. The other was a belief that human society is moving toward realization (even though it may never attain the reality) of the Kingdom of God."

10. It begins to be important to distinguish between "fundamentalists" and "evangelicals" in the 1940s. Evangelicals, represented by the National Association of Evangelicals, are characterized by a less militant, more accommodating approach to secular culture and a softer position on biblical authority (Ammerman 1991:37).

11. Recall also the discussion of Pentecostal women preachers from the previous chapter. Just as social distance from organized inerrancy leads to more variation among these denominations concerning women's ordination, social distance from organized liberalism leads to support of female clergy that is expressed in terms other than the liberal language of gender equality.

12. Compare this with the similar phenomenon identified by Tolbert and Zucker (1983:22) in the diffusion of civil service reform among American cities. They comment: "Early adoption of civil service reform—before 1915—appears to reflect efforts to resolve specific problems confronting municipal administrations, while later adoption is rooted instead in the growing legitimacy of civil service procedures, with the diffusion of societal norms serving to define local structure."

13. A similar argument could be made about gender policy among African-American denominations. Because they are less oriented to the liberal/antiliberal conflicts of white Protestantism, and less concerned with signaling loyalty to either of these (white) camps, it is likely that gender rules among black denominations are less weighted with liberal or antiliberal meaning.

14. See Trapp (1989) for a review of the theological arguments.

15. Catholic antimodernism and antiliberalism are described in detail elsewhere (Daly 1985; Kurtz 1986; Appleby 1992; Burns 1992; Gleason 1995). In this section I will highlight only the points that are directly relevant to the argument I am developing.

16. See Appleby (1992) for examples.

17. In 1864, Errors twelve and thirteen were: "The decrees of the Apostolic See and of the Roman congregations impede the true progress of science" and "The method and principles by which the old scholastic doctors cultivated theology are no longer suitable to the demands of our times and to the progress of the sciences" (Pius IX [1864] 1956: 145).

18. Pius XII endorsed modern methods of biblical exegesis in a 1950 encyclical that also strongly asserted papal authority to define correct teaching (Pius XII 1950). And even if it took until 1996 for a pope to reject creationism firmly and explicitly, biological evolution has been officially acknowledged as a "serious hypothesis" at least since Pius XII (Tagliabue 1996:A1).

19. This is not to say, of course, that opposition to female clergy is completely new to this period. David Noble (1992), for example, documents official Catholic opposition to women's ordination at least as early as Charlemagne. Nor is this to say that opposition to full gender equality was completely absent from Catholic antimodernism before the contemporary period. Roman Catholic bishops in the United States "put themselves solidly on record against women's suffrage." The National Council of Catholic Women officially opposed the Equal Rights Amendment in 1924 and, in 1930, Pius XI "described women's efforts for equality as debasing and unnatural" (Iadarola 1985: 460, 463, 459). Opposing women's ordination and gender equality clearly is a long-standing feature of the Catholic Church. The point here, however, is that this opposition has emerged into prominence as a central marker of Catholic antimodernism only since the 1970s.

20. See Weaver and Appleby (1995) for a sampling of such groups. See also Dillon (1995) for an analysis of the ways in which doctrinally conservative Catholics discuss women's ordination.

21. The issue has similarly threatened ecumenical relations between Anglican and Orthodox churches (Field-Bibb 1991:140).

22. The point can be stated another way: an antiliberal organizational identity obstructs the diffusion of formal gender equality among denominations. This formulation highlights a connection to David Strang's and John Meyer's (1994) argument that literal social ties will not adequately explain diffusion of a culturally meaningful practice. That is, when a diffusing object or practice carries meaning, the dif-

fusion process is likely to be influenced by more than "realist" elements of social structure, such as connectedness, structural equivalence, spatial contiguity, and the like. Strang and Meyer (1994:100) argue that diffusion patterns will also be influenced by "culturally theorized understandings of the nature of social actors and of diffusing practices." Most relevant in the present context is their (p. 103) hypothesis that diffusion "flows are increased where the actors involved are perceived as similar [because] perceptions of similarity provide a rationale for diffusion." I would add the converse point, important to the case of women's ordination, that actors' perceptions of their *dis*similarity (from the "liberal" world, for example) provide a rationale for resisting diffusion (of gender equality, for example). From this perspective, "diffusion processes often look more like complex exercises in the social construction of identity than like the mechanical spread of information" (Strang and Meyer 1994:102).

6. Internal Organizational Factors

1. The ten states scoring lowest on this measure were, starting from the bottom: Alabama, Mississippi, Louisiana, Arkansas, Georgia, South Carolina, Oklahoma, Tennessee, Florida, and North Carolina. Texas, West Virginia, Kentucky, and Virginia were, respectively, twelfth, thirteenth, fifteenth, and sixteenth from the bottom (Beggs 1995:631).

2. Unfortunately, I have no measure of the social class composition of denominations.

3. This result is unchanged when other variables are controlled.

4. See Chaves (1996) for more detail on how denominations' southern and rural composition was measured.

5. The exception is the Salvation Army.

6. Martin Riesebrodt (1993b:259–264), making a similar observation regarding women's organizations in fundamentalist movements, hypothesizes that movements having autonomous women's institutions are more likely to temper the strict patriarchal gender ideology often associated with these groups. He suggests that the much harsher patriarchalism of Iranian Shi'ite fundamentalism compared with American Protestant fundamentalism is attributable in part to the absence of autonomous women's institutions in the former and their presence in the latter.

7. In addition to the political efforts of the female mission leaders, Shadron attributes this stunning turnaround from eight years before to the changed consciousness brought about by World War I. Some who had previously voted against laity rights for women now voted in favor. One said, "We are not going to give the lives and property of this nation to protect democracy from autocracy in civil government and submit like slaves to autocracy in the Church" (quoted in Shadron 1981:273). Formal gender equality now seemed associated with goodness and democracy and progress.

8. Female religious orders within Roman Catholicism are not an exception to the general point that sacramentalist denominations do not encourage autonomous women's organizations. These orders can be considered truly autonomous only after sisters began to increase both their individual autonomy, through higher education, and their institutional autonomy, through charter reform and the development of cross-order organizations such as the Leadership Conference of Women Religious. Furthermore, women's orders became sources of strong pressure toward gender equality in the Catholic Church only after these changes in the direction of greater autonomy. Thus Roman Catholicism is not an exception to the general point that autonomous women's organizations generate advocacy for gender equality. See Weaver (1995:chap. 3) and Burns (1992:chap. 6) for accounts of this transformation.

7. The Changing Nature of Conflicts over Women's Ordination

1. A special word of thanks is due James Cavendish, who helped very substantially with the data collection for this chapter.

2. This account is drawn from Rowe (1974).

3. Anna Howard Shaw's name was presented to this annual conference for ordination on the same day. Anna Shaw, however, left this denomination for the Methodist Protestant Church, leaving Anna Oliver as the test case (Rowe 1974:65–66).

4. This development is not unique to conflicts over women's ordination. Such "special purpose groups" are increasingly present across a wide range of intradenominational conflicts. Moreover, such SMO-like groups also compose an increasing proportion of *inter*denominational organizations (Wuthnow 1988:chap. 6).

5. As is true for the frequency of conflicts, this finding would be even more dramatic if I included post-1970 conflicts over implementing gender equality within denominations that already granted women full clergy rights. Almost every denomination had such conflicts in the 1970s and 1980s, and SMOs were key actors in most every case.

6. It is necessary to place quotes around words like "irregular" and "illegitimate" in this context because, when these events occur, a major aspect of the conflict is almost always whether or not the ordinations are, in fact, legitimate. This issue is further complicated in a denomination such as the Southern Baptist Convention, where congregations traditionally have the autonomy to ordain whomever they please. I nevertheless include the Southern Baptist Convention in this list of denominations experiencing irregular ordinations of women because the legitimacy of these ordinations has been contested by official denominational bodies. Congregations ordaining women or employing ordained women, for example, have been "disfellowshipped" by regional associations and denied financial support by denominational agencies (Stancil 1988:47).

7. See Kniss (1997) for more on extrainstitutional tactics in intra-denominational conflict. In research on a range of conflicts among Mennonites, he found that "unruly" tactics were more likely to occur when challengers directly attacked the legitimacy of established religious authority.

8. This somewhat paradoxical phenomenon—late adopters of an organizational change experiencing harsher conflict than early adopters—can be observed in other arenas. To cite just one example, the harshest conflict over formal race equality was experienced by the latest, not the earliest, U.S. colleges and universities to institutionalize formally equal admissions with respect to race.

8. Conclusion

1. I thank Gerald Marwell for this particular formulation.

2. See Fink (1995) for an attempt to extend Jay's argument by operationalizing patrilineal descent and using that operationalization to analyze cross-denominational variation in women's ordination.

REFERENCES

Allison, Paul D. 1984. *Event History Analysis: Regression for Longitudinal Data*. Newbury Park, Calif.: Sage.

Ammerman, Nancy Tatom. 1987. *Bible Believers: Fundamentalists in the Modern World*. New Brunswick, N.J.: Rutgers University Press.

———— 1991. "North American Protestant Fundamentalism." Pp. 1–65 in *Fundamentalisms Observed,* edited by Martin E. Marty and R. Scott Appleby. Chicago: University of Chicago Press.

Angell, Stephen Ward. 1996. "The Controversy over Women's Ministry in the African Methodist Episcopal Church during the 1880s: The Case of Sarah Ann Hughes." Pp. 94–109 in *This Far By Faith: Readings in African-American Women's Religious Biography,* edited by Judith Weisenfeld and Richard Newman. New York: Routledge.

Anthony, Susan B., and Ida Husted Harper, eds. 1902. *History of Woman's Suffrage.* Vol. 4. Indianapolis: Hollenbeck Press.

Appleby, R. Scott. 1992. *"Church and Age Unite!" The Modernist Impulse in American Catholicism*. Notre Dame, Ind.: University of Notre Dame Press.

Bailey, Fred Arthur. 1979. "The Status of Women in the Disciples of Christ Movement, 1865–1900." Ph.D. dissertation, University of Tennessee, Knoxville.

Bam, Brigalia, ed. 1971. *What Is Ordination Coming To? Report of a*

Consultation on the Ordination of Women, Cartigny, Switzerland, 21–26 September 1970. Geneva: World Council of Churches.

Barfoot, Charles H., and Gerald T. Sheppard. 1980. "Prophetic vs. Priestly Religion: The Changing Role of Women Clergy in Pentecostal Churches." *Review of Religious Research* 22:2–17.

Bassett, Paul Merritt. 1978. "The Fundamentalist Leavening of the Holiness Movement, 1914–1940: The Church of the Nazarene: A Case Study." *Wesleyan Theological Journal* 13:65–91.

Baumgaertner, William L., ed. 1988. *Fact Book on Theological Education, 1987–1988.* Vandalia, Ohio: Association of Theological Schools in the United States and Canada.

Beaver, R. Pierce. 1980. *American Protestant Women in World Mission: History of the First Feminist Movement in North America.* Rev. ed. Grand Rapids, Mich.: William B. Eerdmans.

Bednarowski, Mary Farrell. 1980. "Outside the Mainstream: Women's Religion and Women Religious Leaders in Nineteenth-Century America." *Journal of the American Academy of Religion* 48:207–231.

Beggs, John J. 1995. "The Institutional Environment: Implications for Race and Gender Inequality in the U.S. Labor Market." *American Sociological Review* 60:612–633.

Bendroth, Margaret L. 1984. "The Search for 'Women's Role' in American Evangelicalism, 1930–1980." Pp. 122–134 in *Evangelicalism and Modern America,* edited by George Marsden. Grand Rapids, Mich.: William B. Eerdmans.

———— 1987. "Women and Missions: Conflict and Changing Roles in the Presbyterian Church in the United States of America, 1870–1935." *American Presbyterians* 65:49–59.

———— 1993. *Fundamentalism and Gender, 1875 to the Present.* New Haven: Yale University Press.

Billington, Louis. 1993. " 'Female Laborers in the Church': Women Preachers in the Northeastern United States, 1790–1840." Pp. 166–191 in *History of Women in the United States: Historical Articles on Women's Lives and Activities,* edited by Nancy F. Cott. Munich: K. G. Saur.

Blair-Loy, Mary. 1994. Personal correspondence.

Bliss, Kathleen. 1952. *The Service and Status of Women in the Churches.* London: SCM Press.

Blumhofer, Edith L. 1989a. *The Assemblies of God: A Chapter in the*

Story of American Pentecostalism. Vol. 1: *To 1941.* Springfield, Mo.: Gospel Publishing House.

———— 1989b. *The Assemblies of God: A Chapter in the Story of American Pentecostalism.* Vol. 2: *Since 1941.* Springfield, Mo.: Gospel Publishing House.

Bonner, Thomas Neville. 1992. *To the Ends of the Earth: Women's Search for Education in Medicine.* Cambridge, Mass.: Harvard University Press.

Booty, John E. 1988. *The Episcopal Church in Crisis.* Cambridge, Mass.: Cowley Publications.

Borgatti, Stephen P., M. G. Everett, and L. C. Freeman. 1992. *UCI-NET IV, Version 1.0.* Columbia, S.C.: Analytic Technologies.

Boyd, Lois A., and R. Douglas Brackenridge. 1983. *Presbyterian Women in America: Two Centuries of a Quest for Status.* Westport, Conn.: Greenwood Press.

———— 1992. "Presbyterian Women Ministers: A Historical Overview and Study of the Current Status of Women Pastors." Pp. 289–307 in *The Pluralistic Vision: Presbyterians and Mainstream Protestant Education and Leadership,* edited by Milton J. Coalter, John M. Mulder, and Louis B. Weeks. Louisville, Ky.: John Knox Press.

Brackenridge, R. Douglas. 1980. "Equality for Women? A Case Study in Presbyterian Polity, 1926–1930." *Journal of Presbyterian History* 58:142–165.

Bradley, Martin B., Norman M. Green, Jr., Dale E. Jones, Mac Lynn, and Lou McNeil. 1992. *Churches and Church Membership in the United States, 1990.* Atlanta: Glenmary Research Center.

Brasher, Brenda. 1994. "The Hand That Rocks the Cradle? Ambiguous and Articulated Instances of Women's Authority and Women's Power in Two Christian Fundamentalist Congregations." Paper presented at the meetings of the Association for the Sociology of Religion, Los Angeles.

Bratt, James D. 1992. "Adam, Eve, and the Christian Reformed Church." *Christian Century* 109:805–808.

Braude, Ann. 1981. "The Jewish Woman's Encounter with American Culture." Pp. 150–192 in *Women and Religion in America,* vol. 1: *The Nineteenth Century,* edited by Rosemary Radford Ruether and Rosemary Skinner Keller. San Francisco: Harper & Row.

Brekus, Catherine A. 1996a. "Harriet Livermore, the Pilgrim Stranger:

Female Preaching and Biblical Feminism in Early Nineteenth-Century America." *Church History* 65:389–404.

——— 1996b. "Female Evangelism in the Early Methodist Movement, 1784–1845." Manuscript. University of Chicago Divinity School.

Brereton, Virginia Lieson, and Christa Ressmeyer Klein. 1980. "American Women in Ministry: A History of Protestant Beginning Points." Pp. 171–190 in *Women in American Religion,* edited by Janet Wilson James. Philadelphia: University of Pennsylvania Press.

Brown, George. [1870] 1987. *The Lady Preacher: Or the Life and Labors of Mrs. Hannah Reeves.* New York: Garland.

Brubaker, Pamela. 1986. "Women." Pp. 161–180 in *Church of the Brethren: Yesterday and Today,* edited by Donald F. Durabaugh. Elgin, Ill.: Brethren Press.

Bruce, Deborah A., and John P. Marcum. 1995. "Comparing Female and Male Pastors in the Presbyterian Church (U.S.A.)." Paper presented at the annual meetings of the Society for the Scientific Study of Religion, St. Louis.

Bucke, Emory S. 1962. *The History of American Methodism.* Vol. 3. New York: Abingdon Press.

Buechlein, Daniel. 1994. "Bishops React to 'Ordinatio Sacerdotalis.' " *Origins* 24:56–57.

Buechler, Steven M. 1990. *Women's Movements in the United States.* New Brunswick, N.J.: Rutgers University Press.

Burns, Gene. 1992. *The Frontiers of Catholicism: The Politics of Ideology in a Liberal World.* Berkeley: University of California Press.

Burt, Ronald S. 1987. "Social Contagion and Innovation: Cohesion versus Structural Equivalence." *American Journal of Sociology* 92: 1287–1335.

Carden, Maren Lockwood. 1989. "The Institutionalization of Social Movements in Voluntary Organizations." *Research in Social Movements, Conflict, and Change* 11:143–161.

Carroll, Jackson W., Barbara Hargrove, and Adair Lummis. 1983. *Women of the Cloth: A New Opportunity for the Churches.* San Francisco: Harper & Row.

Carroll, Jackson W., and Robert L. Wilson. 1980. *Too Many Pastors? The Clergy Job Market.* New York: Pilgrim Press.

Carson, Mary Faith, and James J. H. Price. 1981. "The Ordination of Women and the Function of the Bible." *Journal of Presbyterian History* 59:245–265.

Casanova, Jose. 1994. "Transnational Catholicism and Globalization." Paper presented at the annual meetings of the American Political Science Association, New York.

Charlton, Joy. 1995. "What It Means to Go First: Clergywomen of the Pioneer Generation." Paper presented at the annual meetings of the Society for the Scientific Study of Religion, St. Louis.

Chaves, Mark. 1996. "Ordaining Women: The Diffusion of an Organizational Innovation." *American Journal of Sociology* 101: 840–873.

Christian Reformed Church in North America. 1991. *Agenda for Synod*. Grand Rapids, Mich.: Christian Reformed Church in North America.

——— 1994. *Agenda for Synod*. Grand Rapids, Mich.: Christian Reformed Church in North America.

Clemens, Elisabeth S. 1993. "Organizational Repertoires and Institutional Change: Women's Groups and the Transformation of U.S. Politics, 1890–1920." *American Journal of Sociology* 98:755–798.

Coleman, James, Elihu Katz, and Herbert Menzel. 1957. "The Diffusion of an Innovation among Physicians." *Sociometry* 20:253–269.

Collier-Thomas, Bettye. 1996. "Minister and Feminist Reformer: The Life of Florence Spearing Randolph." Pp. 177–185 in *This Far by Faith: Readings in African-American Women's Religious Biography*, edited by Judith Weisenfeld and Richard Newman. New York: Routledge.

Commission on Theology and Church Relations of the Lutheran Church–Missouri Synod. 1985. *Women in the Church: Scriptural Principles and Ecclesial Practice*.

"Conclusions of the Interorthodox Consultation on the Place of the Woman in the Orthodox Church and the Question of the Ordination of Women." [1988] 1989. *Saint Vladimir's Theological Quarterly* 33:392–406.

Cooney, Jonathan. 1988. "Maintaining the Tradition: Women Elders and the Ordination of Women in the Evangelical United Brethren Church." *Methodist History* 27:25–35.

Cott, Nancy F. 1987. *The Grounding of Modern Feminism*. New Haven: Yale University Press.

Crews, Mickey. 1990. *The Church of God: A Social History*. Knoxville: University of Tennessee Press.

Cummings, Mary Lou. 1978. "Ordained into Ministry: Ann J. Allebach (1874–1918)." Pp. 2–11 in *Full Circle: Stories of Mennonite Women,* edited by Mary Lou Cummings. Newton, Kans.: Faith and Life Press.

Daly, Gabriel. 1985. "Catholicism and Modernity." *Journal of the American Academy of Religion* 53:773–796.

Dau, W. H. T. 1916. *Woman Suffrage in the Church: An Opinion Rendered*. St. Louis: Concordia Publishing House.

Davidman, Lynn. 1991. *Tradition in a Rootless World: Women Turn to Orthodox Judaism*. Berkeley: University of California Press.

Davis, Gerald. 1991. "Agents without Principles? The Spread of the Poison Pill through the Intercorporate Network." *Administrative Science Quarterly* 36:583–613.

Davis, James A. 1992. "Changeable Weather in a Cooling Climate atop the Liberal Plateau: Conversion and Replacement in Forty-Two General Social Survey Items, 1972–1989." *Public Opinion Quarterly* 56:261–306.

Davis, James A., and Tom W. Smith. 1994. *General Social Surveys, 1972–1994,* machine-readable data file. Chicago: National Opinion Research Center.

DeBerg, Betty A. 1990. *Ungodly Women: Gender and the First Wave of American Fundamentalism*. Minneapolis: Fortress Press.

Dennis, James S. 1902. *Centennial Survey of Foreign Missions*. New York: Fleming H. Revell Company.

Dillon, Michele. 1995. "Institutional Distinctions, Conservative Reasoning, and the Maintenance of Gender Inequality: 'Orthodox' Catholics Construe the Implications of Women's Ordination." Paper presented at the annual meetings of the Society for the Scientific Study of Religion, St. Louis.

DiMaggio, Paul. 1988. "Interest and Agency in Institutional Theory." Pp. 3–22 in *Institutional Patterns and Organizations,* edited by Lynne G. Zucker. Cambridge, Mass.: Ballinger.

Dinges, William D., and James Hitchcock. 1991. "Roman Catholic

Traditionalism and Activist Conservatism in the United States." Pp. 66–141 in *Fundamentalisms Observed*, edited by Martin E. Marty and R. Scott Appleby. Chicago: University of Chicago Press.

Dodson, Jualynne E. 1981. "Nineteenth-Century A.M.E. Preaching Women." Pp. 276–289 in *Women in New Worlds: Historical Perspectives on the Wesleyan Tradition*, edited by Hilah E. Thomas and Rosemary Skinner Keller. Nashville: Abingdon.

——— 1996. "Women's Ministries and the African Methodist Episcopal Tradition." Pp. 124–138 in *Religious Institutions and Women's Leadership: New Roles Inside the Mainstream*, edited by Catherine Wessinger. Columbia, S.C.: University of South Carolina Press.

Douglas, Mary. 1992. "The Debate on Women Priests." Pp. 271–294 in Douglas, *Risk and Blame: Essays in Cultural Theory*. New York: Routledge.

Dudley, Roger L. 1995. "How Lay Members View Women Pastors." Paper presented at the annual meetings of the Society for the Scientific Study of Religion, St. Louis.

Ferree, Myra Marx, and Beth Hess. 1994. *Controversy and Coalition: The New Feminist Movement across Three Decades of Change*. New York: Twayne Publishers.

Field-Bibb, Jacqueline. 1991. *Women Towards Priesthood: Ministerial Politics and Feminist Praxis*. New York: Cambridge University Press.

Fink, Virginia S. 1995. "The Importance of an Idea for the Ordination of Women in American Denominations." Paper presented at the annual meetings of the American Sociological Association, Washington, D.C.

Finlay, Barbara. 1996. "Do Men and Women Have Different Goals for Ministry? Evidence from Seminarians." *Sociology of Religion* 57:311–318.

Fitzgerald, Maureen. 1993. "The Religious Is Personal Is Political: Foreword to the 1993 Edition of *The Woman's Bible*." Boston: Northeastern University Press.

Flexner, Eleanor. 1974. *Century of Struggle: The Woman's Rights Movement in the United States*. New York: Atheneum.

Fligstein, Neil. 1987. "The Intraorganizational Power Struggle: Rise of Finance Personnel to Top Leadership in Large Corporations, 1919–1979." *American Sociological Review* 52(1):44–58.

Flora, J. R. 1987. "Ordination of Women in the Brethren Church: A Case Study from the Anabaptist-Pietist Tradition." *Journal of the Evangelical Theological Society* 30:427–440.

Freedman, Estelle. 1979. "Separatism as Strategy: Female Institution Building and American Feminism, 1870–1930." *Feminist Studies* 5:512–529.

Galaskiewicz, Joseph, and Ronald S. Burt. 1991. "Interorganization Contagion in Corporate Philanthropy." *Administrative Science Quarterly* 36:88–105.

Geaney, Dennis. 1978. "Dialog with Women on Their Call to Ministry and Priesthood." Pp. 143–155 in *Women and Priesthood: Future Directions,* edited by Carroll Stuhmueller. Collegeville, Minn.: Liturgical Press.

Gifford, Carolyn De Swarte. 1987a. "Introduction." Pp. 1–21 in *The Defense of Women's Rights to Ordination in the Methodist Episcopal Church.* New York: Garland Publishing.

———. 1987b. "Introduction." Pp. 1–16 in *The Debate in the Methodist Episcopal Church over Laity Rights for Women.* New York: Garland Publishing.

Gilkes, Cheryl Townsend. 1985. " 'Together and in Harness': Women's Traditions in the Sanctified Church." *Signs* 10:678–699.

——— 1986. "The Roles of Church and Community Mothers: Ambivalent American Sexism or Fragmented African Familyhood?" *Journal of Feminist Studies in Religion* 2:41–59.

——— 1993. "Church of God in Christ." P. 238 in *Black Women in America: An Historical Encyclopedia,* edited by Darlene Clark Hine. Brooklyn: Carlson Publishers.

Gleason, Philip. 1995. *Contending with Modernity: Catholic Higher Education in the Twentieth Century.* New York: Oxford University Press.

Godfrey, W. Robert. 1994. "Women in Ecclesiastical Offices: Advisory Committee 10-B Majority Report." Grand Rapids, Mich.: Christian Reformed Church in North America.

Goldman, Ari L. 1992. "Catholics Are at Odds with Bishops." *New York Times,* June 19:A8.

Gorrell, Donald. 1981. "A New Impulse." Pp. 233–245 in *Women in New Worlds: Historical Perspectives on the Wesleyan Tradition,* edited by Hilah E. Thomas and Rosemary Skinner Keller. Nashville: Abingdon.

Grindal, Gracia. 1990. "Getting Women Ordained." Pp. 161–179 in *Called and Ordained: Lutheran Perspectives on the Office of the Ministry,* edited by Todd Nichol and Marc Kolden. Minneapolis: Fortress Press.

———— 1996. "Women in the Evangelical Lutheran Church in America." Pp. 180–210 in *Religious Institutions and Women's Leadership: New Roles inside the Mainstream,* edited by Catherine Wessinger. Columbia, S.C.: University of South Carolina Press.

Groves, Richard. 1984. "Southern Baptist Women in Ministry." *Christian Century* 101:202–203.

Guth, James, John C. Green, Corwin E. Smidt, and Lyman A. Kellstedt. 1994. "Women Clergy and the Political Transformation of Mainline Protestantism." Presented at the annual meetings of the Social Science History Association, Atlanta.

Hamilton, Michael S. 1993. "Women, Public Ministry, and American Fundamentalism, 1920–1950." *Religion and American Culture: A Journal of Interpretation* 3:171–196.

Hannon, Vincent Emmanuel. 1967. *The Question of Women and the Priesthood.* London: Geoffrey Chapman.

Hardesty, Nancy A. 1991. *Your Daughters Shall Prophesy: Revivalism and Feminism in the Age of Finney.* Brooklyn, N.Y.: Carlson Publishing.

Hassey, Janette. 1986. *No Time for Silence: Evangelical Women in Public Ministry around the Turn of the Century.* Grand Rapids, Mich.: Zondervan.

Haunschild, Pamela R. 1993. "Interorganizational Imitation: The Impact of Interlocks on Corporate Acquisition Activity." *Administrative Science Quarterly* 38:564–592.

Hawley, John Stratton, ed. 1994. *Fundamentalism and Gender.* New York: Oxford University Press.

Hawley, John Stratton, and Wayne Proudfoot. 1994. "Introduction."

Pp. 3–44 in *Fundamentalism and Gender,* edited by John S. Hawley. New York: Oxford University Press.

Hiatt, Suzanne. 1983. "How We Brought the Good News from Graymoor to Minneapolis: An Episcopal Paradigm." *Journal of Ecumenical Studies* 20:576–584.

Higginbotham, Evelyn Brooks. 1993. *Righteous Discontent: The Women's Movement in the Black Baptist Church, 1880–1920.* Cambridge, Mass.: Harvard University Press.

Hill, Patricia. 1985. *The World Their Household: The American Woman's Foreign Mission Movement and Cultural Transformation, 1870–1920.* Ann Arbor: University of Michigan Press.

Himmelstein, Jerome. 1986. "The Social Basis of Antifeminism: Religious Networks and Culture." *Journal for the Scientific Study of Religion* 25:1–15.

Hitchcock, Helen Hull. 1995. "Women for Faith and Family: Catholic Women Affirming Catholic Teaching." Pp. 163–185 in *Being Right: Conservative Catholics in America,* edited by Mary Jo Weaver and R. Scott Appleby. Bloomington: Indiana University Press.

Hole, Judith, and Ellen Levine. 1971. *Rebirth of Feminism.* New York: Quadrangle Books.

Hout, Michael, and Andrew Greeley. 1997. "The Laity and Reform in the Church: A Six-Nation Study." UC Berkeley Survey Research Center Working Paper. Berkeley, Calif.

Hudson, Mary Lin. 1990. " 'Shall Women Preach?' Louisa Woosley and the Cumberland Presbyterian Church." *American Presbyterians* 68:221–230.

Hunter, Fannie McDowell. [1905] 1985. "Women Preachers." Reprinted in *Holiness Tracts Defending the Ministry of Women,* edited by Donald W. Dayton. New York: Garland Publishing.

Hutchison, William R. 1976. *The Modernist Impulse in American Protestantism.* Cambridge, Mass.: Harvard University Press.

Huyck, Heather Ann. 1981. "To Celebrate a Whole Priesthood: The History of Women's Ordination in the Episcopal Church." Ph.D. dissertation, University of Minnesota.

Iadarola, Antoinette. 1985. "The American Catholic Bishops and Woman: From the Nineteenth Amendment to ERA." Pp. 457–476 in *Women, Religion, and Social Change,* edited by Yvonne

Yazbeck Haddad and Ellison Banks Findly. Albany: State University of New York Press.

Jacquet, Constant H. 1988. "Women Ministers in 1986 and 1977: A Ten Year View." New York: Office of Research and Evaluation, National Council of Churches.

——— 1989. *Yearbook of American and Canadian Churches*. Nashville: Abingdon Press.

Jay, Nancy. 1992. *Throughout Your Generations Forever: Sacrifice, Religion, and Paternity*. Chicago: University of Chicago Press.

John Paul II. [1984] 1986. "Women's Ordination: The Correspondence between Rome and Canterbury." *One in Christ* 22:289–290.

——— 1994. "Apostolic Letter on Ordination and Women." *Origins* 24:49, 51–52.

——— 1995. "Letter to Women." *Origins* 25:137–143.

Jones, David A. 1989. "The Ordination of Women in the Christian Church: An Examination of the Debate, 1880–1893." *Encounter* 50:199–217.

Katzenstein, Mary Fainsod. 1990. "Feminism within American Institutions: Unobtrusive Mobilization in the 1980s." *Signs* 16:27–54.

King, Gail Buchwalter, ed. 1991. *Fact Book on Theological Education, 1990–1991*. Pittsburgh: Association of Theological Schools in the United States and Canada.

——— 1994. *Fact Book on Theological Education, 1993–1994*. Pittsburgh: Association of Theological Schools in the United States and Canada.

Kleinman, Sherryl. 1984. *Equals before God: Seminarians as Humanistic Professionals*. Chicago: University of Chicago Press.

Klingelsmith, Sharon. 1980. "Women in the Mennonite Church, 1900–1930." *Mennonite Quarterly Review*, July:163–207.

Knight, George W., III. 1981. "The Ordination of Women: No." *Christianity Today,* February 20:16–19.

Kniss, Fred. 1997. *Disquiet in the Land: Cultural Conflict in American Mennonite Communities*. New Brunswick, N.J.: Rutgers University Press.

Kurtz, Lester R. 1986. *The Politics of Heresy: The Modernist Crisis in Roman Catholicism*. Berkeley: University of California Press.

Kwilecki, Susan. 1987. "Contemporary Pentecostal Clergywomen: Female Christian Leadership, Old Style." *Journal of Feminist Studies in Religion* 3:57–75.

Lakey, Othal Hawthorne. 1985. *The History of the CME Church.* Memphis, Tenn.: CME Publishing House.

Lawless, Elaine J. 1988. *Handmaidens of the Lord: Pentecostal Women Preachers and Traditional Religion.* Philadelphia: University of Pennsylvania Press.

Lawson, Matthew. 1995. "Women and Ordination within International Seventh-Day Adventism." Paper presented at the annual meetings of the Society for the Scientific Study of Religion, St. Louis.

Lazarus-Yafeh, Hava. 1988. "Contemporary Fundamentalism—Judaism, Christianity, Islam." *Jerusalem Quarterly* 47:27–39.

Lehman, Edward C., Jr. 1980. "Patterns of Lay Resistance to Women in Ministry." *Sociological Analysis* 41:317–338.

——— 1981. "Organizational Resistance to Women in Ministry." *Sociological Analysis* 42:101–118.

——— 1987. "Sexism, Organizational Maintenance, and Localism: A Research Note." *Sociological Analysis* 48:274–282.

———. 1993. *Gender and Work: The Case of the Clergy.* Albany: State University of New York Press.

Liebman, Robert C., and Robert Wuthnow, eds. 1983. *The New Christian Right: Mobilization and Legitimation.* New York: Aldine.

Lincoln, C. Eric, and Lawrence H. Mamiya. 1990. *The Black Church in the African American Experience.* Durham: Duke University Press.

Loveland, Anne. 1993. "Domesticity and Religion in the Antebellum Period: The Career of Phoebe Palmer." Pp. 35–51 in *History of Women in the United States: Historical Articles on Women's Lives and Activities,* edited by Nancy F. Cott. Munich: K. G. Saur.

Lynch, John E. 1975. "The Ordination of Women: Protestant Experience in Ecumenical Perspective." *Journal of Ecumenical Studies* 12:173–197.

Maher, Frances, ed. 1984. *The Ordination of Women in Lutheran Churches: Analysis of an LWF Survey.* Lutheran World Federation.

Marder, Janet R. 1996. "Are Women Changing the Rabbinate? A Reform Perspective." Pp. 271–290 in *Religious Institutions and*

Women's Leadership: New Roles inside the Mainstream, edited by Catherine Wessinger. Columbia, S.C.: University of South Carolina Press.

Marilley, Suzanne M. 1995. *Woman Suffrage and the Origins of Liberal Feminism in the United States, 1820–1920.* Cambridge, Mass.: Harvard University Press.

Marsden, George M. 1980. *Fundamentalism and American Culture: The Shaping of Twentieth-Century Evangelicalism, 1870–1925.* New York: Oxford University Press.

Marsden, Peter V., and Joel Podolny. 1990. "Dynamic Analysis of Network Diffusion Processes." Pp. 197–214 in *Social Networks through Time,* edited by Jeroen Weesie and Henk Flap. Utrecht: Isor.

Marty, Martin E., and R. Scott Appleby. 1993. *Fundamentalisms and Society: Reclaiming the Sciences, the Family, and Education.* Chicago: University of Chicago Press.

McAnarney, Elizabeth R. 1977. "The Impact of Medical Women in United States Medical Schools." Pp. 9–65 in *Women in Medicine,* edited by Carolyn Spieler. New York: Josiah Macy, Jr. Foundation.

McBeth, Leon. 1981. "The Ordination of Women." *Review and Expositor* 78:515–530.

McCarthy, John D., and Mayer Zald. 1977. "Resource Mobilization and Social Movements: A Partial Theory." *American Journal of Sociology* 82:1212–41.

McCarthy, John D., David W. Britt, and Mark Wolfson. 1991. "The Institutional Channeling of Social Movements by the State in the United States." *Research in Social Movements, Conflict, and Change* 13:45–76.

Melton, J. Gordon, ed. 1991. *The Churches Speak On: Women's Ordination.* Detroit: Gale Research.

Meyer, John W., John Boli, and George M. Thomas. 1994. "Ontology and Rationalization in the Western Cultural Account." Pp. 9–27 in *Institutional Environments and Organizations: Structural Complexity and Individualism,* by W. Richard Scott, John W. Meyer, and associates. Thousand Oaks, Calif.: Sage.

Meyer, John W., and Brian Rowan. [1977] 1991. "Institutional Organizations: Formal Structure as Myth and Ceremony." Pp. 41–62 in *The New Institutionalism in Organizational Analysis,* edited by Walter W. Powell and Paul J. DiMaggio. Chicago: University of Chicago Press.

Meyer, John W., W. Richard Scott, and Terrence E. Deal. 1981. "Institutional and Technical Sources of Organizational Structure: Explaining the Structure of Educational Organizations." Pp. 151–179 in *Organization and the Human Services: Cross-Disciplinary Reflections,* edited by Herman D. Stein. Philadelphia: Temple University Press.

Mezias, Stephen J. 1990. "An Institutional Model of Organizational Practice: Financial Reporting at the Fortune 200." *Administrative Science Quarterly* 35:431–457.

Mill, John Stuart. 1869. *The Subjection of Women.*

Mills, Edgar. 1995. "Consequences of the Gender Shift in the Protestant Ministry." Paper presented at the annual meetings of the Society for the Scientific Study of Religion, St. Louis.

Moody, Joycelyn K. 1995. "On the Road with God: Travel and Quest in Early Nineteenth-Century African American Holy Women's Narratives." *Religion and Literature* 27:35–51.

Morello, Karen Berger. 1986. *The Invisible Bar: The Woman Lawyer in America, 1638 to the Present.* New York: Random House.

Mueller, Carol McClurg. 1992. "Building Social Movement Theory." Pp. 3–25 in *Frontiers in Social Movement Theory,* edited by Aldon D. Morris and Carol McClurg Mueller. New Haven: Yale University Press.

Mulder, Edwin G. 1989. "Full Participation—A Long Time in Coming!" *Reformed Review* 42:224–245.

Murnion, Philip J. 1994. "The Potential and Anomaly of the 'Priestless Parish.'" *America,* January 29:12–14.

Nason-Clark, Nancy. 1987a. "Ordaining Women as Priests: Religious vs. Sexist Explanations for Clerical Attitudes." *Sociological Analysis* 48:259–273.

——— 1987b. "Are Women Changing the Image of Ministry? A Comparison of British and American Realities." *Review of Religious Research* 28:330–340.

Nesbitt, Paula D. 1993. "Dual Ordination Tracks: Differential Benefits and Costs for Men and Women Clergy." *Sociology of Religion* 54:13–30.

——— 1997. *Feminization of the Clergy in America: Occupational and Organizational Perspectives.* New York: Oxford University Press.

New York Times. 1996. "Guerillas Take Afghan Capital as Troops Flee." September 28:1, 5.

Noble, David. 1992. *A World without Women: The Christian Clerical Culture of Western Science.* New York: Alfred A. Knopf.

Noll, William T. 1981. "Laity Rights and Leadership." Pp. 219–232 in *Women in New Worlds: Historical Perspectives on the Wesleyan Tradition,* edited by Hilah E. Thomas and Rosemary Skinner Keller. Nashville: Abingdon.

——— 1992. "A Welcome in the Ministry: The 1920 and 1924 General Conferences Debate Clergy Rights for Women." *Methodist History* 30:91–99.

Norwood, Frederick A. 1982. *Sourcebook of American Methodism.* Nashville: Abingdon.

Parvey, Constance F., ed. 1983. *The Community of Women and Men in the Church: The Sheffield Report.* Philadelphia: Fortress Press.

——— 1985. "Stir in the Ecumenical Movement: The Ordination of Women." Appendix 2 in *The Force of Tradition: A Case Study of Women Priests in Sweden,* by Brita Stendahl. Philadelphia: Fortress Press.

Peek, Charles W., George D. Lowe, and L. Susan Williams. 1991. "Gender and God's Word: Another Look at Religious Fundamentalism and Sexism." *Social Forces* 69:1205–1221.

Piepkorn, Arthur C. 1978. *Profiles in Belief: The Religious Bodies of the United States and Canada.* Vol. 2: *Protestant Denominations.* San Francisco: Harper & Row.

Pius IX. [1864] 1956. *Syllabus of the Principal Errors of Our Time, Which Are Censured in the Consistorial Allocutions, Encyclicals, and Other Apostolic Letters of Our Most Holy Lord, Pope Pius IX.* Pp. 143–152 in *The Papal Encyclicals in Their Historical Context,* edited by Anne Fremantle. New York: G. P. Putnam's Sons.

Pius X. [1907] 1954a. "Lamentabili Sane: Syllabus Condemning the

Errors of the Modernists." Pp. 223–228 in *All Things in Christ: Encyclicals and Selected Documents of Saint Pius X,* edited by Vincent A. Yzermans. Westminster, Mo.: Newman Press.

——— [1907] 1954b. "Pascendi Dominici Gregis: The Doctrines of the Modernists." Pp. 86–132 in *All Things in Christ: Encyclicals and Selected Documents of Saint Pius X,* edited by Vincent A. Yzermans. Westminster, Mo.: Newman Press.

Pius XII. 1950. *Humanis Generis: Concerning Some False Opinions Which Threaten to Undermine the Foundations of Catholic Doctrine.* Washington, D.C.: National Catholic Welfare Conference.

Powell, Walter W., and Paul J. DiMaggio, eds. 1991. *The New Institutionalism in Organizational Analysis.* Chicago: University of Chicago Press.

Prichard, Rebecca B. 1996. "*Grandes Dames, Femmes Fortes,* and *Matrones:* Reformed Women Ministering." Pp. 39–57 in *Religious Institutions and Women's Leadership: New Roles inside the Mainstream,* edited by Catherine Wessinger. Columbia, S.C.: University of South Carolina Press.

Redekop, Gloria Neufeld. 1990. "The Understanding of Woman's Place among Mennonite Brethren in Canada: A Question of Biblical Interpretation." *Conrad Grebel Review,* Fall:259–274.

Reskin, Barbara, and Irene Padavic. 1994. *Women and Men at Work.* Thousand Oaks, Calif.: Pine Forge Press.

Reumann, John H. P. 1987. *Ministries Examined: Laity, Clergy, Women, and Bishops in a Time of Change.* Minneapolis: Augsburg Publishing House.

Riesebrodt, Martin. 1993a. *Pious Passion: The Emergence of Modern Fundamentalism in the United States and Iran.* Berkeley: University of California Press.

——— 1993b. "Fundamentalism and the Political Mobilization of Women." Pp. 243–271 in *The Political Dimensions of Religion,* edited by Said Amir Arjomand. Albany: State University of New York Press.

Riley, Janet. 1989. "The Ordination of Disciple Women: A Matter of Economy or Theology?" *Encounter* 50:219–231.

Roberts, B. T. [1891] 1985. "Ordaining Women." Reprinted in *Ho-*

liness Tracts Defending the Ministry of Women, edited by Donald W. Dayton. New York: Garland Publishing.

Rose, Susan D. 1987. "Women Warriors: The Negotiation of Gender in a Charismatic Community." *Sociological Analysis* 48:245–258.

Rossi, Alice, ed. 1973. *The Feminist Papers: From Adams to de Beauvoir.* New York: Columbia University Press.

Rowe, Kenneth E. 1974. "Discovery: The Ordination of Women: Round One: Anna Oliver and the General Conference of 1880." *Methodist History* 12:60–72.

Royle, Marjorie H. 1987. "Using Bifocals to Overcome Blindspots: The Impact of Women on the Military and the Ministry." *Review of Religious Research* 28:341–350.

Ruether, Rosemary Radford, and Rosemary Skinner Keller, eds. 1981. *Women and Religion in America.* Vol. 1: *The Nineteenth Century.* San Francisco: Harper & Row.

———— 1986. *Women and Religion in America.* Vol. 3: *1900–1968.* San Francisco: Harper & Row.

Sacred Congregation for the Doctrine of the Faith. [1976] 1991. "Declaration on the Question of the Admission of Women to the Ministerial Priesthood." Pp. 1–10.

Schoenherr, Richard A., and Lawrence A. Young. 1993. *Full Pews and Empty Altars: Demographics of the Priest Shortage in United States Catholic Dioceses.* Madison, Wisc.: University of Wisconsin Press.

Scott, Anne Firor. 1991. *Natural Allies: Women's Associations in American History.* Chicago: University of Illinois Press.

Scott, W. Richard, John W. Meyer, and associates. 1994. *Institutional Environments and Organizations: Structural Complexity and Individualism.* Thousand Oaks, Calif.: Sage.

Sexton, Lydia. [1882] 1987. *Autobiography of Lydia Sexton.* New York: Garland Publishing.

Shadron, Virginia. 1981. "The Laity Rights Movement, 1906–1918." Pp. 261–275 in *Women in New Worlds: Historical Perspectives on the Wesleyan Tradition,* edited by Hilah E. Thomas and Rosemary Skinner Keller. Nashville: Abingdon.

Simon, Rita J., and Pamela S. Nadell. 1995. "In the Same Voice or Is

It Different?: Gender and the Clergy." *Sociology of Religion* 56:63–70.

Skocpol, Theda. 1992. *Protecting Soldiers and Mothers: The Political Origins of Social Policy in the United States.* Cambridge, Mass.: Harvard University Press.

Smith, Frank. 1989. "Petticoat Presbyterianism: A Century of Debate in American Presbyterianism on the Issue of the Ordination of Women." *Westminster Theological Journal* 51:51–76.

Smith, Tom W. 1990. "Liberal and Conservative Trends in the United States since World War II." *Public Opinion Quarterly* 54:479–507.

Snow, David A., E. Burke Rochford, Jr., Steven K. Worden, Robert D. Benford. 1986. "Frame Alignment Processes, Micromobilization, and Movement Participation." *American Sociological Review* 51:464–481.

Sommers, Elaine. 1983. *Mennonite Women: A Story of God's Faithfulness, 1683–1983.* Scottsdale, Penn.: Herald Press.

Stancil, Bill. 1988. "Divergent Views and Practices of Ordination among Southern Baptists since 1945." *Baptist History and Heritage* 23:42–49.

Stanley, Susie C. 1997. "Wesleyan/Holiness Churches: Innocent Bystanders in the Fundamentalist/Modernist Controversy." Forthcoming in *Beyond Two Parties: Reclaiming a Nonpartisan History of American Protestantism,* edited by William Vance Trollinger, Jr., and Douglas Jacobsen. Grand Rapids, Mich.: Eerdmans. (Page reference is to manuscript.)

Stanton, Elizabeth Cady. [1895] 1972. *The Woman's Bible.* New York: Arno Press.

Stanton, Elizabeth Cady, Susan B. Anthony, and Matilda Joslyn Gage, eds. 1881. *History of Woman Suffrage.* Vol. 1: *1848–1861.* Rochester, N.Y.: Charles Mann.

Steinfels, Peter. 1992. "New Fire in Bishops' Debate over Document on Women." *New York Times,* November 18:A13.

Stendahl, Brita. 1985. *The Force of Tradition: A Case Study of Women Priests in Sweden.* Philadelphia: Fortress Press.

Stouffer, Austin H. 1981. "The Ordination of Women: Yes." *Christianity Today,* February 20:12–15.

Strang, David. 1991. "Adding Social Structure to Diffusion Models:

An Event History Framework." *Sociological Methods and Research* 19:324–353.

Strang, David, and John W. Meyer. 1994. "Institutional Conditions for Diffusion." Pp. 100–112 in *Institutional Environments and Organizations: Structural Complexity and Individualism,* by W. Richard Scott, John W. Meyer, and associates. Thousand Oaks, Calif.: Sage.

Strang, David, and Nancy Brandon Tuma. 1993. "Spatial and Temporal Heterogeneity in Diffusion." *American Journal of Sociology* 99:614–639.

Sutton, John R., Frank Dobbin, John W. Meyer, and W. Richard Scott. 1994. "The Legalization of the Workplace." *American Journal of Sociology* 99:944–971.

Tagliabue, John. 1996. "Pope Bolsters Church's Support for Scientific View of Evolution." *New York Times,* October 25:A1, A4.

Tarrow, Sidney. 1994. *Power in Movement: Social Movements, Collective Action, and Politics.* New York: Cambridge University Press.

Taylor, Marvin J., ed. 1976. *Fact Book on Theological Education, 1975–1976.* Vandalia, Ohio: Association of Theological Schools in the United States and Canada.

——— 1980. *Fact Book on Theological Education, 1979–1980.* Vandalia, Ohio: Association of Theological Schools in the United States and Canada.

Todd, Mary. 1996. "Not in God's Lifetime: The Question of the Ordination of Women in the Lutheran Church–Missouri Synod." Ph.D. dissertation. University of Illinois at Chicago.

Tolbert, Pamela S., and Lynne G. Zucker. 1983. "Institutional Sources of Change in the Formal Structure of Organizations: The Diffusion of Civil Service Reform, 1880–1935." *Administrative Science Quarterly* 28:22–39.

——— 1995. "Institutional Analyses of Organizations: Legitimate but Not Institutionalized." Paper presented at the annual meetings of the American Sociological Association, Washington, D.C.

Trapp, Daniel J. 1989. "The Discussion of the Ordination of Women to the Priesthood among Roman Catholics in the United States, 1977–1987." Doctoral dissertation, Pontificium Athenaeum S. Anselmi De Urbe Facultas Sacrae Theologiae.

Tucker, Cynthia Grant. 1990. *Prophetic Sisterhood: Liberal Women Ministers of the Frontier, 1880–1930*. Bloomington: Indiana University Press.

———— 1996. "Women and the Unitarian-Universalist Ministry." Pp. 79–100 in *Religious Institutions and Women's Leadership: New Roles inside the Mainstream,* edited by Catherine Wessinger. Columbia, S.C.: University of South Carolina Press.

Tyrrell, George, trans. 1908. *The Programme of Modernism: A Reply to the Encyclical of Pius X, Pascendi Dominici Gregis*. New York: Putnam's Sons.

Vance, Laura. 1995. "The Struggle for Ordination: Women and the Adventist Ministry." Paper presented at the annual meetings of the Society for the Scientific Study of Religion, St. Louis.

Wallace, Ruth A. 1992. *They Call Her Pastor: A New Role for Catholic Women*. Albany: State University of New York Press.

Walsh, Mary Roth. 1977. *"Doctors Wanted: No Women Need Apply": Sexual Barriers in the Medical Profession, 1835–1975*. New Haven: Yale University Press.

Ward, Gary L. 1991. "Introductory Essay: A Survey of the Women's Ordination Issue." Pp. xiii–xxxv in *The Churches Speak On: Women's Ordination,* edited by J. Gordon Melton. Detroit: Gale Research.

Warner, R. Stephen. 1990. "Woman's Place, Women's Space." Paper presented at the annual meetings of the American Sociological Association. Washington, D.C.

Weaver, Mary Jo. [1985] 1995. *New Catholic Women: A Contemporary Challenge to Traditional Religious Authority*. Bloomington: Indiana University Press.

Weaver, Mary Jo, and R. Scott Appleby, eds. 1995. *Being Right: Conservative Catholics in America*. Bloomington: Indiana University Press.

Weisberg, D. Kelly. 1977. "Barred from the Bar: Women and Legal Education in the United States, 1870–1890." *Journal of Legal Education* 28:485–507.

Welter, Barbara. 1966. "The Cult of True Womanhood, 1820–1860." *American Quarterly* 18:151–174.

Wessinger, Catherine, ed. 1993. *Women's Leadership in Marginal Reli-*

gions: *Explorations outside the Mainstream.* Urbana: University of Illinois Press.

————— 1996. *Religious Institutions and Women's Leadership: New Roles inside the Mainstream.* Columbia, S.C.: University of South Carolina Press.

West, Candace, and Donald Zimmerman. 1987. "Doing Gender." *Gender and Society* 1:125–151.

Will, Jim. 1980. "The Ordination of Women—The Development in the Church of the United Brethren in Christ." Pp. 27–40 in *"Woman's Rightful Place": Women in United Methodist History,* edited by Donald K. Gorrell. Dayton, Ohio: United Theological Seminary.

Wuthnow, Robert. 1988. *The Restructuring of American Religion.* Princeton: Princeton University Press.

Yamaguchi, Kazuo. 1991. *Event History Analysis.* Newbury Park, Calif.: Sage.

Zald, Mayer, and Michael Berger. 1978. "Social Movements in Organizations: Coup d'Etat, Insurgency, and Mass Movements." *American Journal of Sociology* 83:823–860.

Zikmund, Barbara Brown. 1981. "The Struggle for the Right to Preach." Pp. 193–206 in *Women and Religion in America,* vol. 1: *The Nineteenth Century,* edited by Rosemary Radford Ruether and Rosemary Skinner Keller. San Francisco: Harper & Row.

————— 1986. "Winning Ordination for Women in Mainstream Protestant Churches." Pp. 339–350 in *Women and Religion in America,* vol. 3: *1900–1968,* edited by Rosemary Radford Ruether and Rosemary Skinner Keller. San Francisco: Harper & Row.

————— 1996. "Women's Ministries within the United Church of Christ." Pp. 58–78 in *Religious Institutions and Women's Leadership: New Roles inside the Mainstream,* edited by Catherine Wessinger. Columbia, S.C.: University of South Carolina Press.

Zikmund, Barbara Brown, Adair T. Lummis, and Patricia M. Y. Chang. 1997. *An Uphill Calling: Ordained Women in Contemporary Protestantism.* St. Louis: Westminster John Knox (forthcoming).

INDEX

World Council of Churches, 28. *See also* External pressure, World Council of Churches as

World Pentecostal Conference. *See* Pentecostals

World's Christian Fundamentals Association, 108, 110, 113

Zahm, John, 123